EUROPEAN POLITICAL ECONOMY

A Paolo

European Political Economy

Political Science Perpectives

LEILA SIMONA TALANI

ASHGATE

Published by
Ashgate Publishing Limited
Gower House
Croft Road
Aldershot
Hampshire GU11 3HR
England

Ashgate Publishing Company
Suite 420
101 Cherry Street
Burlington, VT 05401-4405
USA

Ashgate website: http://www.ashgate.com

British Library Cataloguing in Publication Data
Talani, Leila Simona
    European political economy : political science perspectives
    1.European Union 2.Europe - Economic integration -
    Political aspects 3.Europe - Economic integration - Social
    aspects
    I.Title
    320.9'4

Library of Congress Cataloging-in-Publication Data
Talani, Leila Simona.
    European political economy : political science perspectives / Leila Simona Talani.
        p. cm.
    Includes bibliographical references.
    ISBN 0-7546-3651-8
    1. European Union countries--Economic policy. 2. European Union countries--Economic
    conditions. I. Title.

    HC240.T342 2004
    330.94--dc22

                                                                2004041041

ISBN 0 7546 3651 8

Printed and bound by Athenaeum Press, Ltd.,
Gateshead, Tyne & Wear.

Contents

List of Figures

List of Tables

Acknowledgements

The second book, they say, is more difficult than the first: there is less enthusiasm and you are no longer a student. But, luckily enough, this time I could count on the support of the same people who were around the first time. First and most importantly, my ex-supervisor, mentor, academic point of reference, and, above all, friend, Prof. Alan Cafruny (Hamilton College, US) who not only read and edited the whole book, but also never said I should change job. Then, Prof. Mike Artis (European University Institute, Florence), Prof. Colin Crouch (EUI, Florence), Prof. Henk Overbeek (Free University, Amsterdam) and Prof. Bob Leonardi (London School of Economics). Not to forget my department at the University of Bath which not only sustained me, but also provided me with a friendly and interesting environment! Last but not least, my friends (too many to list, I hope) my family, and, mainly, my 'mamma' (I am Italian after all!).

To the next one,

Simona

Preface

This book aims to provide a useful didactic tool for all scholars and students interested in a non-formalised political economy approach to European economic integration. To be sure, political scientific approaches to political economy have made a major contribution to the study of European economic phenomena. Yet there have been few attempts to systematise the concepts, assumptions, and methods of political scientific interpretations of political economy and to apply them to the key economic events taking place in Europe during the last two decades.

The book begins with a theoretical orientation to European economic issues and European political economy and shows that political scientific approaches to political economy are capable of generating new and important insights into the nature and dynamics of the European Union (EU). The chapters collectively present a statement of political scientists' definitions of political economy and apply the concepts, theories, and insights to contemporary developments in the EU. The book derives its distinctive focus from the emphasis on different approaches to the study of European economic and political developments.

The book is divided, for didactic purposes, into two parts. The first part provides an overview of political scientific approaches to European political economy, both mainstream and critical ones. As such, it contributes directly to the current debate among scholars of political science and International Relations concerning the nature of the process of European integration amongst scholars of political science and international relations. The second part provides for alternative explanations of some European economic policy events allowing the reader to assess the explanatory value of competing approaches.

In the Introduction (Chapter 1) and Part I of this volume the author analyses the competing definitions of political economy and identifies the theoretical assumptions, methodologies and concepts used by both mainstream theorists (Chapter 2) and critical ones (Chapter 3) to conceptualise the process of European economic integration.

Indeed, the theoretical debate among mainstream scholars over the process of European integration is nowadays characterised by two overlapping dichotomies. The first is the traditional divide between 'neofunctionalism' and 'intergovernmentalism'. The second is given by the necessity to integrate systemic or outside-in analysis with inside-out domestic politics approaches. Chapter 2 analyses these overlapping debates by making reference to the most relevant theoretical contributions. It also assesses the heuristic value attributed within mainstream accounts of European political economy to interests, ideas and institutions.

Critical political economy, by contrast, seeks to develop a historical understanding of the interstate and market systems, emphasising how these systems are interpenetrated. Critical political economists contend that mainstream theory ignores relations of power and interest that are contained within the market-integration process itself. In particular, they assert that mainstream theory fails to adequately conceptualise and historicise the role of the State in processes of integration, or to link changes in the nature of the State and inter-state relations to hypotheses concerning class formation and dissolution. Chapter 3 of the book contains an in-depth overview of the main critical approaches to European political economy.

Since the establishment of European Monetary Union (EMU) has undoubtedly represented one of the most important steps in the process of European integration in the last decade, the second, more issue-oriented part of the book starts (Chapter 4) with an exploration of the competing political economy explanations of the making of EMU, from intergovernmentalist accounts, to neoconstructivist or neofunctionalist ones. It seeks not to offer a definitive answer to the process of European monetary integration, but rather to emphasise the explanatory value of different theoretical paradigms.

Chapter 5 assesses the performance of the ECB in the context of the theoretical frameworks set in the first part of the volume. Given the centrality of EMU to all European political and economic developments, the ECB is an important institution, which deserves greater attention, especially from a theoretical standpoint. It becomes therefore imperative to conceptualise its analysis within the different theoretical perspectives, though not all the approaches provide an adequate problematisation of its role and functions. The chapter indeed mainly relies on inside-out and critical accounts of the ECB performance in its first period of activity.

Chapter 6 addresses the issue of mass unemployment in Europe over the last decade. It compares neofunctionalist and neo-Gramscian explanations for the employment policy adopted by the EU commission from 1993 until the introduction of the new chapter on employment in the core treaties of the EU in 1996. It then moves to the analysis of the Italian flexibilisation of labour markets in the last 20 years as a case study.

A comparison between neofunctionalist and interest-based approaches is made in Chapter 7, which focuses on the issue of social policy and the role of social partners in the European decision-making process.

Finally, Chapter 8 analyses the creation of a 'fortress Europe' and the development of a very strict migratory policy in the EU area in the light of considerations relating to the nature of globalisation and its impact on the international division of labour with all that it implies in terms of illegal migration.

The conclusion to the volume sets the debate relating to European integration within the broader context of globalisation and analyses the impact of globalisation on both the nation state and the process of regionalisation taking place at the European level. The chapter addresses the two interrelated debates of the definition of globalisation and its impact on the nation state from different perspectives, the realist (or sceptical one), the institutionalist and the transnationalist one.

Chapter 1

European Political Economy: At the Crossroads between Political Economy and International Political Economy

The study of European political economy (EPE) allows for numerous definitions and perspectives because its subject matter lies at the crossroads of many interrelated disciplines. Because it is inserted within the broader field of political economy it is necessary at the outset to provide a definition of the term 'political economy'. While political economy can be defined in various ways, perhaps the key distinction is between approaches to the subject which begin from an economic standpoint, and those which proceed from the perspective of political science.

I have chosen to approach the study of political economy from the perspective of political science. I hasten to add, however, that such an approach does not deny the existence of a flourishing economic school of 'political economy' featuring a number of different approaches and perspectives. Even when restricting the field of analysis to the 'political science approaches' to European political economy, the area is crowded with different contributions ranging from public choice, to European integration theories, comparative politics approaches and policy-making theories. In the first part of this book I seek to offer a comprehensive review of the many theoretical perspectives approaching the analysis of 'European political economy'. As the ensuing sections of the book make clear, my own account of the subject relies mainly on the vocabulary and tradition of international relations[1] or, better, international political economy and it is therefore set within the context of the evolution of the latter, to which I turn in the next section.

1.1 Evolution of International Political Economy

From the seventeenth-century mercantilists[2] to twentieth-century Marxists, the relationship between economics and politics has been a subject of considerable debate. Yet, during the first half of the twentieth century the study of the international political economy fell into relative neglect.[3] As a result, the disciplines of economics and politics were artificially separated from each other. The reasons why this occurred have been traced by different scholars in different events.[4]

In her best-selling book of the late 1970s *The Politics of International Economic Relations*, Joan Edelman Spero analysed in a very thorough way the main causes of the decline in the use of political-economical variables to explain international events. Spero blamed the divorce on the liberal heritage in western academia which has rejected the old age concept of a unified political and economic order, replacing it with two separate orders. Starting from the assumption of the natural harmony of the economic system and of the absence of any natural law or harmony in the political sphere, liberal theorists argued that the two fields should not interfere with one another.[5] Such theoretical separation has led to, and has been reinforced by, the specialisation of modern academia in which economics and politics have been treated as different disciplines, interested in different processes and studying different systems with different rules.

Furthermore, argued Spero, this formal division of analysis was reinforced by two political and economic developments following World War II. The first one was the agreement on post-war international economic relations, given in the west by the Bretton Woods system and in the east by the Soviet hegemony, which tended to limit conflicts over economic issues. The second was the emergence of the Cold War, which led international relation theorists to focus on 'high' politics, security and security-related issues (as the success of the realist perspective during this period clearly shows).[6]

However, by the mid-1970s the two factors which shaped the study of international politics in the post-war decades (economic consensus and security conflict) were becoming less salient. It became increasingly evident that an integrated analysis of the economic and political issues in the study of international relations was necessary and the study of 'the politics of international economic relations' (PIER) was founded.

The PIER approach favoured by Spero and other scholars did not, however, meet with widespread approval. As Roger Tooze argued, given the predominance of the realist perspective in the 1950s–60s US international relation theories, the development of 'orthodox'[7] IPE, defined by the author as a branch of international relations, was characterised from the beginning by the realist conceptual separation of economics and politics and of the international and the domestic, a separation that the realists borrowed from the concept of a 'liberal' economic order, that is an order in which economic activity is separated from political activity, both from a prescriptive and a descriptive point of view, for the purpose of maximising the common wealth.[8] Moreover, realism not only borrowed its conception of the relations between politics and economics from liberal thought, but also helped support the liberal elements of the international economic order which was established over the western bloc and the dependent third world after World War II, so that one can recognise a dynamic relation between the predominant theoretical perspective and the actual shaping of economic policies.[9]

Indeed, it was the crisis of the liberal world economic order that produced the need for orthodox IPE to bring back together the academic fields of political science and economics analysing the 'politics of the international economic relations' (PIER), or the 'political economy of international relations' (PEIR), in order to find a new body of rules and norms that would preserve the actual division between the political and the economic and keep the world economy functioning as it had in the 1950s and 1960s.[10]

An example of this US-centred orthodox conception of IPE is given by Gilpin's renewed attention to the interaction between economics and politics from a neorealist point of view,[11] as expressed in most of his 1970s works and confirmed in his *Political Economy of International Relations*. Gilpin traces the need for an integrated approach to the study of international relations to the alleged relative decline of American economic leadership of the post-war liberal international economy, in the ongoing shift in the locus of the core of the world economy from the Atlantic to the Pacific, and in the increasing integration of the American and Japanese economies.[12]

On the other hand, starting from the criticism of both the realistic perspective and its PIER/PEIR subsequent development, Tooze proposed a new IPE whose purpose was 'to bring IPE back into the mainstream of social science as a whole', an aim which had already been argued for by Stephen Gill and David Law in their global approach to political economy.[13] According to these authors, although the roots of the political economy approach to international relations go back centuries and may already be traced in the analyses of the mercantilists, the emergence of international political economy as a self-conscious field of study only took place in the 1970s with an historical gap during the early twentieth century which is to be explained by the increasing specialisation of social science disciplines. The upsurge in the literature in the 1970s, particularly in the United States, was the consequence of the changes in the world economics, with the breakdown of the Bretton Woods order and the constraints which interdependence was placing on US policy.

The academic sources of the resurgence of international political economy were, in the categorisation by Gill and Law, varied in character, ranging from: i) the emergence of neoclassical political economy analysis; ii) the revival of Marxist analysis; iii) the emergence of 'development studies' and concern over north-south relations; iv) the analyses of international constraints on national policies as expressed by interdependence and dependency theories; and v) the comparative socio-historical approach.

Given this multitude of approaches and the lack of agreement in the definition of 'political economy' itself, as shown by the variety of different definitions collected in Whynes's work *What is Political Economy*, the boundary of the field is so confused that Gill prefers to abandon the use of the term international political economy in favour of the more comprehensive expression 'Global political economy' which he believes could facilitate a better communication among the rival theoretical frameworks and increase interdisciplinary exchanges.[14]

Gill further clarifies his new IPE position in the essay 'Historical materialism, Gramsci and international political economy'[15] where he argues for a new historical materialist IPE analysis as opposed to the positivist approach, criticised for its ahistorical nature, lack of a dynamic, dialectical quality, narrowness and incompleteness of abstractions, and tendency to extreme parsimony in explanation relative to the infinite complexity of its object of analysis, namely, the international system.[16]

The last development in the field of IPE is, thus, characterised by an increasing opposition between the orthodox stream of thought, enriched by the contribution of the public choice school,[17] and the growing new IPE perspective, trying to provide a common language in which to preserve the insights of otherwise separate research traditions, supporting multiple points of synthesis among different perspectives and avoiding the establishment of one, unitary, all-encompassing theory of IPE.[18]

At this point it is necessary to go deeper into the analysis of the different definitions of 'political economy'.

1.2   Definitions of Political Economy: Economists vs Political Scientists

The very meaning of the term 'political economy' is still a matter of great scholarly debate.[19]

As the late Susan Strange reminded us,[20] there is an intrinsic link between the two concepts of 'politics' and 'economics'; the term 'economics' originated from the Greek word *oikonomia*, which meant a household in the ancient, patriarchal sense, whose management, including the management of people and lands, was more a matter of politics than of economics. However, the term 'political economy' achieved the status of a current expression in Italy, France or Great Britain only during the eighteenth century, when it was used in a more narrow and specific sense as 'that part political management that related to the prosperity of the State and the ordering of the 'economic' affairs'.[21]

Indeed, the core of the whole question is exactly whether there exists or not any substantial difference between the connotations and the semantic contents of the word 'economics' and 'political economy', which implies the broader question whether the study of political economy is separated and autonomous from the study of 'economics'. The answer to that question is a very controversial matter.

Adam Smith,[22] whose *Wealth of Nations* appeared in 1776, and the other classical economists, used the term 'political economy' in a restricted sense to mean what today is called the science of economics[23] and, clearly, that implies that they did not recognise any difference among the two disciplines.

On the other hand, certain contemporary economists see economics and political economy as being the opposite side of the same coin. An example is given by Lord Robbins[24] who interprets political economy as the application of economic science to problems of policy. To Robbins, it seems, 'economics' is the central body of a scientifically established doctrine whereas 'political economy' embraces 'all the modes of analysis and explicit or implicit judgements of value, which are usually involved when economists discuss the assessment of benefits and the reverse or recommendations for policy'.[25]

This definition of 'political economy' is very widespread among the economists who, at various time, have designated this area, called either normative, welfare, applied, or economic policy, as a branch of economics: one is the application of the other.

Recently, a number of scholars such as Gary Becker,[26] Anthony Downs and Bruno Frey, have defined political economy as the application of the methodology of formal economics, that is the so-called rational actor model, to all types of human behaviour and, particularly, to socio-political behaviour.

As Frey puts it,[27] international political economy provides an analysis of the interplay of economic and political factors in the international relations, using the standard tools of economics. From his point of view, the economic theory of politics, often called public choice, may be used to integrate economic and political studies of international relationships since public choice is part

of a larger endeavour which seeks to apply the 'rational behaviour' approach
to areas beyond (traditional) economics.[28]

The 'rational behaviour' approach to social problems and 'public choice'
theory includes three main features. First, the individual is taken as the unit
of analysis. He is assumed to be rational in the sense of responding in a
systematic and hence predictable way to incentives; he is also assumed to
choose courses of action that yield the highest net benefits according to his
own evaluation (utility function). Secondly, an individual's behaviour is
assumed to be consistent (the conditions of 'non reversal of preferences')
and explained by concentrating on changes in the constraints to which he is
exposed. Therefore, changes in behaviour are not attributed to (unexplained)
shifts in preferences. Finally, individuals are assumed to be capable of
comparing alternatives, recognising substitution possibilities, and making
marginal adjustments.[29]

Public choice is based on the contributions of Kenneth Arrow, Antony
Downs, James Buchanan, Gordon Tullock, Mancur Olson[30] and William
Niskanen, with Joseph Schumpeter as an important forerunner.[31] Until Frey,
however, the public choice approach had been applied only to a very limited
extent to international economics. Forerunners include Albert Hirshman with
his *National Power and the Structure of Foreign Trade*,[32] where the link
between economics and politics in the international sphere focuses primarily
on the classical concept of gains from trade, and Charles Kindleberger with
his *Power and Money* whose subtitle, *The Economics of International Politics
and the Politics of International Economics*, clearly indicates the attempt to
widen the range of issues treated by economics.

At the roots of their effort to apply the economic methodology to the study
of political economy and international political economy lies a substantial
criticism of the political science conception of IPE. From the public choice
point of view, political scientists' international political economy is deficient
in various respects: its structure is not analytical, the approach is descriptive,
historical (if not, sometimes, even anecdotal), and no empirical econometric
testing is ever attempted. From this perspective, political science approaches
are useful only in pointing out problems and giving general insights.[33]

Public choice arguments in favour of the application *sic et simpliciter*
of the economic method to the study of political economy are criticised by
those contemporary political economy theorists who come from the tradition
of international relations and who, therefore, tend to put more emphasis on
the central role of the socio-political structures in their definition of political
economy.

According to Gilpin,[34] for example, although approaches to political economy based on the application of the method and theory of economic science are very helpful, they are as yet unable to provide a comprehensive and satisfactory framework for scholarly inquiry. A unified methodology or theory of political economy would require a general comprehension of the process of social change, including the ways in which the social, economic and political aspects of society interact. Thus, Gilpin defines the term 'political economy' simply as 'a set of questions to be examined by means of an eclectic mixture of analytic methods and theoretical perspectives'.[35]

On this definition of political economy as a set of questions there is now a widespread agreement, at least among social science scholars. For example, according to Tooze[36] 'International Political Economy denotes an area of investigation, a particular range of questions and a series of assumptions about the nature of the international "system" and how we understand this "system"'. Also in Susan Strange's *States and Markets* there is implicit the definition of IPE as a set of questions where she criticises the PIER perspective for 'posing a too narrow set of questions'.[37]

Of course, people still debate what exactly should be included in the set of questions that define IPE.

Gilpin's neorealist definition of IPE assumes that the relevant questions concern the relationships between the State and the market because: 'The tensions between these two fundamentally different ways of ordering human relationships has profoundly shaped the course of modern history and constitutes the crucial problem in the study of political economy.'[38] The interaction between the State and the market influence the distribution of power and wealth in international relations.

This definition of political economy, coincides with the definition given by intergovernmentalist approaches to European political economy and establishes their theoretical background.[39] States are the main actors in an international system which is conceptualised as 'anarchical'[40] and lacking a supranational source of legitimacy and power. International institutions (as well as European institutions for that matter) only provide the framework within which states bargain to maximise their utility functions and deals are struck at the minimum common denominator in order to minimise the loss of sovereignty.

Neorealist approaches are, therefore, 'systemic' or 'outside-in' perspectives, analysing the role of an 'individualised' state in the international system according to the standard tools of the rational actor model. Indeed, the prevailing model for systemic analysis in politics comes from economics, in particular from microeconomics theory, which assumes the existence of firms with given utility functions, and attempts to explain their behaviour on the basis of environmental factors such as competitiveness of the markets. It is systemic rather than unit-level theory because its propositions depend on variations in attributes of the system and not on the modification in the behaviour of the single units of analysis. States are assumed to act as rational egoists, which means that they have consistent ordered preferences and that they calculate costs and benefits of alternative courses of action in order to maximise their utility in view of those preferences. Making these assumptions implies that rationality and conceptions of self-interest are constants rather than variables in the systemic approach, i.e., states are assumed to be rational and interest-oriented.

Robert Keohane's neo-institutionalist position in IPE can be derived from Gilpin's pathbreaking work.[41] Keohane argues that Gilpin has offered a helpful working definition of the phrase 'world political economy' but the concepts of power and wealth have a common deficiency as the basis for explanations of behaviour: to estimate the power of actors, or whether a given product, service, or raw material constitutes wealth, one has to observe their behaviour in power relationships or in markets, i.e., it is necessary to insert the behaviour of actors in their institutional context.

As an alternative, according to Keohane:

> We can view international political economy as the intersection of the substantive area studied by economics – production and exchange of marketable means of want satisfaction – with the process by which power is exercised that is central to politics. Wherever, in the economy, actors exert power over one another, the economy is political.[42]

This area of intersection can be contrasted with 'pure economics' in which no actor has any control over others but faces an externally determined environment.

Therefore, according to Keohane, thinking about IPE in terms of wealth and power does not help to construct a strong explanatory model of behaviour. However, focusing on the *pursuit of wealth* and the *pursuit of power* does contribute to insightful interpretation, since it provides working hypotheses about the motivations of actors that emphasise specific interests within a given institutional framework. Defining international political economy in terms of the pursuit of wealth and power leads neo-institutionalists to analyse co-operation in the world political economy and the institutional form it takes less as an effort to implement high ideals than as a means of attaining self-interested economic and political goals.[43]

As a matter of fact, wealth and power are sought by a variety of actors in world politics, but states are, in Keohane's thought, crucial actors. This is why his analysis of international cooperation and regimes, focuses principally on states. At the same time, however, contrary to neorealist perspectives, in the neo-institutional conceptualisation states do not act in a vacuum or in an anarchical system, but are constrained by the international institutional structure.[44]

However, like the neorealists, neo-institutionalists adopt a distinctive 'outside-in' or systemic level of explanation, i.e., an explanation which accounts for State behaviour on the basis of attributes of the system as a whole.[45] Their 'outside-in' perspective is indeed very similar to that of systemic form of realist theory, or structuralist realism[46] the only distinguishing feature being the emphasis on the effects of international institutions and practices on State behaviour.[47] This distinguished feature is shared by neofunctionalist accounts of European political economy and is the one feature which allows us to recognise the theoretical continuity between neo-institutionalist IPE perspectives and neofunctionalist EPE approaches.

Indeed, the most important recent development from within the orthodox or mainstream approaches to IPE/EPE, as further elaborated in the next chapters, has been the shift from a prevailing outside-in/systemic approach, to a new attention to inside-out or domestic politics accounts.[48] Ultimately, an integrated domestic politics/international system approach to both international and European phenomena has been proposed taking the form of double/multi-level game theories.[49] However, similar developments have maintained a distinct focus on the role of the politician and the decision-maker has the trait d'union between the national and the international level of analysis, leaving the criticism of the assumption of the centrality of the State and its decision-makers to the theoretical interventions of critical theorists.[50]

The contributors to the critical school deviate from the orthodox perspective on theory and methodology in three ways. First, they are willing to recognise and confront the necessary subjectivity of the social sciences as opposed to their subordination to the economic methodology or approach. Second, they are all open to considering a wide variety of forms of historical and social explanation as well as their combination. Third, they put the explanatory primacy not only on states or institutions, but also on interests and ideas.

Accordingly, the issues analysed by critical theorists are to a great extent different from those of the orthodox authors. Critical theorists study not only

US statecraft and of the presumed decline of its hegemonic power, but also the historical development and influence of concrete 'private' interests in the world economy such as firms and representatives of sectoral interest groups. They also seek to understand the evolution of intellectual paradigms and their role in shaping political outcomes.

It is into this context that Susan Strange's eclectic definition of IPE should be inserted.[51] The first stage in her definition of IPE was expressed in the preface to a collection of essays entitled *Paths to International Political Economy* in which she strongly argued for openness to insights from other disciplines in the development of a field, IPE, that was still considered as a branch of international relations. As her work progressed she began to stress the need to go a step beyond in the development of a truly eclectic approach to international political economy, i.e., to find a way to effect a synthesis of some kind, to provide some unifying concepts that would allow connections to be made and dialogues to be initiated between the disciplines in order to overcome the conventionally accepted paradigm of the politics of international relations (PIER).

Strange argued that such a synthesis could be achieved by identifying the main 'enveloping'[52] structures that, rather than the rational, conscious decision of any actor, determine the range of options within which 'States and other groups and individuals contest all the major who-gets-what issues of politics', both at the national and at the international level.

Apart from the importance, already stressed by Marxist and Gramscian authors,[53] of the production structure in international political economy, Strange draws to the attention of IPE scholars the role of the financial structure,[54] the security structure and the knowledge structure, represented, at the abstract level, by the belief systems, and at the operational level, by the management of information.[55] Moreover, two other major factors, technology and markets, both exogenous to the international political system and both ignored by the orthodox scholars, are added to states as the determinants of change in the major structures: thus an eclectic analytical framework for the study of IPE is set. The final stage in the clarification of Strange's position is the insertion of a new variable in the evolution of structures and bargaining relationships: firms. Firms, like states with which they undertake an incessant bargaining process, play a role in markets and technological development. Like states and markets they are affected by changes in any of the four major structures and, above all, they exercise power in many ways, both domestically and internationally. Thus, argues Susan Strange, if we want to achieve the main aim of IPE, which is to look for the sources of power and the consequences of the exercise of it, we cannot rationally exclude firms from our analysis.[56]

Besides Susan Strange's eclectic contribution to a new definition of IPE, the development of a new Gramscian definition of IPE, based on the works of Cox[57] and well explained by Gill[58] should not be neglected since it has formed the basis of a number of studies of European political economy from a distinctive critical IPE perspective.[59]

Starting from the assumptions that the central task of social science is to express social action, structure and change, that, epistemologically, 'there is no symmetry between the social and natural sciences with regard to concept formation and the logic of inquiry and explanation' and that there is not, and logically cannot be, a single language of scientific explanation, Gill develops a historically integrated, dialectical form of IPE analysis with the explicit aim to transcend the subject/object and agent/structure dichotomies that undermine the plausibility of the generally positivist epistemologies and ontologies at the roots of the majority of studies in IPE.[60]

At a preliminary level of analysis, it is possible to underline three main differences between the Gramscian and the orthodox IPE. First of all, in international studies the Gramscian approach criticises the empiricist and positivist assumptions of the prevailing orthodox tradition to which it contrasts a specific form of 'non structuralist historicism'.[61] Second, the Gramscian approach is also critical of the methodological individualism and the methodological reductionism, typical of both public choice approaches to political economy and orthodox accounts of IPE. For Gramsci, it is *la situazione* (the situation), defined as the 'ensemble of social relations configured by social structure', that is the basic unit of analysis rather than any individual actor as in modern public choice theory.[62] Third, the approach inserts an ethical dimension to the analysis of social events establishing the normative goal of the move towards a 'good society' and thus, politically, the construction of an 'ethical' state and a unitary society in which 'personal development, rational reflection, open debate, democratic empowerment, and economic and social liberation can become widely available'.[63] Finally, neo-Gramscian approaches adopt a materialist interpretation of history and put the explanatory primacy of their analyses on economic factors. In particular, the role of transnational economic actors and the power relations among the different interest groups representing them in the societal and political context is recognised as the main heuristic tool to approach the study of international and European events.[64]

Whereas neo-Gramscians stress the role of socioeconomic interests, and of the power relations between transnational interest groups as historically determined, in accounting for international phenomena, neoconstructivists underline the role of ideas as key explanatory variables.[65]

The emphasis on ideas and ideological paradigms to explain choices in economic policy-making is not exclusive to neoconstructivist perspectives, being a distinguished feature of some institutionalist approaches to comparative politics, particularly historical institutionalism.[66] However, neoconstructivist definitions of political economy differ from more institutionalist ones in that they attribute explanatory primacy to the autonomous role of ideas in shaping the choices of policy-makers, *independently* from the institutional structure where the policy-making takes place. Therefore, ideas matter, no matter what the rules or institutions are.

Constructivist approaches are also explicitly cautioning against the importance attributed in some international political economy literature to private economic interests, like multinationals and firms, as the driving forces for international cooperation within the context of globalisation.[67] In their accounts, on the contrary, interests are defined by the prevailing ideological framework. For example, McNamara (a leading figure in the neoconstructivist panorama providing for a well-known application of the approach to European economic integration) explicitly rejects the primacy of economic interests in shaping international events in favour of the argument that the process of interest redefinition has historically been dependent on policy-makers shared beliefs.

Ultimately, therefore, the approach stresses the autonomous role of policy-makers in deciding upon international political economy issues, independently from both the institutional and the economic structures, while embedding it in the prevailing ideological context. This is in turn treated as the ultimate heuristic factor.

1.3   Conclusion

This chapter has tried to show that at the core of the whole debate about the definition and content of 'political economy' as well as of, of course, 'European political economy', lies a set of epistemological, if not philosophical, questions about the role and definition of political-science theories and their prescriptive, predictive, or only descriptive value.[68] The chapter concludes with two observations concerning theory.

First, as Susan Strange has noted, the role of a theory in social science, and, therefore, also in international relations, is, first of all, to explain some aspect of the international system that is not easily explained by 'common sense'. Thus the rational approach, from classical Adam Smith to contemporary rational choice and public choice theorists, has only limited explanatory power in the sense that it simply confirms what common sense already tells us, that is that individuals are apt to act selfishly. Rationalists offer powerful simplifying devices that nevertheless stop well short of a theory of social behaviour since they do not explain the actions of socio-political actors, such as interest or pressure groups, parties or states, in a global political economy.[69]

Secondly, a theory of social science need not necessarily aspire to predict anything, and when it does happen the social scientist has to bear in mind that the irrational factors involved in human relations are infinite and infinite are their possible combinations and implications. As Karl Popper points out, the chain of 'unintended social repercussions of intentional human actions'[70] is infinite and it is absolutely impossible to predict all of them. Therefore, it is not possible to identify causal, deterministic relations in any human or social action. Here is where the boundary between social and natural science is drawn.[71] With respect to the prescriptive value of social science theories, this is only a question of subjective choice of the scientist who decides, on the basis of a set of personal value judgements, whether or not to apply his theory to the policy-making process. Finally, the scientific value of a social theory is given, by the respect of the scientific virtues of rationality and impartiality in the aspiration to the systematic formulation of explanatory propositions.

In this context, any genuine attempt to explain socio-political reality using variables taken from different, even opposed, scientific paradigms, should be openly welcomed, while any abstract model clearly inconsistent with the real events of the real world, should be relegated to the realm of pseudo-scientific hypotheses.

As Hargreaves-Heap and Hollis remind us:

> shoppers do not adjust the utility of the mth apple to that of the nth pear; businessmen do not skate along cost curves in a finely tuned zest for profit; preferences are not fully ordered, information perfect and calculations faultless; markets do not clear to the mutual benefit of firms and households.

Reality is much more complex, and, for this reason, maybe, much more interesting.[72]

Scheme
Theoretical approaches to European political economy

Economists:

1   Application of economic theories
2   Applied branch of economics to question of public policy (transport policy, budgetary policy, etc.)
3   Application of the economic methodology (methodological individualism; rational actor model) to the political process and policy-making issues:
    • rational choice – public choice (intersection with political science)
    • game theory

Political scientists:
(IR/IPE tradition)

A   *Mainstream approaches:*

1   Neorealist/intergovernmentalist approach:
    • the State is the main actor of the international system
    • the international system is characterised by a situation of anarchy
    • application of the rational actor model to the State's behaviour
2   Neo-institutionalist/neofunctionalist approach:
    • the State is embedded in a web of international institutions and is constrained by the international system – criticism of the assumption of anarchy in international relations
    • the rational actor model still applies to the behaviour of the State

Compromise solutions:

Multi-level games
Continuum between
intergovernmental and
neo-instutionalist
explanations

B   *Critical approaches: (criticism of the rational actor assumption)*

•   Neoconstructivist – ideological paradigms are the main explanatory variable
•   Neo-Gramscian – power relation samongst national and trasnational socioeconomic groups as historically defined are the main explanatory variable
•   Neo-Marxist – class struggle is the main explanatory variable
•   Eclectic – many different variables from different context are used as the main explanatory variables

Notes

1 For a similar theoretical setting of the field of European political economy within the context of international relation/IPE theories see Laursen (1995); see also Rosamond (2000). A different view is expressed by Hix (1996).

2 Friedrich List, a late mercantilist, defines 'political economy' as: 'the policy which each separate nation had to obey in order to make progress in its economical conditions'. See List (1885).

3 See Strange (1970).

4 See Blake and Walters (1976).

5 For readings on the classical liberal school, see Adam Smith, *An Inquiry into the Nature and Causes of the Wealth of Nations*; James Mill, *Elements of Political Economy*; John Stuart Mill, *Principles of Political Economy*.

6 See Spero (1977).

7 See Murphy and Tooze (1991), p. 4.

8 See Murphy and Tooze (1991), p. 3.

9 On the influence of perspectives in shaping policies see also Gill and Law (1988).

10 Some meaningful exceptions to this are represented, for example, by Strange (1970), Cooper (1972) and Paarlberg (1976).

11 In his preface to *The Political Economy of International Relations*, Gilpin writes: 'I had returned to a realist conception of the relationship of economics and politics that had disappeared from postwar American writings, than almost completely devoted to more narrowly conceived security issues'. Moreover, Gill and Law define Gilpin's approach as being a realist one. See Gill and Law (1988), preface, p. xvii and Gilpin (1987).

12 See Gilpin (1987), Preface.

13 See Gill and Law (1988).

14 See Gill and Law (1988), p. 15.

15 Included in Murphy and Tooze (1991).

16 For more details on this criticism, see Murphy and Tooze (1991), Ch. 1.

17 See Frey (1984).

18 See Murphy and Tooze (1991), p. 29.

19 For an argument with the one set here see Hall, P., Interests, ideas or institutions ....

20 See Strange (1988), p. 19.

21 See Strange (1988), p. 20.

22 However, already in the nineteenth century there was a great debate on the nature and content of the term 'political economy' as is shown by the criticism of Friedrich List to the Smith's cosmopolitical definition of 'political economy' to which he opposes a national definition of 'political economy': 'Which teaches how a given nation in the present state of the world and its own special national relations can maintain and improve its economical conditions' while '... cosmopolitical economy (sustained by A. Smith, n.d.r.) originates in the assumption that all nations of the earth form but one society living in a perpetual state of peace'. See Crane and Amawi (1991), p. 50.

   From the mercantilist point of view: '... from the political union originates the commercial union. All examples which history can show are those in which the political union has led the way and the commercial union has followed.' See Crane and Amawi (1991), p. 51.

23 See Gilpin (1987), p. 8; Whynes (1984), p. 2.

24   See Whynes (1984), p. 3.
25   See Whynes (1984), p. 4.
26   See Becker (1976).
27   See Frey (1984), Preface, p. vii.
28   For further explanation of the concept, see Becker (1976).
29   See Frey (1984), p. 4.
30   See Olson (1965).
31   See Frey (1984), p. 4.
32   Frey makes reference to Hirshman (1945). See Frey (1984), p. 4.
33   See Frey (1984), p. 4.
34   See Gilpin (1987), p. 8.
35   See Gilpin (1987), p. 8.
36   See Murphy and Tooze (1991), p. 1.
37   See Strange (1988), p. 12.
38   See Gilpin (1987), p. 11.
39   See Part 1, Chapter 1 of this book.
40   Milner (1993).
41   See Keohane (1984), p. 18.
42   See Keohane (1984), p. 22.
43   See Keohane (1984), p. 25.
44   See Keohane (1986), p. 7.
45   See Waltz (1979), pp. 67–73; see also Waltz (1986), p. 47.
46   See Krasner (1983).
47   Keohane (1986), p. 18.
48   Frieden explicitly makes reference to new domestic politics approaches to IPE in Frieden and Lake (2000), Introduction.
49   See, for example, Putnam (1988); see also Evans, Jacobson and Putnam (1993).
50   See Murphy, and Tooze (1991), Introduction, p. 6.
51   See Strange (1991), p. 33.
52   See Strange (1991), p. 34.
53   See Cox (1981); see also Gill (1991).
54   '... the system under which credit is created, allocated and put to use'. See Strange (1991), p. 35.
55   See Gill and Law (1988), p. 11: '... perspectives are not merely explanations of the global political economy, but are part of it'.
56   Though admittedly Susan Strange did not directly address the issues of European political economy, her thought has profoundly influenced the research and intellectual development of many scholars of the EU and many have adopted her theoretical framework to effect their analysis.
57   See Cox (1983).
58   See Gill (1991).
59   See, for example, Overbeek (2002); Cafruny and Ryner (2002); Bieler and Morton (2001).
60   See Gill (1991), p. 51.
61   Gramsci's historicism is characterised by three components: a) transience, i.e., history and social change are cumulative, endless, yet non repetitive processes; b) historical need, i.e., social interaction and political change take place within the 'limiti del possibile' (limits of the possible), limits that, however, are not fixed and immutable, but exist within the

dynamics of a given social structure; c) a dialectical variant of philosophical realism which identifies the intellectual process as a creative, practical, yet open-ended and continuous engagement to explain an intractable social reality, not an ordered, perfectly rational one. Moreover, this process is a dialectical one, and is thus part of the historical process: it does not stand outside it. See Gill (1991), p. 56.

62   See Frey (1984).
63   See Gill (1991), p. 59.
64   Overbeek (2002); Cafruny and Ryner (2002); Bieler and Morton (2002).
65   The role of ideas in international relations has been given emphasis in the contribution of Woods (1995); an application to European studies is to be found in Risse-Kappen (1996); and Risse (1998).
66   For example Hall (1992, 1989).
67   This argument is made by McNamara (1999); see also Risse (1998).
68   See Laursen (1995).
69   Here is again the concept of a 'global political economy' already argued for by Gill and Law (1988).
70   See Popper (1963), p. 342.
71   On a similar point see Keohane (1986), p. 5.
72   See Hargreaves-Heap and Hollis (1984), p. 7.

References

Baldwin, D.A. (1993), *Neorealism and Neoliberalism: The Contemporary Debate*, New York: Columbia University Press.

Becker, G.S. (1976), *The Economic Approach to Human Behaviour*, Chicago: University of Chicago Press.

Bieler, A. and Morton A.D. (eds) (2001), *Social Forces in the Making of the New Europe : The Restructuring of European Social Relations in the Global Political Economy*, London: Palgrave.

Blake, D.H. and Walters, R.S. (1976), *The Politics of Global Economic Relations*, Englewood Cliffs, NJ: Prentice Hall Inc.

Cafruny, A. and Ryner, M. (2002), *The Political Economy of the European Union*, New York: Rowman and Littlefield.

Cooper, R.N. (1972), 'Trade Policy is Foreign Policy', *Foreign Policy*, 9 (Winter 1972–73).

Cox, R.W. (1981), 'Social Forces, States and World Orders: Beyond International Relations Theory', *Millennium: Journal of International Studies*, 10 (2).

Cox, R.W. (1983), 'Gramsci, Hegemony and International Relations: An Essay in Method', *Millennium: Journal of International Studies*, 12 (2).

Crane, G.T. and Amawi, A. (1991), *The Theoretical Evolution of International Political Economy: A Reader*, New York and Oxford: Oxford University Press.

Evans, P.B., Jacobson, H.K. and Putnam, R.D. (1993), *Double-edged Diplomacy: International Bargaining and Domestic Policy*, Berkeley: University of California Press.

Frey, B.S. (1984), *International Political Economy*, Oxford: Basil Blackwell.

Frieden, J. and Lake, D. (2000), *International Political Economy: Perspectives on Global Power and Wealth*, New York: St Martin's Press.

Gill, S. and Law, D. (1988),*The Global Political Economy: Perspectives, Problems and Policies*, Brighton: Harvester-Wheatsheaf.

Gill, S. (1991), 'Historical Materialism, Gramsci and International Political Economy', in C.N. Murphy and R. Tooze (eds) (1991), *The New International Political Economy*, Boulder, CO: Lynne Rienner Publishers.

Gilpin, R. (1975), *US Power and Multinational Corporation*, New York: Basic Books.

Gilpin, R. (1987), *The Political Economy of International Relations*, Princeton, NJ: Princeton University Press.

Hall, P. (ed.) (1989), *The Political Power of Economic Ideas: Keynesianism across Nations*, Princeton, NJ: Princeton University Press.

Hall, P. (1992), 'The Movement from Keynesianism to Monetarism: Institutional Analysis and British Economic Policy in the 1970s', in S. Steinmo, K. Thelen and F. Longstreth (eds) (1992), *Structuring Politics: Historical Institutionalism in Comparative Analysis*, New York: Cambridge University Press.

Hargreaves-Heap, S. and Hollis, M. (1984), 'Bread and Circumstances: The Need for Political Economy', in D.K. Whynes (ed.), *What is Political Economy? Eight Perspectives*, Oxford: Basil Blackwell.

Hirshman, A. (1945), *National Power and the Structure of Foreign Trade*, Berkeley,CA: University of California Press, reprinted 1969.

Hix, S. (1996), 'CP, IR and the EU! A rejoinder to Hurrel and Menon', *West European Politics*, 19 (4).

Kegley, C.W. (1995), *Controversies in International Relations Theory: Realism and the Neo-liberal Challenge*, New York: St Martin's Press.

Keohane, R.O. (1984), *After Hegemony: Cooperation and Discord in the World Political Economy*, Princeton, NJ: Princeton University Press.

Keohane, R.O. (1986), *Neorealism and its Critics*, New York: Columbia University Press.

Kindleberger, C. (1970), *Power and Money*, New York: Basic Books.

Krasner, S.D. (1983), *International Regimes*, Ithaca: Cornell University Press.

Laursen, F. (1995), *The Political Economy of European Integration*, Amsterdam: Kluwer Law International.

List, F. (1885), 'Political and Cosmopolitical Economy', in G.T. Crane and A. Amawi (1991), *The Theoretical Evolution of International Political Economy: A Reader*, New York and Oxford: Oxford University Press.

McNamara, K. (1999), *The Currency of Ideas*, New York: Cornell University Press.

Murphy, C.N. and Tooze, R. (1991), *The New International Political Economy*, Boulder, CO: Lynne Rienner Publishers.

Olson, M. (1965), *The Logic of Collective Action*, Cambridge, MA: Harvard University Press.

Overbeek, H. (ed.) (2002), *The Political Economy of European Unemployment. European Integration and the Transnationalisation of the Employment Question*, London: Routledge.

Paarlberg, R.L. (1976), 'Domesticating Global Management', *Foreign Affairs*, Vol. 54 (3) (April).

Popper, K.R. (1963), *Conjectures and Refutations: the Growth of Scientific Knowledge*, London: Routledge.

Putnam, R. (1988), 'Diplomacy and Domestic Politics', *International Organization*, Vol. 42.

Risse-Kappen, T. (1996), 'Exploring the Nature of the Beast: International Relation Theory Meets the European Union', *Journal of Common Market Studies* (1996), pp. 53–80.

Risse, T. (1998), 'The Euro or not the Euro? The EMU and identity politics in the European Union', *Robert Shuman Centre Working Papers*, pp. 98–99.

Rosamond, B. (2000), *Theories of European Integration*, New York: St Martin's Press.

Spero, J.E. (1977), *The Politics of International Economic Relations*, London: George Allen and Unwin.

Strange, S. (1970), 'International Economics and International Relations: a Case of Mutual Neglect', *International Affairs*, London, Vol. 46 (2) (April).

Strange, S. (1988), *States and Markets*, London: Pinter.

Waltz, K. (1979), *Theory of World Politics*, Reading, MA: Addison Wesley.

Whynes, D.K. (1984), *What is Political Economy? Eight Perspectives*, Oxford: Basil Blackwell.

Woods, N. (1995), 'Economic Ideas and International Relations: Beyond Rational Neglect', *International Studies Quarterly* (June).

PART 1
THEORETICAL CONCERNS

Chapter 2

Mainstream Approaches to European Political Economy

This chapter provides an overview of mainstream theoretical approaches to European political economy. The overview includes three dimensions, as indicated in Figure 2.1.

First, the focus is on theories addressing European integration issues at the macro level of analysis, i.e., only theories addressing changes in the wider political/economic environment.[1] Second, an attempt is made to choose those theories seeking to analyse mainly the relations between politics and economics in the process of European integration. Finally, the last dimension is given by the necessity to integrate the international or systemic level of analysis with the domestic politics approaches.[2]

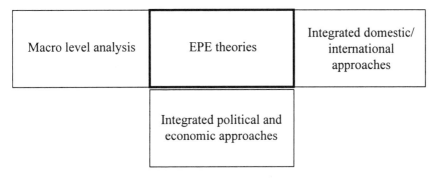

Figure 2.1   The realm of European political economy

To sum up, European political economy theories are defined here as those theories addressing history making events in the process of European economic integration from an integrated international/domestic politics perspective. Clearly, however, also other theories will be considered to the extent to which they contribute to the definition of the actual status of the debate within the discipline.

2.1   The Neofunctionalist/Intergovernmentalist Dichotomy

The theoretical mainstream debate of European political economy is characterised by the dichotomy between neofunctionalist and inter-governmentalist approaches.

2.1.1 Neofunctionalist Explanations

Neofunctionalist integration theory finds direct expression in the European Community since it was the community itself in its early stage that inspired the thesis in the form in which it was originally offered by E.B. Haas in his study *The Uniting of Europe*.[3]

The conceptual origins of the approach are identifiable in classical functionalist theories of international integration and cooperation.[4] The neofunctionalist interpretation of European integration lies within the institutionalist (later on neo-institutionalist school) of international relations/ international political economy for the emphasis attributed to the proactive role of international institutions in the process of international integration. This is in contrast with the classical realist/neorealist interpretations that attribute only to the nation state the role of 'agent' in the international arena.[5]

Neofunctionalist explanations of integration rest on the following conceptual propositions:

1   an ideal-type analysis of the process of integration leading to the creation of a supranational political community;
2   a liberal pluralist conception of society in which interest groups/political parties and other national actors progressively shift their loyalty from the national to the supranational level;
3   a conceptualisation of regional integration resting on the notion of spill-over.

The analysis will turn now to each of these propositions to clarify their conceptual content and their consequences for the process of European economic integration.

The ideal-type of the supranational political community The starting point of neofunctionalist analysis of European integration is the identification of the ideal-type of the 'political community', the approximation to which defines the success of the process of integration. In the words of Haas:

> Political Community ... is a condition in which specific groups and individuals show more loyalty to their central political institutions than, to any other political authority, in a specific period of time and in a definable geographic space.[6]

The political community as defined by Haas does not coincide with the notion of the federal State, though this may clearly be a possibility, since the constitutional form taken by the central institutions of the supranational political community is not particularly relevant. It may be a unitary, a federal, or even, in certain circumstances highlighted by the author, a confederate arrangement.[7]

Haas argues that the extent to which the process of European integration is leading to a supranational political community, can be measured by the degree to which a number of indicators of the community sentiment are met. Such indicators, as listed by Haas,[8] are:

1   the level of endorsement of supranational action by national interest groups and political parties in preference to action by their national government;
2   the level of supranational organisation of interest groups and political parties and the level of supranational definition of their interests;
3   the level of supranational coalition of interest groups and political parties on the basis of common ideologies and interests;
4   the level of creation of a supranational doctrine (supranationalism) from interest groups and political parties' conflict at the supranational level;
5   the level of recognition of a supranational rule of law by interest groups, political parties and governments;
6   the level of willingness by the government to overcome national interests in supranational negotiations.

In order to qualify as a genuine supranational political community all the above indicators must be positively established. Therefore, the scholar interested in assessing progress towards a supranational political community should utilise those indicators to reach appropriate conclusions.

Shift of loyalties of societal actors Haas' approach assumes that the assessment of the creation of a supranational political community relies not so much on 'objective criteria' but on the conduct of groups, individuals and governments. In particular, it requires their shift of loyalty from the central authorities of the nation state to the supranational political institutions. Indeed, the definition of 'political integration' given by neofunctionalists is precisely that of a process in the course of which this shift of loyalties gradually takes place, or, in the words of Haas:

> Political integration is the process whereby political actors in several distinct national settings are persuaded to shift their loyalties, expectations and political activities toward a new centre, whose institutions possess or demand jurisdiction over the pre-existing national states.[9]

Also in the case of the process of political integration neofunctionalists identify a set of specific indicators, each of which corresponds to a different stage of development toward the end of political community.

1   The first stage is the assessment of the degree of commitment of key interest groups, political parties and governments to integration and the assessment of their motivations.
2   The second stage is the assessment of the degree to which political actors shift their demands from the national to the supranational level once new central institutions are established.
3   The third stage is the assessment of the degree to which the conditions of the political community have been fulfilled.

What is important, however, for the inclusion of neofunctionalism amongst the theories of European political economy, is the recognition by Haas of the primacy of the process of economic integration in Europe over the process of political integration. Economic integration in Europe precedes political integration, though the level of economic success achieved does not necessarily correspond to political success.[10]

A conceptualisation of regional integration resting on the notion of spill-overs
In order to clarify the role of economic integration in the process of European integration it is necessary to specify the dynamics of the integration process from the neofunctionalist perspective. How does integration take place?

The neofunctionalist approach to integration is based on the notion of spill-overs, that is, the assertion that integration in one issue area will reveal functional linkages to other issue areas. As a result, the desire to obtain the full benefits of integration in the first area would lead to pressures for integration in a second linked area.

Haas identifies two sorts of spill-overs. The first, functional spill-over, is economic and occurs when incomplete integration undermines the possibility of achieving all the benefits of the existing policies, both in the areas that are already integrated and in related sectors of economy, thus automatically creating the need for further cooperation among the EC countries. The second, political spill-over is linked to the fundamental role of existing supranational institutions in giving impetus to a self-reinforcing process of institution building.

Each of these spill-overs deepens and widens integration by working through interest groups pressure, public opinion, elite socialisation, or other domestic actors and processes. All the original states of the European Community were advanced, industrial, pluralist democracies with highly developed party organisations, and with pressure groups, representing almost every conceivable sphere of activity and interest which might exert an influence upon governments. These, argued Haas, were the background conditions most favourable to the strategy of integration by spill-overs, that is, by concrete economic achievements which build up *de facto* linkages of one national political and economic system with another.

Pressure groups and political parties are, he claims, 'singled out as significant carriers of values and ideologies whose opposition, identity or convergence determines the success or failure of a transnational ideology'.[11] Moreover, in Haas' conception interest groups are more important than parties: they are the dynamic element of political process in advanced pluralist democracies, and this is especially true of the groups which operate in the economic sector. Haas argues that 'almost universally economic groups seem to be in the forefront of those who clamour for the recognition of common needs'.[12]

Moreover, groups may or may not be ideologically oriented. Groups with long-range expectations, for example, are likely to possess well-developed bodies of doctrine, whose implementation is closely associated with the positions taken toward further integration. However, those who entertain short range expectations, whether negative or positive, are less likely to be sharply motivated by ideology and are commonly driven by their immediate needs.[13]

Although the demands for task-expansion expressed by pressure groups and parties would be felt originally at the national level, as regional and central institutions are given more power and functions in response to pressures, the demands, the expectations, and the loyalties of groups and parties will gradually shift to the new centre of decision-making. Supranational institutions will then respond and thereby become the driving force or motor of community development.

Summing up, on the one hand national political actors will be inevitably driven to further integration by the existence of spill-overs stemming from already established supranational policies and institutions, while on the other hand, supranational institutions serve to exploit the political expectations of groups to increase supranationalism.

The evolution of neofunctionalism The central dependent variable in Haas theory was the hypothesised evolution of new supranational institutions, rather than specific policy developments, and the intellectual heirs of his theory, such as Nye and Keohane, were much more interested in the study of international interdependence and transnationalism than in the analysis of the role and impact of domestic factors which slipped more and more out of focus.[14]

In fact, the concept of spill-over was undermined by the failure of the European integration to advance steadily and by the variation in integration across issues, time periods, or countries.[15] Neofunctionalist theorists, then, provided for a revision of the approach.[16]

Lindberg, in particular, graphically represented the ups and downs of the process of European integration until the beginning of the 1970s, along a gradually ascending slope, to signify that, even though its pulse was irregular, the Community was progressing towards an ever closer union.[17] Flux and stress, contradiction and crisis were considered as basic conditions of the process of integration. Quoting the author:

> The growth of the Community implies change, and change is usually attended by stress and conflict ... We would go so far as to argue that when there are no more crises the system will have ceased to grow.[18]

Late neofunctionalists even foreshadowed the possibility of the collapse of the integration process:

> It cannot be at all excluded that too much stress and too many crises will overload the system ability to cope with them. Under such circumstances the very real advantages of going on with integration might be overwhelmed by the manifest risks of losing control of domestic and foreign policy choices.[19]

This, of course, put under discussion the whole inherently expansive logic of spill-overs which had characterised earlier versions of neofunctionalism, and required a new formulation of the dynamics of Community integration and change, one that provided also for the possibility of failure and collapse.

Whereas Haas and Schmitter focused on the universalisation of the neofunctionalist integration model by proposing a study on the general circumstances under which efforts at economic union would lead to political integration,[20] Lindberg proposed a new neofunctionalist basic model of system change in the European Community.[21]

The idea of functionalist spill-overs was not abandoned, but no more assumptions were made as to 'the inevitability or automaticity of the direction of actor response to a perceived functional relationship'.[22] On the contrary the notion of automaticity was combined with other mechanisms of coalition formation to increase integration. Those ranged from log-rolling and side payments, actor socialisation and feedback mechanisms.[23]

Finally, the outcomes of the Community dynamics included not only further steps towards integration (what Lindberg comes to define as *forward linkages*) but also situations of stalemate (*equilibrium*), failure to integrate after the achievement of an agreement (output failure), withdrawal from already taken obligations (*spill-back*) and treaty renegotiations (*system transformations*).

Conclusions: neofunctionalism as a theory of European political economy
Neofunctionalism went through a substantial process of transformation from its original formulation by Ernst Haas, a process of transformation, which is somehow related to the ups and downs of the process of European integration itself. Neofunctionalism is indeed the 'one' theory whose origins and developments are mostly entangled with the building of supranational institutions and the implementation of common European policies. This is the result both of the original connection of its formulation with the birth of the European integration process and of its conceptual content which relies on the propulsive role played by supranational institutions themselves.

Despite the attempts made by neofunctionalists to adapt their claims to the failure of Europe to proceed steadily and firmly towards unity,[24] however, this school of thought lost much of its appeal as a macro-theory of integration. Even those who originally proposed it have now turned to different theoretical paradigms.[25]

On the one hand, neofunctionalism has been limited in its scope and some of its claims have been applied at a lower level of analysis, to explain, for example, institutional change or European policy-making. This is the case of theories stressing the role of political entrepreneurs in supranational policy-making or theories of policy networks,[26] particularly those underlying the role of epistemic communities[27] or, in general, technocratic networks, in giving impulse to further integration.

On the other hand, as underlined above, the neo-institutionalist heirs of neofunctionalists, like Keohane and Nye, have turned away from the

Table 2.1   Lindberg's alternative output models

Obligations	Outcomes		
	Fulfilment	*Retraction*	*Extension*
To participate in a joint decision-making process (i.e., to make new policy)	Forward linkage model	Output failure model	Systems transformation
To implement agreements and the routine enforcement of specific rules (i.e., to administer a previously agreed area of joint activity)	Spill-back model	Equilibrium model models	

Source: Lindberg and Scheingold (1970), p. 136.

analysis of the process of regionalisation, to focus on interdependence at the transnational level.[28]

Finally, part of the decline of neofunctionalism as a grand-theory is explained by the parallel rise of intergovernmentalism as 'the' theoretical paradigm capable of addressing all the main issues of European political economy.

Before turning to the analysis of intergovernmentalism, however, it is worth summarising the main characteristics of neofunctionalism, which put this theory firmly within the realm of European political economy theories.

First, in its original formulation and in many of its later adaptations, neofunctionalism is a theory that directly addresses the macro-level of the integration process, asking questions about the nature of integration, its dynamics and mechanisms, the goals of the process and the consequences for the nation states and its societal components. It is therefore, almost by definition, a macro-theory.

Secondly, neofunctionalism belongs to the liberal tradition and relies on a pluralist conception of society in which interest groups and political parties are singled out as substantial carriers of values and needs. Moreover, their demands are ultimately the motor of further integration through the mechanism of spill-overs. It is true that neofunctionalists focused their analysis more on the functioning of supranational institutions than on domestic dynamics, but the domestic level was clearly conceptualised and its role in the whole process of integration was substantially elaborated.

Finally, and this is most important, neofunctionalists attributed a primary role to economic integration and to the analysis of economic interests and interest groups. Not only are economics and politics inextricably linked in neofunctionalist accounts, but economics precedes politics; economic 'interdependence' amongst European states precedes their decision to move towards further political cooperation, at least from a purely chronological point of view. The analysis is thus, undoubtedly, a political economy one.

Let us now move on to the other macro-theory of European political economy to investigate its main tenets and its position within the discipline.

2.1.2 *Intergovernmentalist Explanations*

The intergovernmentalist approach to European economic integration finds its intellectual origins in realist theories of international relations. It postulates that nation states dominate EC politics and that outcomes directly reflect the interests and relative power of the member states.

It is however important to note that, contrary to traditional realist accounts of world politics, intergovernmentalists put the emphasis on 'low politics' and, in particular on the economic interests pursued by nation states in the international/regional arena as opposed to geopolitical considerations.[29] Indeed, realist explanations of international economic cooperation would assume that security or geopolitical strategic considerations dominate state's economic choices.[30] On the contrary, intergovernmentalists put the emphasis on specific economic interests to account for state's preferences in foreign economic policy. In this respect their analysis resembles IR neorealist approaches.[31]

Thus intergovernmentalist theory seeks to analyse the process of European economic integration as the result of strategies pursued by rational governments acting on the basis of their preferences and power, assuming that national preferences in foreign economic policies are dictated by specific economic interests.

Finally, the latest versions of intergovernmentalism introduce an explicit theory of domestic politics to account for the set of economic interests states choose to pursue in international arena as well as an explicit theory of bargaining in international negotiations.

Institutional intergovernmentalism   Andrew Moravcsik in his article 'Negotiating the Single European Act', proposes an intergovernmental institutional approach to European economic integration.[32]

The author demonstrates empirically that the primary source of integration lies in the interests of the states themselves and in the relative power each brings to Brussels, although he also recognises the important role played by supranational institutions in cementing existing interstate bargaining as the foundation for renewed integration.

Intergovernmental institutionalism is based on three principles:

1   intergovernmentalism;
2   lowest common denominator bargaining;
3   strict limits on future transfer of sovereignty.

First of all, claims Moravcsik, from its inception the EC has been based on interstate bargaining between its leading member states acting according to their policy preferences.

Secondly, and this is the notion of the lowest common denominator bargaining, without a 'European hegemon' capable of providing universal incentives or threats to promote regime formation and without a widespread use of linkages and log-rolling, the bargains struck in the EC reflect the relative power positions of the member states. The small states' interests are satisfied through side payments and bargaining tends to converge toward the lowest common denominator of large states' interests. Given this assumption, the only tool that can compel a state to accept an outcome on a major issue when it prefers the status quo is the threat of exclusion: if two major states can isolate the third and credibly threaten it with exclusion, and if such exclusion undermines the substantive interests of the excluded state, then the coercive threat may allow the achievement of an agreement at a level of integration above the lowest common denominator.

Finally, protection of sovereignty implies that policy-makers safeguard their countries against the future erosion of sovereignty by demanding the unanimous consent of regime members to sovereignty related reforms and that they avoid granting open-ended authority to central institutions that might infringe on their sovereignty, preferring instead to work through intergovernmental institutions, such as the Council of Ministers.

As the author himself claims,[33] intergovernmental institutionalism is founded on realist assumptions: states are the principal actors of the international system; interstate bargains reflect national interests and relative power; international regimes shape interstate politics by providing a common framework that reduces the uncertainty and transaction costs of interstate interactions.

Liberal intergovernmentalism   More recently, Moravcsik has built on his preceding institutional intergovernmentalist approach to create a new 'liberal intergovernmentalism', which refines the theory of interstate bargaining and institutional compliance and adds an explicit theory of national preference formation grounded in liberal theories of international interdependence.[34]

At the core of liberal intergovernmentalism are three essential elements:

1   the assumption of rational state behaviour;
2   a liberal theory of national preference formation;
3   an intergovernmentalist analysis of interstate negotiation.

As a starting point, state action at any particular moment is assumed to be minimally rational, that is, to be purposively directed toward the achievement of a set of consistently ordered goals or objectives.

So far, nothing has changed from the previous, neorealist version of his theory, but this new approach adopted by Moravcsik departs decisively from the preceding one because it no longer takes domestic preferences as given. On the contrary, following liberal theories of international relations, the foreign policy goals of national governments are viewed as varying in response to shifting pressures from domestic conflicting socioeconomic groups whose preferences are aggregated through political institutions. Thus, the model of rational state behaviour, on the basis of domestically constrained preferences, implies that international conflict and cooperation can be modelled as a process that takes place in two successive stages: governments first define a set of interests, then bargain among themselves in an effort to realise those interests. As noted above, those interests are assumed to be of an economic nature.

This shift towards a two-level approach to the study of international relations is completed by Moravcsik in his introduction to Evans, Jacobson and Putnam's *Double-edged Diplomacy: International Bargaining and Domestic Politics*[35] where the author acknowledges that the question facing international relation theorists today is no longer whether to combine domestic and international explanations into a theory of double-edged diplomacy, but how best to do it.

The solution to this problem, is, in turn sought by the author in a further contribution to this debate to which we turn in the following section.

A rationalist framework of international cooperation An integrated domestic/international theorisation of European integration from an intergovernmentalist point of view is contained in Moravcsik's *The Choice for Europe*. The central argument of the book is that European integration can be best conceptualised as:

> ... a series of rational choices made by national leaders. These choices responded to constraints and opportunities stemming from the economic interests of powerful domestic constituents, the relative power of each state in the international system, and the role of international institutions in bolstering the credibility of interstate commitments.[36]

Therefore, the process of European integration needs to be tackled within a *rationalist framework of international cooperation*, which implies the division of major EC negotiations into three stages. These start from the domestic level and move to the international level passing through the analysis of international negotiations as the meeting point between the national and the supranational arenas. The three stages, as devised by the author, are the following:

Stage 1: national preference formation;
Stage 2: interstate bargaining;
Stage 3: the choice to delegate sovereignty to international institutions.

In the first stage states formulate a specific set of policy preferences, by preferences meaning not only policy goals but also a set of underlying national objectives independent of the international system. In the second stage, states bargain with the other states in the international system to maximise their chances of achieving their preferences. In the third stage, and on the basis of the outcomes of international negotiations, states decide whether or not to delegate sovereignty on that particular issue to an international institution.

Within this macro-level *framework*,[37] as opposed to *theory* or *model*, it is possible to explain each stage in the EC negotiations using different *meso-theories*. In particular, the first stage needs theories of domestic politics able to explain why states decide to push at the international level certain preferences and not others. After having discarded theories attributing explanatory primacy to geopolitical interests, Moravcsik chooses to use theories stressing the primacy of economic interests in defining national preferences, i.e., political economy theories.[38]

In terms of explaining the outcomes of interstate bargaining processes, in Moravcsik's opinion, the theoretical framework more suitable is represented by game theoretical approaches, ranging from Putnam's two-level game to more sophisticated ones.[39]

Finally, according to the author, the explanation for the governments' choice to pool and delegate sovereignty should be sought not so much in theories stressing the importance of ideology, as with federalist theories, or the necessity to improve technocratic management, but in theories underlining the need to obtain a credible commitment by the other nation states.

Summing up, according to this interpretation, states act in international negotiations as rational actors to further the economic interests of powerful domestic groups and accept international institutional constraints to ensure compliance with the agreement by the other nation states.

Of course this tripartite framework is not theoretically neutral. It embodies important assumptions that constrain possible explanations. In the words of the author:

> The framework assumes above all that the primary political instrument by which individuals and groups in civil society seek to influence international negotiations is the nation state which acts externally as a unitary and rational actor on behalf of its constituents.[40]

Table 2.2   International cooperation: a rationalist framework

Stages of negotiations	1 National preference formation	2 Interstate bargaining	3 Institutional choice
Basic question to answer	What is the source of underlying national preferences?	Given national preferences, what explains the efficiency and distributional outcomes of interstate bargaining?	Given substantive agreement, what explains the transfer of sovereignty to international institutions?
Alternative theoretical approaches to answer the basic question (meso–theories)	Economic interests or geopolitical interests?	Asymmetrical interdependence or supranational entrepreneurship?	Federalist ideology or centralised technocratic management or more credible commitment?
Moravcsik's preferred explanation	Economic interests	Asymmetrical interdependence	More credible commitment
Observed outcome at each stage	Underlying national preferences $\longrightarrow$	Agreements on substance $\longrightarrow$	Choice to delegate or pool decision-making in international institutions

Source: Derived from Moravcsik (1998), p. 24.

Therefore, this framework is based on the two strong assumptions that the states are *unitary*, i.e., act in the international context with a single voice, and *rational*, i.e., in international negotiations they seek to maximise the achievement of a ranked set of preferences. Both assumptions, as we will see in Chapter 3, are strongly criticised by critical theorists.

Conclusions: intergovernmentalism as a theory of European political economy
In contrast to neofunctionalism, the definition of intergovernmentalism as a theory of Political Economy is explicit,[41] particularly in its latest version, and this is what distinguishes the approach from early realist interpretations of the process of European integration.[42] It is indeed clear in Moravcsik's conceptualisation of Europe that the interests member states bring to Brussels are of an economic nature and therefore the process of European integration responds to economic interests and not to geopolitical or ideological considerations.

Furthermore, similar economic interests are not taken for granted, but derive from the competition at the domestic level amongst the different societal groups, in a typical pluralist conception of society. Of course, different societal groups are mobilised in a different way according to the issues at stake. Therefore the theories of domestic politics necessary to reconstruct the process of states' preferences formation differ according to the issues at stake.

However, the domestic level of analysis is indispensable to understand the positions adopted by the states in international negotiations. Moreover, similar domestic considerations actually represent the very reason why states decide to engage in an international bargaining process in the first place. From this point of view, intergovernmentalism is indeed a theory trying to integrate the domestic level of analysis with the international one, to the extent that Moravcsik's rational framework include in the three stages to reach an international cooperation agreement the analysis of the domestic origins of states' preferences. As Chapter 3 shows, critical theorists ask what extent states interests derive exclusively from a domestic process of preferences formation, thus completely overlooking the transnational dimension. It is also unclear why certain groups interests prevail over the others, unless a theory explicitly tackling the issue of power relations is introduced in the analysis.

Finally, intergovernmentalism, although lately defined as a 'framework of analysis', is addressing the 'macro' events of the process of European integration, focusing on its major turning point with special attention to the most important rounds of negotiations, as stated by Moravcsik, from

'Messina to Maastricht'. It is therefore classifiable within the so-called 'macro' approaches.

2.1.3 A Synthesis Approach between Neofunctionalism and Intergovernmentalism

Stone and Sandholtz have proposed an interesting criticism of the intergovernmentalist approach from within the framework of mainstream theory.[43] They point out three major deficiencies of the model. The first is that some EU policy-making does not resemble interstate bargaining. The second is that the two-level metaphor cannot fully account for supranational institutions that exercise an autonomous influence on EU policy-making, such as the Commission or the Court of Justice. The third is that the two-level game approach pays too little attention to the emergence of transnational society.

Instead they propose a continuum between the two poles of the intergovernmentalist approach and the supranational one in the EU. They argue that, unlike most regimes, which tend to organise interstate cooperation in one or few closely related sectors, the EU possesses differing degrees of competence across a diverse range of policy areas.

The continuum is capable of situating these policy sectors comparatively, thus, policy sector A may be located at a two level politics while policy sector B may, on the contrary, exhibit strong features of supranationalism.

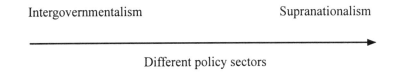

Figure 2.2   Continuum between intergovernmentalism and supranationalism

Such an approach is a clear compromise solution that seeks to overcome the dichotomy between intergovernmentalism and supranationalism ecumenically, but without any elaboration of a real alternative. It is however worth mentioning before turning to the analysis of other attempts to integrate the domestic with the international level of analysis.

2.2 Integrated Domestic/International Models

2.2.1 From an Intergovernmentalist Point of View: Putnam's Two-level Game Approach

According to intergovernmentalists, one of the most useful attempts to find an integrated domestic-international politics model has been proposed by Robert Putnam in his article 'Diplomacy and Domestic Politics'[44] in which, having defined a new conceptual framework applicable to all kinds of issues including foreign economic policy ones, he tries to answer the questions 'when' and 'how' domestic politics and international relations become entangled.

Putnam's approach to the problem rests on the metaphor of the two-level game for domestic-international relations: at a national level, domestic groups pursue their interests by pressuring the governments to adopt favourable policies, and politicians seek power by constructing coalitions among these groups; at the international level, national governments seek to maximise their own ability to satisfy domestic pressures, while minimising the adverse consequences of foreign developments. Since each national political leader appears at both game boards, international relation scholars can ignore neither of the two games.

Formal analysis of any game, however, requires well-defined rules, choices, payoffs, players and information. Therefore Putnam's effort is to define an analytic framework for two-level games that can motivate further empirical research.

It is convenient, analytically, to break down the process into two stages: first, the bargaining between the negotiators leading to an international agreement, called by the author 'Level I'; second, the separate discussions within each group of constituents about whether to ratify an agreement, called 'Level II'.

Putnam defines the 'win-set' for a given Level II constituency as the set of all possible Level I agreements that would 'win', that is, gain the necessary majority among the constituents. In his opinion, the contours of the Level II win-set are very important for understanding Level I agreements for two quite different reasons. First, larger win-sets make Level I agreements more likely, *ceteris paribus*, in other words, the greater the domestic support for an international agreement, the more likely is its success and, in turn, the smaller the win-set, the greater the risk of involuntary defection.[45]

The second reason why the win-set size is important is that the relative size of the respective Level II win-sets will affect the distribution of joint gains from the international bargain: the larger the perceived win-set of a negotiator, the more he can be 'pushed around'[46] by the other Level I negotiators. Conversely, in this respect, a small domestic win-set can be a bargaining advantage, because the absence of domestic consensus to an agreement implies more bargaining power in the negotiation phase. Thus the win-set is double edged: on one hand, the larger the win-set, the easier it is to implement at a domestic level; on the other hand, the larger the win-set, the lower the bargaining power during the negotiations phase.

In order to determine the size of the win-set, three sets of factors are especially important: Level II preferences and coalitions; Level II institutions; Level I negotiator strategies.

First of all, the size of the win-set depends on the distribution of power, preferences, and possible coalitions among Level II constituents. Thus, any testable two-level theory of international negotiations must be rooted in a theory of domestic politics, that is, a theory about the power and preferences of the major domestic actors.

The national interest will be the sum of the preferences of different interest groups as weighted by their access to policy-making institutions. Moreover, because these societal groups play such a central role, they can limit the international strategies available to a state and policy-makers may depend heavily on these groups to negotiate the agreements since their preferences will be the key to implementing their terms and, thus, not incurring in an 'involuntary defection'.[47]

Finally, in Putnam's model the size of the win-set depends also on the strategies of the level one chief negotiator who is the only formal link between Level I and Level II. Despite the fact that the policy-maker is constrained by the pressures of the domestic constituents on one side and by the international environment on the other side, in the model analysed, the chief negotiator is assumed to have his own independent policy view and preferences which may diverge from those of his constituents. The motives of the chief negotiator include enhancing his standing in the Level II game by increasing his political resources or minimising potential losses as well as shifting the balance of power at Level II in favour of domestic policies that he prefers and pursuing his own conception of the national interest in the international context. This expanded conception of the role of the chief negotiator implies, according to the author, that he has, in effect, a veto over possible agreements.

As a matter of fact, Putnam's emphasis on the special responsibilities of central executives is a point of affinity between the two-level game model and the state-centric literature even though his approach highlights several significant features of the links between international and domestic politics.

Moreover, the idea that the policy-maker is ultimately responsible for the decision-making at both the national and the international level, inserts this approach amongst the mainstream intergovernmentalist tradition. Below attention is turned to a more institutionalist approach to finding a convincing synthesis between the domestic and the international level of analysis.

2.2.2 An Institutionalist Interpretation of the Integrated Domestic/ International Approach

Starting from the criticism of the assumption of anarchy in international political economy, Helen Milner has identified two theoretical reasons for the neglect of domestic policy in the recent US debate: one is the centrality of anarchy as the condition for differentiating between domestic and international politics, the other is the use of game theory with its assumption of unitary, rational actors.[48] This almost exclusively international focus of the systemic approaches is problematic because it rests upon a series of unexamined assumptions about domestic politics that are crucial to the result.

Important assumptions are made mainly about three areas: the determination of the pay-off structures, or national interests of states, the strategies available to states to alter systemic conditions, and the capacity of states to ratify and implement cooperative arrangements.

Considerations of domestic politics help to solve the problem of unfounded assumptions on these areas in the following three important respects. First, a domestic politics approach allows us to determine how preferences are aggregated and national interests defined since, whether the focus is on absolute gains or on relative gains, a theory of domestic politics is the only means to calculate gains and losses and thus answer the basic IPE questions. Second, an analysis of the domestic situation can help explain the strategies that states adopt to realise their goals. It is true that strategies may be suggested by a state's structural position in the international environment, but the nature of its political system, bureaucratic politics, the influence of special interest and pressure groups and, in some issues, even public opinion may ultimately determine which strategies states can pursue internationally. Third, internationally agreed terms must always be enforced internally to become effective.

Thus, since domestic ratification is essential, when negotiating internationally, policy-makers must always anticipate domestic reactions: international agreements can always be reached, but they can only be implemented if the domestic actors concur. For these reasons domestic politics are essential in order to understand international cooperation and international economic cooperation in particular.

The following section provides an account of some of the most well-known domestic politics approaches to foreign policy-making, foreign economic policy-making, European integration and European economic integration.

2.3 Inside-out/Domestic Politics Approaches

2.3.1 Domestic Determinants of Foreign Politics

One of the first US scholars to draw attention to this area and to claim that domestic forces of foreign policy are no less crucial to its content and conduct than are the international situations towards which it is directed, was James Rosenau. His main aim was to back up such conviction conceptually and empirically.[49]

In order to understand the relationship between domestic and international politics, the author collected insights from many disciplines, ranging from sociology to psychology, from economics to political science, and used a variety of analytic techniques. However, the unifying factor of his effort was represented by the adoption of an original approach resting on the idea of the 'issue area', that is, the idea of deriving both the distinguishing characteristics and the boundaries of a set of activities from the values that are being sought or contested, rather than from the nature of the units to which the actors belong.[50] In this way Rosenau sought to overcome the traditional distinction between systemic and unit level analysis, at least for certain kinds of issue areas.

For Rosenau, the functioning of the political system depends on the nature of the issues at stake and therein lies an important conceptual challenge: how to cope with issue generated differences without permitting their multitude to overwhelm analysis and reduce it to a fragmented and 'idiographic' description. The solution is found in the elaboration of a typology of issue areas, of categories of issues that affect the political process in sufficiently similar ways to justify their being clustered together. In fact, claims Rosenau, if the entire range of issues that are processed by a political system could be classified into a manageable number of mutually exclusive areas, with each area distinguished by the political dynamics it generates, then it would be possible to analyse the political process without being paralysed by idiographic description.

However, not much would be achieved if 'issue area' came to mean more or less what is conventionally designated as an 'issue', namely 'any conflict over values or interests among identifiable individuals or groups'.[51] Instead, a typology of issue areas must be seen as comprised of certain kinds of actors whose values and interests are such that they can be expected to engage in certain kinds of behaviour when issues are activated in that area. It follows that several aspects of the political process can be connected to the nature of the issues at stake.

The problem is, at this point, to determine whether domestic policy issues are different from foreign policy ones, in other words, to assess whether foreign policy is a different universe of issues, and if it is, whether it is a unified world or one divisible into several distinctive areas. Rosenau's theoretical effort consists precisely in studying the foreign-domestic distinction in a detailed and systematic way. By 'foreign policy as an issue area' the author comes to mean, after a very thorough analysis, all the controversies within society that, at any moment in time, are being posed over the way in which the society is attempting to maintain or alter its external environment. More specifically, it is the attempt to exercise control over the external environment that constitutes 'foreign policy' whereas the controversies engendered by the attempt represent the 'issue area'.[52] Rosenau's focus, thus, is on national political systems and not on international systems. He is interested in the process through which national systems undertake to cope with their external environment, and not in the process, which is transmitted in the environment itself.

Summing up his analysis, it seems clear that the author has developed an affirmative answer to his original question of whether foreign and domestic areas are distinguishable from each other. In terms of the motives, roles and interaction sequences they activate, foreign and domestic issues do seem to differ in significant ways.[53] There does remain, however, the question of whether or not the boundaries between foreign and domestic areas are rigid. The answer seems clear to the author: there are foreign policy issues that develop themselves in ways typical of the domestic rather than the foreign area, given the definition of domestic issues as those that involve the allocation of scarce resources or the arrangement of historic relationships.

The crucial point of this synthesising formulation is that some foreign policy issues unfold in a similar way to domestic policy ones because they imply, for a variety of reasons, the utilisation of a society's personnel and wealth. That is to say that certain efforts to allocate resources or rearrange relationships in the external environment cannot be carried out without domestic resources or relationships also undergoing change. In short, although most foreign policy issues may not involve the diversion of substantial resources from the internal to the external environment, some do and these are the ones that exhibit the characteristics of the domestic issues and should be processed like them. The manner of analysing an issue is thus a function of the degree to which a society's resources or relationships are affected.

Indeed, in order to account for the exceptional issues that transgress the boundaries between the areas one can pose a conclusion in terms of a single over-all hypothesis: the more an issue encompasses a society's resources and relationships, the more it will be drawn into society's domestic political system and the less it will be processed through the society's foreign political system.

2.3.2 Domestic Institutionalism and Foreign Economic Policy

Peter Katzenstein has also studied the existence of an entanglement between domestic politics and foreign economic policy.[54] His volume *Between Power and Plenty* analyses how the domestic structures of advanced industrial states shape political strategies in the international political economy resting on the assumption that the domestic structure of the nation state is a critical intervening variable without which the interrelation between international interdependence and political structure cannot be understood. According to Katzenstein, differences in the domestic structures of the advanced industrial states and the international context in which they are situated have dictated the adoption of different strategies of foreign economic policy. The rationale of each strategy is to establish a basic compatibility between domestic and international policy objectives but, since the domestic structures in the industrial states differ in important ways, so do the strategies of foreign economic policy that these states pursue.

Given this starting premise, namely that the main purpose of all strategies of foreign economic policy is to make domestic politics compatible with the international political economy, Katzenstein, unlike Rosenau, puts little value on a clear-cut distinction between domestic and foreign politics. He does not join the debate over whether domestic politics really determine international economic relations or the reverse. The two processes are clearly interlinked and thus both must be analysed in order to render international phenomena intelligible.

Moreover, this reorientation of international political economy towards a more integrated foreign-domestic politics approach is urged by the process of accelerating change in the international security and economic systems connected to the decline of the US hegemonic position in world politics. In fact, argues Katzenstein, although international and domestic factors have been closely intertwined in the historical evolution of the international political economy since the middle of the nineteenth century, the relative weight of domestic structures in the shaping of foreign economic policy increased in periods of hegemonic decline. The gradual shift from security issues to economic concerns during the 1970s reinforced this process.[55]

With respect to the theoretical orientation of the book which shapes both the problems in foreign economic policy worth explaining (the dependent variables) and the political and economic forces operating at home and abroad which make these problems intelligible (the independent variables), Katzenstein tries to overcome the dualism the 'societal' and the 'State-centric' interpretations of foreign economic policy. Thus he recognises the importance of political and economic interest groups in the formulation and implementation of policy, but also inserts State's autonomy in decision-making as a key variable of the analysis.

His comparative approach is indebted to that tradition of political research which postulates the State as a central actor in all governing coalitions and a critical institution in all policy networks.[56] It is true that State strength and power differ from country to country and vary according to whether one analyses the definition of objectives or the implementation of foreign economic policy, but the autonomy of the State remains a central assumption which cannot be overlooked.

It is exactly this identification of State-strength as a key variable of interests which is criticised by many scholars interested in an integrated domestic-foreign policy approach. Given the difficulties of measuring State-strength, claims Putnam,[57] for example, this approach risks tautology while efforts to locate individual countries on this ambiguous continuum have proved problematic.[58] Moreover, because State structures vary little from issue to issue and from year to year, such explanations are ill suited to account for differences across issues and across time. A more adequate account of the domestic determinants of foreign economic policy and international relations must stress 'politics': parties, social classes, interest groups (both economic and non economic), legislators and even public opinion and elections, not simply executive officials and institutional arrangements.[59]

2.3.3 A Domestic Politics Approach to European Integration

Moving out of US academic circles toward the European debate over the issue of European integration it is necessary to give account of the attempt made by Simon Bulmer to transfer Katzenstein's integrated international-domestic politics approach from foreign economic policy issues to the problems of European policy-making.[60] In fact, already in the early 1980s, Simon Bulmer proposed a domestic politics approach to the study of European integration based on five fundamental assumptions.

First, the national polity is the basic unit in the European Community since it is the level at which governments, interest groups, parliamentary bodies and political parties derive their legitimacy and their power. Second, each national polity has a different set of social and economic conditions that shapes its national interest and policy content. Third, European policy only represents one facet of a national polity's activity and, therefore, it is somewhat artificial to separate a member state's European policy from the rest of its domestic behaviour. Fourth, although in formal terms the national governments hold a key position at the junction of national politics and community politics, whether governments are really as powerful as the intergovernmentalists claim can only be determined by specific examination. Finally, the concept of 'policy style', defined as 'the interaction between (a) the government's approach to policy-making and (b) the relationship between government and other domestic actors in the policy process', is the analytic device for structuring the examination of a member state's behaviour in the EC given the author's underlying assumption that it is possible to identify whether a member state has a coherent, single 'policy style' in connection with the disparate areas of the EC activity.

2.3.4 A Domestic Politics Approach to Foreign Economic Policy-making: The Case of Exchange Rate Regimes

Jeffry Frieden focuses on the role of national economic sectors interests and preferences in shaping foreign economic policy-making and, in particular, exchange rate agreements and regimes.[61]

According to Frieden, two interrelated dimensions of policy choice are especially important in an environment of increasing capital mobility that has characterised the European Community over the last twenty years:[62] the degree of exchange rate flexibility and the level of the exchange rate itself. With regard to the first dimension, in a Mundell-Fleming world[63] with full capital mobility, a country faces something of a trade-off between exchange rate stability and monetary policy autonomy.[64] the more the country's exchange rate is held constant, the less its monetary policy can deviate from that of the rest of the world. In fact, although without capital mobility, national authorities can adopt and sustain macroeconomic policies that differ from the rest of the world and can hold their exchange rates constant, with mobile capital the attempt will be contravened by financial flows.[65]

Thus, while some actors will favour a low degree of exchange rate flexibility, such as a system of pegged but adjustable exchange rates as the European Monetary System or fixed rate regime as the European Monetary Union despite the loss of monetary policy autonomy, others will be willing to accept a higher degree of exchange rate flexibility, ranging from a freely floating rate solution to a two-tier EMU, in exchange for policy-making autonomy. With respect to the second dimension, which is the preferred level of exchange rates itself, some fixing of exchange rate is assumed, as in the EMS before the crisis. However, some actors will prefer a high, more appreciated, exchange rate, while others will prefer a low, more depreciated, one. The first dimension involves the desired degree of exchange rate flexibility, which can be presented, in a simplified way, as whether the rate should be fixed or flexible and is relevant for the negotiating phase of any exchange rate arrangement.

Fixing the rate in a world of mobile capital implies foregoing national monetary policy autonomy, at least to a certain extent, in favour of greater certainty about the value of the currency. In other words, it gives priority to a stable exchange rate over the ability of national policy to affect domestic macroeconomic conditions.

This is especially attractive to two groups of actors whose economic activities directly involve international trade and payments and who, therefore, are highly sensitive to currency fluctuations: first, international traders and investors, second, the producers of export-oriented tradable goods who tend to suffer from exchange market volatility, since it makes their business riskier, the only exception being the producers of tradable goods in which competition is not primarily on price, and is instead, for example, on quality.[66] In turn, these actors are relatively unconcerned about domestic macroeconomics conditions, because they can respond to depressed local demand by shifting their business to other countries. Conversely, two other groups of actors tend to be greatly concerned about domestic macroeconomics conditions and thus favour the national monetary policy autonomy made possible by a flexible exchange rate. The first of these groups consists of producers of non-tradable goods and services: since their business does not involve the use of foreign exchange and since currency volatility has at best only indirect effects on them, they tend to have no clear preferences for stable exchange rates. The second group consists of producers of import-competing tradable goods for the domestic market, who tend to be relatively indifferent about exchange rate volatility, which may even reduce import pressure inasmuch as it makes importing riskier, and who are primarily concerned about policy-making autonomy.

In contrast, in the implementing phase of monetary arrangements, in which the actors are much more concerned about the level of exchange rates, the political cleavages are likely to change since the interests of the various economic sectors will integrate the impact of the relative price changes involved in depreciation or appreciation of the currency. From a differential distributional point of view, the lower, that is, more depreciated, the exchange rate, the higher is the price of tradable goods relative to non-tradable ones.[67] This, in turn, tends to favour the producers of tradable goods, whose output prices rise more than the prices of the non-tradable inputs they use, and to hurt producers of non tradable goods. Producers in the tradable sector, therefore, gain from depreciation that makes their products more competitive in home and foreign markets, while producers in the non-tradable sector generally benefit from currency appreciation, which raises the domestic relative price of their products and lowers the domestic relative price of tradable goods. Moreover, international traders and investors, who are interested in purchasing assets abroad, favour a strong currency.

These varying exchange rates level preferences, in turn, affect preferences about different macroeconomic policies: the actors who gain from a strong currency will prefer macroeconomic policies consistent with the commitment to the ERM which caused, from its outset, an overvaluation of the weakest currencies,[68] while producers of tradable goods will prefer a depreciation of the currency.

From an operational point of view, it is possible to identify the import competing producers of tradable goods for domestic market with the producers of standardised manufactures, that is, with the manufacturing sector. The export oriented producers of tradable goods can be identified with the big, international companies, the producers of non-tradable goods and services with the public sector and finally the investors with the financial and banking systems.[69]

Thus, the constellation of interests involved in the negotiating and implementing phase of monetary arrangements, according to Frieden's model, can be simplified as follows:

Table 2.3   Frieden's model

	Floating exchange rates	Fixed exchange rates	
Depreciation of the currency	Manufacturing, small companies	Export-oriented, big companies	Manufacturing, small companies + export-oriented, big companies
Appreciation of the currency	Public sector	Financial and banking sector	Public sector + financial and banking sector
	Manufacturing, small companies, + public sector	Export-oriented, big companies + financial and banking sector	

2.4   Conclusions: What is Mainstream in European Political Economy

Concluding the survey of the main mainstream theories of European political economy it is important to note the characteristics that render similar approaches mainstream. Although, as the next chapter will show, critical theorists identify a varity of weaknesses in mainstream formulations, both neofunctionalism and intergovernmentalism, as well as the various compromise solutions proposed in the literature, do indeed present some common elements.

First and foremost, mainstream theorists tend to deny heuristic value to subjects or actors placed outside the formal institutional system, whether it is represented by the national state system or by regional/international institutions. This is not to say that these types of actors are not considered at all. Indeed in the latest versions of both neofunctionalist and intergovernmentalist approaches the attention to interest groups, political parties and public opinion at both the national and the international level is substantially greater than before. The problem is that those actors are not viewed as having an independent explanatory role.

Moreover, the analysis of their behaviour is instrumental to understanding the developments of the attitude of formal institutions, whether they are represented by the states or by international institutions. For example, even in the most recent version of intergovernmentalism, interest groups' preferences are used to explain the preferences of the state which ultimately remains the only actor of change in the international system: they do not produce change autonomously. Similar considerations apply also to neofunctionalist explanations, with the difference that, in this case, states are constrained in their international actions by existing supranational/international institutions and these supranational institutions may acquire a proactive role in the process of integration, like in the case of political spill-overs. As further elaborated in the next chapter, critical theorists all agree in overcoming this explanatory focus on formal institutions and introduce different heuristic variables, which range from ideological paradigms to transnational non-state actors.

Another common element amongst mainstream approaches is recognisable in the adoption of the rational actor model: actors in the international system are rational in the sense that they strive to maximise the achievement of a stable and ranked set of preferences. This is clearly states in the intergovernmentalist approach, and it is actually one of its fundamental assumptions, but also in the latest, neo-institutionalist versions of neofunctionalism the use of rational choice is explicit.

This aspect of mainstream is being scrutinized by critical theorists. In some cases, as with neo-Gramscian or neoconstructivist approaches, the rational actor method is rejected in favour of alternative explanatory logics in which the subject/object dichotomy is overcome altogether.

The following chapter is dedicated to the analyses of these alternative paradigms.

Notes

1 It is common practice to distinguish theories of European integration according to the level of analysis. Theories addressing changes in the wider political/economic environment are defined macro-theories and coincide with IR/IPE theoretical approaches to European Integration. Those theories addressing issues related to institutional change or policy setting decisions, like new instutionalism(s) are used at a lower level of analysis while policy-shaping decisions are tackled through theories acting at the lowest level of analysis, like policy network theories (Peterson (1995), pp. 69–93).

2 Note that in this context the systemic level is the international system, not the European system. For a similar interpretation See Frieden and Lake (2000), Introduction.

3 See Haas (1968).

4 See Taylor (1994). For a thorough discussion of the differences and affinities between classic functionalist approaches to international integration and neofunctionalism see Rosamond (2000).

5 See Introduction to this book for a more detailed explanation of the differences between neo-institutionalist and neorealist approaches to IR/IPE.

6 See Haas (1968), p. 5.
7 See Haas (1968), p. 8.
8 See Haas (1968), p. 10.
9 See Haas (1968), p. 16.
10 For a similar interpretation see Rosamond (2000), p. 60.
11 See Haas (1968), p. 5.
12 See Haas (1968), p. 5.
12 See Haas (1968), pp. 287–9.
13 See Keohane and Nye (1977).
14 For a neofunctionalist account of the ups and downs of European Integration see Lindberg and Scheingold (1970).
15 See Schmitter (1970) and Lindberg and Scheingold (1970).
16 See Lindberg and Scheingold (1970), p. 104.
17 See Lindberg and Schcingold (1970), p. 106.
18 See Lindberg and Scheingold (1970), p. 106.
19 See Hass and Schmitter (1964). For a complete account of this effort see Rosamond (2000), pp. 68–72.
20 See Lindberg and Scheingold (1970), p. 106.
21 See Lindberg and Scheingold (1970), p. 118.
22 For more details see Lindberg and Scheingold (1970), pp. 117–21.
23 For more information on the developments of neofunctionalism see Rosamond (2000), ch. 4.
24 Haas remained within IR/IPE but shifted its interest from Europe to world politics and interdependence theories, while Lindberg narrowed its interest to the study of European policy-making. See Rosamond (2000), p. 97.
25 See, for example, Peterson (1995).
26 See Haas (1992). See also Verdun (1999).
27 For more details on this approach and its relationship with neofunctionalism see Rosamond (2000), pp. 94–6.
28 See Moravcsik (1998), p. 26.
29 For realist interpretations of the process of European integration see Hoffman (1966). See also Milward (2000).
30 See Gilpin (1987), p. 11. See elsewhere, Introduction.
31 See Moravcsik (1991).
32 Moravcsik (1991), p. 27.
33 See Moravcsik (1993a), p. 474.
34 See Moravcsik (1993b).
35 See Moravcsik (1998), p. 18.
36 The author defines the term framework as 'a set of assumptions that permit us to disaggregate a phenomenon we seek to explain, in this case successive rounds of international negotiations, into elements each of which can be treated separately'. See Moravcsik (1998), p. 19.
37 See Moravcsik (1998), p. 35. One example is Frieden's theory of exchange rate preferences formation explained below in this chapter.
38 See Moravcsik (1998), p. 50. Other theories of international bargaining quoted by Moravcsik are, for example, Lax and Sebenius (1986).
39 See Moravcsik (1998), p. 22.
40 See Moravcsik (1998).

41 For a different interpretation of the differences between realism and intergovernmentalism see Rosamond (2000).
42 See Stone and Sandholtz (1994).
43 See Putnam (1988).
44 Putnam (1988, p. 438) distinguishes among 'voluntary defection', which occurs when new interests overcome preceeding agreement, and 'involuntary defection', defined as the lack of credibility of an agreement from the outset because it is not supported by a domestic actor, that is, because its win-set is too small.
45 See Putnam (1988), p. 440.
46 See Milner (1988), Introduction.
47 See Milner (1992). For further details on the subject, see also Milner (1993).
48 See Rosenau (1967).
49 See Rosenau (1967), p. 7.
50 See Rosenau (1967), p. 16.
51 See Rosenau (1967), ch. 2.
52 See Rosenau (1967), Table 3, p. 46.
53 See Katzenstein (1977) and Katzenstein (1976).
54 See Katzenstein (1977), p. 4.
55 See Katzenstein (1977), p. 19.
56 See Putnam (1988).
57 See Milner (1987).
58 See Putnam (1988), p. 432.
59 See Bulmer (1983), p. 354.
60 For further explanation of the concept of 'policy style' see Bulmer (1983), p. 361.
61 See Frieden (1991); see also Frieden (1994).
62 Incidentally, the issue of European Monetary Union has been addressed for the first time in the context of the European community exactly at the beginning of the 70s, with the Werner plan, since the Treaty of Rome, in its original version, did not contain any reference to the goal of monetary union. Although many authors, like Padoa Schioppa (see Padoa Schioppa (1988)), claim that this was due to the collapse of the Bretton Wood system, some evidence may be found that this debate over monetary arrangements was urged by the growing impact of greater capital mobility. See, for references on this subject, Bank for International Settlement (BIS) (1990).
63 The Mundell-Fleming model is a macroeconomic model which links together the monetarist economic equilibrium, that is, the equilibrium of monetarist variables, given by the equilibrium between the money supply and demand, summarised in the so-called L/M curve, and the real variables equilibrium, the equilibrium between investments and savings, summarised by the so-called I/S curve. The model does include also the equilibrium of the external economic relationships in the form of the balance of payments equilibrium, summarised in the so-called B/P curve. See Chapter 4 of this book.
64 See also Padoa Schioppa (1988).
65 In fact, in the Mundell-Fleming model, if the exchange rates are held constant, any monetary expansion causes the interest rates to decrease and the capital, given the assumption of its freedom of movement, to outflow till the interest rates reach their original level without any rise in the domestic demand. Thus, if the exchange rates are fixed, any expansionary monetary policy is ineffective in stimulating national economy, while, monetary policy can be effective if the value of the currency is allowed to vary.

The reverse is true for fiscal policies, since, given capital mobility, in a fixed exchange rates regime, bonds floated to finance increased government spending are bought by international investors and there is no effect on interest rates which are set globally. If exchange rates vary, as foreigners buy more government bonds the resultant capital inflow causes a currency appreciation that tends to reduce domestic demand for domestically produced goods and thus to dampen the fiscal expansion. Therefore, In conclusion, any autonomous national macroeconomic policy in a world of capital mobility, does not affect interest rates, i.e., does not produce any effective change in domestic economy, which can result in changes in the exchange rates.

66 It is true that it is possible to cover exchange rates risks by recurring to the forward exchange rate market, but this is neither costless nor feasible for all currencies. See CEC (1990).

67 In fact, the real exchange rate can be expressed as the relationship between the price of non-tradable goods and that of tradable one: P\P*xe.

By assumption, the price of tradables, P*, is set on world markets and cannot be changed, in foreign currency terms, by national policy. Depreciation makes tradables relatively more expensive in domestic currency terms, while non-tradables become relatively cheaper; appreciation has the opposite effect.

68 See Walters (1990), ch. 5.

69 See Frieden (1991).

References

Alt, J. and Eichengreen, B. (1989), 'Parallel and Overlapping Games: Theory and Application to the European Gas Trade', *Economics and Politics*, Vol. 1.

Bank for International Settlement (BIS) (1990), *Sixtieth Annual Report*, Basle: BIS.

Bulmer, S. (1983), 'Domestic Politics and European Community Policy-making', *Journal of Common Market Studies*, Vol. XXI (4), June, p. 354.

Eichenberg, R.C. and Dalton, R.J. (1993), 'The Europeans and European Community: The Dynamics of Public Support for European integration', *International Organization*, Vol. 47.

Frieden, J.A. and Lake, D.A. (2000), *International Political Economy: Perspective on Global Power and Wealth*, 4th edn, Bedford: St Martin's Press, Introduction.

Frieden, J. (1991), 'Invested Interests: The Politics of National Economic Policies in a World of Global Finance', *International Organization*, 45, Autumn.

Frieden, J. (1994), 'The Impact of Goods and Capital Market Integration on European Monetary Politics', preliminary version.

Gilpin, R. (1987), *The Political Economy of International Relations*, Princeton, NJ: Princeton University Press.

Goldstein, J. and Keohane, R.O. (1993), *Ideas in Foreign Policy*, Ithaca, NY: Cornell University Press.

Gourevitch, P.A. (1986), *Politics in Hard Times: Comparative Responses in International Ecomomic Crisis*, Ithaca, NY: Cornell University Press.

Haas, E.B. (1968), *The Uniting of Europe: Political, Social and Economic Forces*, 2nd edn, Stanford, CA: Stanford University Press.

Hass, E.B. and Schmitter, P.C. (1964), 'Eonomics and Differential Patterns of Political Integration: Projections about Unity in Latin America', *International Organization*, Vol. 18 (Autumn), pp. 705–37.

Haas, P. (1992), 'Introduction: Epistemic Communities and International Policy Co-ordination', *International Organization*, Vol. 46 (1).

Hoffman, S. (1966), 'Obstinate or Obsolete? The Fate of the Nation State and the Case of Western Europe', *Daedalus* (Summer), pp. 862–915.

Katzenstein, P.J. (1976), 'International Relations and Domestic Structures: Foreign Economic Policies of Advanced Industrial States', *International Organization*, Vol. 30 (Winter), pp. 1–45.

Katzenstein, P.J. (ed.) (1977), *Between Power and Plenty: Foreign Economic Policies of Advanced Industrial States*, Madison: University of Wisconsin Press.

Keohane, R.O. and Nye, J.S. (1977), *Power and Interdependence*, Boston: Little Brown.

Lax, D.A. and Sebenius, J.K (1986), 'The Manager as Negotiator: Bargaining for Co-operation and Competitive Gain', in R.E. Walton and R.B. McKersie, *A Behavioural Theory of Labor Negotiations: An Analysis of a Social Interaction System*, New York.

Lindberg, L.N. and Scheingold, S.A. (1970), *Europe's Would-be Polity: Patterns of Change in the European Community*, Englewood Cliffs, NJ: Prentice-Hall.

Martin, L. (1993), 'International and Domestic Institutions in the EMU Process', *Economics and Politics*, Vol. 5 (2).

Milner, H. (1987), 'Resisting the Protectionist Temptation: Industry and the Making of Trade Policy in France and the United States during the 1970s', *International Organization*, Vol. 41 (Autumn), pp. 639–65.

Milner, H. (1988), *Resisting Protectionism*, Princeton, NJ: Princeton University Press, Introduction.

Milner, H. (1992), 'Theories of Cooperation', *World Politics*, Vol. 44.

Milner, H. (1993), 'The Assumption of Anarchy in International Relations Theory: A Critique' in D.A. Baldwin (1993), *Neo-realism and Neo-liberalism: The Contemporary Debate*, Columbia University Press.

Milward, A.S. (2000), *The European Rescue of the Nation State*, London: Routledge.

Moravcsik, A. (1991), 'Negotiating the Single European Act: National Interests and Conventional Statecraft in the European Community', *International Organization*, Vol. 45 (1), Winter.

Moravcsik, A. (1993a), 'Preferences and Power in the EC: A Liberal Intergovernmentalist Approach', *Journal of Common Market Studies*, Vol. 31 (4), December, p. 474.

Moravcsik, A. (1993b), 'Integrating International and Domestic Theories of International Bargaining' in P.B. Evans, H.K. Jacobson and R.D. Putnam (eds), *Double-edged Diplomacy: International Bargaining and Domestic Policy*, Berkeley: University of California Press.

Moravcsik, A. (1998), *The Choice for Europe: Social Purpose and State Power from Messina to Maastricht*, London: UCL Press.

Murphy, C.N. and Tooze, R. (1991), *The New International Political Economy*, Boulder, CO: Lynne Rienner Publishers.

Peterson, J. (1995), 'Decision-making in the European Union: Towards a Framework for Analysis', *Journal of European Public Policy*, Vol. 2 (1), March, pp. 69–93.

Putnam, R. (1988), 'Diplomacy and Domestic Politics', *International Organization*, Vol. 42.

Rogowsky, R. (1989), *Commerce and Coalitions: How Trade Affects Domestic Political Alignments*, Princeton: Princeton University Press.

Rosamond, B. (2000), *Theories of European Integration*, London: Macmillan.

Rosenau, J. N. (1967), *Domestic Sources of Foreign Policy*, New York: The Free Press.

Rosenthal, G. (1975), *The Men Behind the Decisions*, Lexinngton: D.C. Heath.

Sandholtz, W. (1993), 'Choosing Union Monetary Politics and Maastricht', *International Organization*, Vol. 47.

Schmitter, P.C. (1970), 'A Revised Theory of Regional Integration', *International Organization*, Vol. 24 (Autumn), pp. 836–68.

Spero, J. (1977), *The Politics of International Economic Relations*, London: George Allen and Unwin.

Stone, A. and Sandholtz, W. (1994), 'European Integration and Domestic Politics: A Framework Research Protocol', October.

Taylor, P. (1994), 'Functionalism: The Approach of David Mitrany', in A.J.R. Groom and P. Taylor (eds), *Frameworks for International Co-operation*, London: Pinter.

Wallace, H., Wallace, W. and Webb, C. (1977), *Policy-making in the European Communities*, London: John Wiley.

Walters, A. (1990), *The Sterling in Danger*, London: Collins.

Verdun, A. (1999), 'The Role of the Delors Committee in the Creation of EMU: An Epistemic Community, *Journal of European Public Policy*, Vol. 6 (2).

Chapter 3

Critical Approaches to European Political Economy

Some scholars have sought to analyse the process of European economic integration using the conceptual, analytical and theoretical tools provided by the critical approaches to international political economy.[1]

Before moving to their substantive contributions, it is worth noting that, as in the case of mainstream approaches, this chapter also focuses on macro-level theories addressed specifically to the explanation and interpretation of key turning points in the process of European economic integration. The only exception is represented by the eclectic approach to political economy proposed by Susan Strange, an author who rarely tackled directly the issues relating to European integration but whose contribution influenced too many scholars and students of European studies to be ignored here.

Generally speaking, critical approaches to European political economy differ from mainstream ones on methodological, epistemological and substantive grounds.

First of all, in substantive terms, critical theorists focus not only on formal institutions such as the nation states or international organisations, but also on different socioeconomic actors, including firms, socioeconomic interest groups, NGOs, political parties, ideological paradigms or public opinion.

From an epistemological point of view, some critical analysts, particularly neoconstructivists and neo-Gramscians, seek to overcome the positivist distinction between the subject and the object of analysis, rejecting the notion of the objectivity of the social reality and therefore recognising the possibility for it to be modified by the subjective evaluations of the scholar. In practical terms this means that critical theorists prefer contextual social or historical explanations to causal ones. They prefer to 'reconstruct' the social reality under scrutiny (hence the use of the term 'constructivism') within a particular social or historical or ideological context. Social reality is not a 'datum' (something which is given), it is a 'factum' (something which has been 'constructed').

Hence critical theorists reject methodological individualism based on the rational actor model and focus more on the analysis of the situation in which that particular event took place. Of course, each different critical approach would reconstruct the situation on the basis of different philosophical premises and different assumptions about which are the most important explanatory variables.

Finally, some critical theories, like neoconstructivism or Susan Strange's eclectic approach, stress the role of explanatory variables other then material interests, like ideas or shared beliefs, to explain why certain social events took place.

3.1 An Eclectic Approach to EPE

3.1.1 Susan Strange's Analytical Framework

The identification of an analytical framework within which to analyse political economy issues represents the second stage in the development of Susan Strange's eclectic approach to IPE.[2] Reliance on such a framework allows the author to reject rational actors models and related causal explanations, providing instead for the contextualisation of the events under consideration.

In order to overcome the problem of causality in political economy explanation, Susan Strange reverted to the notion of 'enveloping structures' that, in her words:

> rather than the overt conscious decision or action of any actor in the system, set the agendas and determined the range of options within which states and other groups and individuals contested all the major who-gets-what issues of politics, within the state and in the world economy.[3]

'Enveloping structures' are therefore the contexts within which political economy events take place and must be analysed. They are also the contexts within which certain structural power relations are formed and within which structural changes occur.

The first enveloping structure is obviously represented by the 'productive structure', i.e., by the system in which relations of production are formed. In Susan Strange's words, the 'productive structure' is given by 'whatever or whoever determines what is to be produced, by what combination of labour, land, capital and technology; by what productive methods; where and on what terms and conditions for the workers'.[4] Analysis of the productive structure allows the scholar to identify those power relations stemming from the relation of production. These relations represent the background of many political economy issues and may provide for a decisive argument to explain them.

However, according to Strange, structural power relations do not stem only from the relation of production, as Marxists or Gramscians would argue. Other types of structural power must also be analysed before proposing any convincing explanations.

The second enveloping structure is represented by the 'financial structure', which is defined by the author as whoever or whatever determines financial relations, especially relations between creditors and debtors, savers and investors, or, better: 'The system under which credit is created, allocated and put into use'.[5]

Modifications in such a system would indeed create new power relations, new winners and losers, a new allocation not only of financial power but also of political power. The financial structure produces changes in the political economy environment and must therefore be analysed to account for them.

Equally important for the determination of the losers and winners in international/European political economy issues are two other structures. They too influence not only the trade-off of the choices in the system as a whole, but also the allocation of the benefits and costs amongst the different societal groups or individuals. These remaining structures are the 'security structure' and the 'knowledge structure'.

The 'security structure' is clearly represented by the military system, i.e., by the structural power stemming from military relations. However Susan Strange agrees with the attempts made by scholars of strategic issues to redefine the notion of security to include food security, energy security or even environmental security. Consequently, the actors in this more broadly defined security system are not only the nation states, but also NGOs, political parties and movements, public opinion and, especially, firms.

Finally, the last structure in which relational power is sought is the 'knowledge structure'. This is defined on the one hand as the system of shared beliefs and ideas (value system) and, on the other hand by the systems through which information are communicated and exchanged (information system).

Both the first, abstract definition of the knowledge structure and the second, more operational one, modify the options available to social actors and therefore influence their actions and the outcomes of social events.

Moreover changes in both the value system and the technologies available to exchange information produce different power relations at the societal level and must therefore be considered as significant sources of social change.

Thus, following Strange, it is possible to draw a diagram of the analytical framework in which contemporary political economy events have to be analysed.

This diagram includes the four enveloping structures within which social change takes place. It also represents graphically the major sources of structural change, i.e., what or who produces changes in the four enveloping structures. Similar sources are identified by the author not only in the states, but also in the markets and in the technology.

The purpose of the diagram is:

> to show how the choices of actors, whether governments, corporate enterprise, social classes, age, sex or occupational groups, or just individual human beings, have the range of choices open to them determined by the basic structures of the international political economy and how the system of states is not the prime factor, the sole source of significant change ....[6]

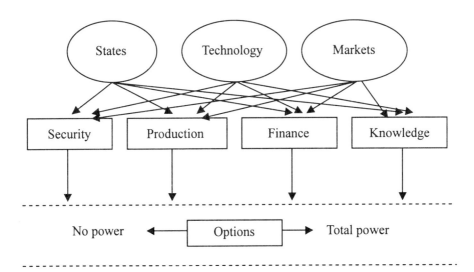

Figure 3.1   Determinants of choice

Source: Strange (1991), p. 39.

Concluding, it is important to notice that in Strange's analysis there is no hierarchical order amongst the different enveloping structure. This means that there is no heuristic primacy of one structural context over another, as, for example, in Marxist or neo-Gramscian reconstructions of socioeconomic events where the structure of production 'determines' changes in, for example, the knowledge structure (in the Marxist terminology a 'superstructure').

Moreover, according to Susan Strange, not all phenomena are to be analysed within all enveloping structures. In some cases, say, relations of productions explain it all, while in some other cases it is necessary to introduce other structural relations to give account of the social event under consideration. In other words, within this analytical framework there is no preordained way to decide which structure counts more in which specific case.

3.1.2 The Role of Firms

One of the most important distinguishing features of Susan Strange's contribution to political economy studies is her recognition of the role played by firms in the evolution of structures and as actors of the international political economy system.[7] Firms are considered important to states both in alliance with governments and in conflict and competition with them.[8] In a context of increased competition for world market shares, states and firms relations increase and diversify[9] and international political economy scholars have to reconsider their theoretical frameworks to give account of this new reality.

This international role of firms is explained by the phenomenon of the reallocation of production abroad, through foreign direct investments or mergers and acquisitions. According to Strange, firms are compelled to move abroad not to pursue higher profits, but to survive. Three major structural changes brought about such a development.

The first structural change was in the method of production and was due to the accelerated pace of technological change. Accelerating technical change meant that new productive enterprises would cost more and would therefore require the firm to look for new markets abroad. On similar grounds, by the way, it is possible to explain the European bid for the creation of the Internal market and of the European Monetary Union.[10]

The second structural change was in the greater transnational mobility of capital, making it much easier for the foreign owned firm (FOF) to get ready access to the capital needed to keep up in the technical race in whatever country it chose to locate production or part of it.

Finally, this new international role of firms has been allowed by changes in the transport and communication spheres, producing a relevant reduction of costs for the re-allocation of production abroad.

The result of this new role of the firm has been to add two new dimensions to the practice of diplomacy in the international political economy. Alongside the traditional negotiation process amongst the states, scholars of IPE/EPE have now to consider also the negotiation dynamics going on between states and firms and also amongst firms alone.

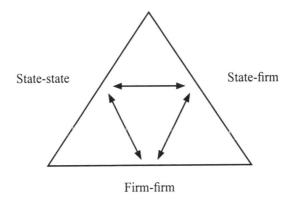

State-state

State-firm

Firm-firm

Figure 3.2   Dimensions of diplomacy

Source: Strange (1991), p. 45.

The new role of firms changes the balance of power between states and firms. Firms are now in a far better bargaining position *vis-à-vis* governments. Governments cannot any longer dictate to national firms where to locate production nor even how much tax they should pay, since they can always react by moving their production abroad. Moreover, states are competing amongst themselves to attract a relevant share of firms investment, and this reduces their bargaining power.

Summing up, according to Strange, in the new international political economy, as well as in the new European political economy, no scholar can afford to ignore the role of firms.

3.1.3 Susan Strange as a Critical European Political Economy Theorist

The importance of Susan Strange for critical European political economy is clearly given by her shift from the traditional mainstream focus on state and institutions as the determinants of change in the international/European political economy context.

Particularly relevant is also her stress on the role of firms as the main actors of the new international political economy context and the repercussions that this has both in terms of bargaining process and power, and in terms of policy outcomes. Susan Strange herself utilises this notion to explain the establishment of the Single Market in Europe. This came about as the necessary outcome of European firms need to gain new markets in Europe, as a consequence of the technological changes in the structure of production. In her words:

> It was the strongest European-based firms who pushed hard on national governments and in Brussels through organisations like the European Round table for the European Single Market Initiative (ESM) in the 1980s.[11]

Finally, the notion of enveloping structures contextualises political economy explanations in a way that overcomes the need to identify causal relations, thus nullifying the heuristic value of the rational actor model.

3.2   Neoconstructivist Reconstructions of Europe

3.2.1   Neoconstructivism as a Critical Approach

Neoconstructivists[12] criticise mainstream assumptions of the rational actor model, state-centrism, the distinction between integration in 'low politics' and integration in 'high politics'.

The criticism of the rational actor model is effected by reverting to social constructivism. In particular, neoconstructivist scholars argue that social action does not only and necessarily follow an 'instrumental rationality', by this meaning the logic of rationally maximising a utility function. According to neoconstructivists, in explaining social behaviour it is imperative to consider the impact of ideas and shared beliefs, therefore rejecting the logic of instrumentality in favour of a logic of communicative action. In other words, in their decision making, social actors are moved by their values, beliefs and their views of the world and not necessarily by their material interests rationally ranked according to their utility functions. Therefore, to understand why certain actors take a certain decision it is important to understand the values or ideas pursued by the actors in question and how they have been communicated to them (which is the analysis of the communicative action).

The criticism of state-centrism is effected by reverting to transnationalism and transgovernmentalism.[13] Transnational relations are defined as 'trans-boundary relations that include at least one non-governmental actor'.[14] Trans-governmental relations are instead defined as 'cross-boundary relations among sub-units of national governments in the absence of centralised decisions by state executives'.[15] By means of these two concepts neoconstructivists reject the notion of the State as the only actor in the international arena ('trans-nationalism') and of the State as a unitary, monolithic actor ('transgovernmentalism').

Finally, neoconstructivists do not accept the mainstream proposition that integration in 'low politics' (economic issues) is easier than integration in 'high politics' (foreign, defence and security policy) and this is mainly due to the recessive role they assign to material interests in explaining social action in general and international or European integration in particular. Indeed, if the vectors of integration are represented by the profound beliefs of policy-makers and by the degree of transnationalisation and transgovernmentalism of the issue to be integrated, and not by the maximisation of an economic or material interest, the distinction between low and high politics becomes irrelevant.

3.2.2 A Neoconstructivist Approach to European Integration

Starting from neoconstructivist premises, Thomas Risse devised an analytical framework in which to study the process of European integration and decision-making from a critical perspective.[16]

The author's main assumption is that policy-making in the EU does not take place in an institutional void, but is embedded in both the domestic and the European institutional context and therefore is influenced by both the domestic structures and the EU institutions.

The impact of domestic structures on EU decision-making By domestic structures the author means not only the structure of the political institutions, societal interests formation and aggregation structures and State-society relations, but also the norms and values embedded in the political culture. All these vary according not only to the member state in question, but also with regard to the issue areas involved.

The domestic structure influences the extent to which the State is autonomous from societal constraints, the extent to which governments can act as unitary actors, the possibility for transnational or transgovernmental networks to overcome the government's level of decision making, the effectiveness of the latter in implementing EU policy circumventing the central level of governance, and the level of internalisation of EU principles and norms in the domestic polity.

Three hypotheses on the impact of the domestic structure on the EU decision making stem from such a framework:[17]

1   the more fragmented and decentralised the political institutions, the stronger the organisation of societal interest representation, and the greater the consensus requirements in state-society relations, the less capable are national governments to pursue independent and autonomous policies at the EU level;
2   the more fragmented and decentralised the political institutions and the stronger the organisation of interest representation in society, the less likely are national governments to behave as unitary actors in the EU policy-making process and more likely are they to externalise the lack of domestic consensus in a given policy area at the EU level;
3   the more fragmented the political institutions and the stronger the organisation of societal interest representation, the more likely are transnational policy networks to emerge among EU institutions and political as well as societal actors in the Member States, and the more likely are these networks to affect EU policies.

The impact of EU institutions on EU decision-making On the other hand, the impact of European institutions on the EU policy-making depends on the degree of transnationalisation of a given issue area. In turn, transnational coalition building would prevail over the intergovernmental bargaining process depending on the degree to which:

• the respective issue area or policy sector is regulated by EU policies;
• the respective policy area is governed by majority rather than consensus rule in the Council.

The related hypothesis is the following:

4   the more a particular policy sector has been integrated and the more decisions in this area are governed by majority rule, the more likely is that the policy-making process is characterised by transnational and transgovernmental coalitions among private, sub-national, national and supranational actors rather than intergovernmental bargaining.

Summing up, the degree of transnationalisation/transgovernmentalisation of a decision-making process as opposed to the adoption of an inter-governmental bargaining system would depend on the level of fragmentation of the domestic structure and the level of Europeanisation of the issue area under consideration.

The role of ideas and communicative action on EU decision-making But what is the role of ideas and shared values and knowledge in this framework?

As Risse states:

> The power of ideas in such instances is linked to their consensuality. Ideas become consensual when actors start believing in their value and become convinced of their validity. In other words, communicative processes are a necessary condition for ideas to become consensual.[18]

In terms of EU policy-making this leads to the following propositions:

5   the more policy-making processes are characterised by informality and non-hierarchy, the more space is open for communicative action ... one would expect processes of argumentation and persuasion the more informal transnational and transgovernmental network are involved in preparing and implementing decisions;

6   the internal cohesion of such networks and coalitions depends to a large degree on collectively shared beliefs and understandings rather then convergence of exogenously defined preferences.

This means that the higher the degree of Europeanisation of a decision-making process, the higher is the possibility for coalition based on ideas or shared values, rather than common interests, to inform it through communicative action rather than instrumental action.

Communicative action, which in few words can be defined as the activity of persuasion performed by groups sharing the same values and vision of the world, is in turn more likely to influence macro-events, like history making or policy setting EU decisions.

Concluding, in the words of the author:

> If we start conceptualising the EU as an emerging polity of collectively shared values and norms, we must incorporate communicative rationality in our efforts at theorising about the nature of the beast.[19]

3.3 Neo-Gramscian Approaches to European Political Economy: A Transnational Historical Materialist Theory of European Integration[20]

One of the most recent attempts to translate neo-Gramscian approaches to international political economy into a fully-fledged theory of European political economy is represented by Ryner, Van Apeldoorn and Overbeek's transnational historical materialist theory of European integration.[21]

This theory rotates around three concepts: *historical materialism, transnationalism and neo-Gramscianism.*

3.3.1 Historical Materialism

As defined by the authors, the historical materialist approach consists of:

1   a materialist conception of history. This means a conception of history in which the material forces of production as well as the relations of production represent the determinants of social action and change;
2   a rejection of the separation between the subject and object and its substitution with a dialectic understanding of reality as a dynamic totality;
3   a rejection of the rational actor model and its substitution with the so-called 'method of abstraction', consisting in the reconstruction of the social phenomenon under analysis within its historical and social context.

The process of European Integration, as any other social reality, is therefore interpreted in the light of the historically defined power relations stemming from the structure of production. Moreover, it is conceived as a phenomenon that is a relatively autonomous regional expression of an emerging capitalist global political economy.[22]

In this context social scientific knowledge is not generated by the positivist identification of invariant laws, but rather through an intellectual conceptual 'mapping' ('reconstruction') of contradictory social formations and their movements.

3.3.2 Transnationalism

This version of historical materialism portrays social relations as being constituted at the transnational level, i.e., in a context which transcends national boundaries. Social relations, particularly class relations, are therefore formed and held neither 'outside' the national boundaries (i.e., in the 'international' arena) nor inside them (i.e., in the 'domestic' arena) but they do exist at the same time at both levels. This enables the authors to transcend the distinction between the national and the international.

Such a more dialectical view of the relation between the 'external' and 'internal' factors is considered essential for a better understanding of the nature of international relations and European integration.

3.3.3 *The Essential Gramscian Dimension*

The most important characteristic of this critical approach to European Integration is, however, its reliance on Gramsci's sociology of power.

Gramsci's sociology of power starts from the Macchiavelli's distinction between rule by 'force' and rule through 'consensus'. Gramsci puts this distinction in his own terms contrasting two ideal types of supremacy: 'domination', the exercise of power without the critical, reflective consent of the governed, and 'ethical hegemony', i.e., intellectual and moral direction. However, the Gramscian distinction is not ontologically equivalent to Macchiavelli's one, since 'force' as the source of power is not quite the same as domination, even though 'consensus' always characterises hegemony. However, when consensus is obtained through fraud and deception, hegemony is not 'ethical', and indeed is not hegemony at all, on the contrary it is considered as a form of domination. Moreover, Gramsci notes that, in the real world, there is not a radical separation between force and consensus and that these two forms of rules are mutually supportive and often combine in ambiguous ways.

The domains where force and consent operate to consolidate power are the three levels of society: the structural one, i.e., 'economic structure', and the two superstructural levels, 'civil society', represented by the private sector social actors, and 'political society', the state and with its institutional and public actors.

Gramsci's 'civil society' consists of the various forms of voluntary associations and constitutes the moment of transition from economic structure to political society, the social realm in which mere corporate interests, defined by a group position in the mode of production, can be transformed into broader political aspirations. For Gramsci, civil society is the primary political realm, the realm in which all of the dynamics of identity formation, ideological struggle, the activities of intellectuals and the construction of hegemony, whether 'ethical' or based on fraud, take place. Civil society is the context in which one become conscious and first engages in political action. Civil society is where the aggregation of interests takes place, where narrow interests are transformed into more universal views as ideologies are adopted or amended and alliances formed.

Gramsci locates 'political society', the institutions regulating society, above civil society. What Gramsci calls political society is equivalent to what many realists consider the 'state', however Gramsci considers it important to differentiate between 'political society' or the 'state proper' and what he calls the 'state in the organic, wider sense', i.e., the polity, the overall structure of the superstructure. Understood thus, the state is neither the external expression of society, merely an 'actor in international relations, nor is it located above society: the state is a characteristic of society constituted by the articulation of political and civil society.

Though there is a tendency for there to be a coincidence between force and the realm of the state proper and between rule by consensus and the realm of civil society, this cannot be considered, in Gramsci, as a rule since both force and policies aimed at achieving consensus can be applied in any of the three social realms. Furthermore, the three social realms are also the context for the consolidation of power leading to supremacy.

To achieve supremacy a social group, a corporate actor, must be able to establish 'hegemony' among a group of allies where hegemony is defined as the ability of a social group to exercise a function of political and moral direction.

A hegemon leads by responding to its allies 'interests', i.e., their motivations that derive from their positions in the mode of production, and by both responding to and helping to shape their 'ideal aspirations'. 'Interests' and 'ideal aspirations' are the two basic motivations of human action in civil society recognised by Gramsci. In industrial societies only social groups performing an essential role in the mode of production can become hegemonic unlike, for example, in feudal societies where religious groups have exercised political and moral direction. This essential role in the world of production is what first confers prestige on a leading social group and makes its dominant social and political role acceptable to others.

The path to hegemony comprises three fundamental steps.

- No group can become hegemonic without first understanding its own interests and developing its own hegemonic aspirations: members of a potentially hegemonic group must attain self-awareness of the economic role they perform and of the political role they could fulfil.

- Secondly, on the basis of this critical self-understanding, the potential hegemon can make alliances, taking a step beyond defending its economic-corporate interests, i.e., immediate and narrow selfish interests of a particular category[23] in order to link itself to other groups involved in society's key political struggles. This the process that Gramsci, using Sorel's language, calls the establishment of a 'historical economic-political bloc', not just an alliance, but a dialectical unit of base and superstructure, of theory and practice, of intellectuals and masses. Here the work of intellectuals becomes essential given that the role of intellectuals is to represent the ideas that constitutes the terrain where hegemony is exercised.
- The intellectuals organically tied to the hegemonic class must demonstrate in every field of knowledge that the aspirations of the group they serve coincide with the interests of the society as a whole. The intellectuals of the hegemonic class must produce a philosophy, political theory and economics which together constitute a coherent worldview.
- Finally, Gramsci hypothesises that to further reinforce the solidarity of its immediate bloc of allies and go beyond it to extend the hegemony of the leading social group to the popular masses the potential hegemon must ensure economic development, satisfying the narrower interests of its allies. This is a second reason why hegemons in modern industrial societies can only come from classes that play an essential role in the economy.

Thus in Gramsci's view, a corporate actor that wants to achieve hegemony today must fulfil the following requirements: developing a critical self-understanding, making alliances and capturing the ideological realm, and, if it intends to extend its hegemony to a larger public, ensuring development.

A society in which any one of these requirements is absent experiences a crisis of authority and a hegemonic group that fails to maintain at least those requirements that ensure its social alliance, loses its hegemony.

Hegemony, however, is only one side of supremacy, i.e., of the process of consolidation of power, the other side is domination, both through force or fraud, of those social groups outside the alliance.

Thus supremacy is maintained through hegemony over social allies and domination over social antagonists, but if hegemony is not ethical, if it based on fraud and does not take into account the interests of allied groups, is eventually bound to fail and is doomed to be replaced either by force or by true, ethical hegemony.

3.3.4 *Transnational Historical Materialism as a Theory of European Political Economy*

Relying on Gramsci's sociology of power the authors in question understand the relaunch of European integration in the 1980s and the 1990s as a:

> shift from an international configuration of historic blocs based on Fordism, Keynesianism and 'embedded' or 'corporate' liberalism to a transnational neoliberalism.[24]

The nature of this transnational/neoliberal hegemony in Europe is then described by five propositions:

1   that there is a dialectic relation between neoliberalism as a hegemonic project and neoliberalism as a process and therefore there is scope for social struggle in the implementation of the neoliberal project;
2   the process of implementation of neoliberalism implies the following phases:

  * Neoliberalism and a deconstructive project (neoliberalism emerges as the concept with the most convincing analytical and prescriptive framework of the crisis of Keynesianism and defeats corporate liberalism and social democracy in one country after another).
  * Neoliberalism as a constructive project (the phase of the imposition of structural adjustment, liberalisation, deregulation, privatisation; corporate liberalism is discredited, no new alternative can be articulated, and the tenets of neoliberalism are increasingly accepted as valid and legitimate).
  * Neoliberalism in its consolidation phase (internationally as well as within the countries of the advanced capitalist world, any notion of an alternative to the global rule of capital has become utterly 'unrealistic' and discredited and neoliberal reforms are 'locked in' or 'normalised' in the Foucauldian sense).[25]

3   the process of European integration is not autonomous from the formation of a transatlantic hegemonic bloc, but is one of its regional manifestations;
4   this hegemonic bloc is a 'transnational' one, in the sense that it acts simultaneously in both the domestic and the international arena;
5   finally, the conceptualisation of transnationality must also be brought into a fundamental rethinking of the concepts of sovereignty, governance and statehood in the era of globalisation.

3.4 Neo-Marxist Interpretations of Europe

As neo-Gramscians, also Marxist authors criticise mainstream accounts of European integration as ahistorical and failing to understand the roots of present European political arrangements.

One of the most well known neo-Marxist interpretation of the process of European integration is the one suggested by Peter Cocks.[26] In his theoretical contribution Cocks underlines how European political integration dates back to the sixteenth century and has retained to date its objective of state-building at both the national and the international level.

To understand this claim, it is fundamental to remind the reader about the Marxist conception of the state as instrumental to the exercise of power by the dominant capitalist class. The whole process of nation-state building is interpreted within the Marxist paradigm as a process of legitimating of the power of the capitalist class, and state institutions as the agencies through which such a power can be imposed on the rest of society.

Consistently, the *raison d'être* of the whole process of European integration is identified in the necessity to respond to the problems arising from the growth of capitalism. As capitalism grows behind the nation state, the capitalist class needs to identify new institutional referents to fulfil the functions previously performed by the state. Therefore, the European institutions are interpreted as functional to providing the political infrastructure for the expansion of productive forces and legitimising the power of the capitalist class. In the words of the author:

> I contend that integration in Europe was and is a significant way of realizing the spread of authority (State functions) across larger and larger territorial areas so that the fundamental features of capitalism will remain intact. ... Political and economic integration are methods of providing the institutional conditions for the expansion of capital, while social integration is the process of legitimising the new institutions.[27]

Summing up:

> Integration refers to the geographical spread of state functions in response to the exigencies of capital accumulation and the realization of surplus value on the one hand, and their associated legitimation problems, on the other.[28]

Concluding, the notion of political integration from Cocks' perspective is contiguous to the notion of state-building whereas state-building essentially means reproducing the conditions for the survival of the capitalist class and its legitimation at the social level. The process of European integration is consistently interpreted in the historical context of state-building at both the national and international level since the sixteenth century and represents the present institutional response to the traditional needs of the capitalist class.

A completely different Marxist interpretation of the process of European integration is the one proposed by Hazel Smith.[29] The starting point of this approach is Marx's criticism of liberal constitutionalism as expressed in his pamphlet 'On the Jewish Question'.[30] Such a critique is based on the idea that political emancipation, as the one provided by liberal constitutionalism or, nowadays, by liberal democracy, is distinguished from human emancipation and is indeed functional to the needs of capitalism.

In fact, political emancipation aims at attributing to individuals, defined as selfish monads, equal rights to participate to the political process. However, this form of equality is not substantial, in that it does not tackle real inequalities, which are of a socioeconomic nature. The elimination of socioeconomic inequalities would allow for human emancipation but this is by no means an aim of liberal democracy. Moreover, political emancipation is functional to capitalism in that capital needs men to be attributed the right to enter into contractual relationships both as consumers and as workers. Therefore, Marx's historical materialism implies that increasing political liberalisation is likely to accompany expanding capitalist relations of production.

Smith interprets the process of European integration, and, in particular, the rights' agenda of the Amsterdam Treaty, within the Marxian framework examined above. Her analysis locates the discussion in the context of two relationships. The first is that of the dynamic relationship of European integration, as a process that involves the progressive opening of markets, to the institutionalisation of political rights. The second, is the contradiction inherent to 'a capitalist logic which limits individual rights to a politics which is about facilitating capitalist exchange and, at the same time, provides the conditions of possibility for emancipation through the collective exercise of those rights'.[31]

The main questions asked by the author are why did capitalist elites grant social policy rights to workers in the Amsterdam Treaty? Why did they bother? Why did capital accept restrictions on its powers in production?

First of all, discriminatory practices implied in the lack of social policy rights represent a limit to the maximisation of surplus value. Second, the commodification of labour is facilitated by the promotion of the worker as an 'unindividuated individual'. Finally, social policy rights for workers limit the scope for social dumping which is the possibility for some EU states to be unfairly competitive by offering cheaper and more easily exploitable labour.

The problem of the use of this analysis as the basis for the interpretation of the process of European integration is that the latter can be hardly defined as mainly a process of attribution of rights. Indeed, political and social policy rights are still the prerogative of nation states and even the Treaty of Amsterdam is only to a very limited extent concerned about the issue of 'rights'. In other words, it is difficult to use the Marxian concept of political emancipation as opposed to human emancipation as the basis to explain why the process of European integration took place, simply because political emancipation is only a marginal item in the European agenda.

3.5   Conclusions: Critical Approaches as European Political Economy Contributions

In the introduction to Chapter 1 EPE has been defined as those theories addressing history-making events in the process of European economic integration from an integrated international/domestic politics perspective. It could be legitimate, at this point, to ask to what extent the critical approaches reported above correspond to such a definition.

As already mentioned, the eclectic approach devised by Susan Strange to analyse international political economy does not directly address European political and economic integration. It does, however, definitely provide a macro analytical framework within which to address contextually the political and economic dimensions of international events. It is also helpful in identifying the domestic sources of social change by pointing to the role played by a wealth of national actors, from single individuals, to political parties and PO, as well as of transnational actors (particularly multinational firms), though the role played by each actor is not specified in any systematic way.

The neoconstructivist interpretation of Europe proposed in this chapter, on the other hand, does clearly identify the nature of the interrelations between the domestic and the European level of analysis and provide for precise hypotheses on their possible outcomes.[32] Neoconstructivists, moreover, address the issues of integration within the macro framework provided by IR/comparative approaches to European integration, thus focusing mainly on history making or macro events, more than on the day to day running of the European policy-making. However, their stress on the primary role of ideas and shared beliefs to explain policy-makers' decisions, and their related neglect of the distinction between 'low' and 'high' politics in the process of integration, is indicative of a tendency to sideline the economic dimension in favour of more ideological/institutional one. It is true that in some cases the ideological paradigm invoked to explain decision making at the European level is an economic one,[33] but in many other cases the notions invoked are related to, say, national identity or to political ideology.[34] Therefore, the economic dimension is not always central in neoconstructivist reconstructions of European events rendering it sometimes difficult to define them as 'political economy' theories.

This is clearly not the case with both Marxist and neo-Gramscian approaches to European events for the primacy attributed by them to the relations of production as the sources of the social relations shaping both the political and the ideological superstructures. In both cases, moreover, the dichotomy between the national and the international level of analysis is overcome by making reference to the notion of transnationality. Actors, and, in particular, the social groupings arising from the underlying relations of production, are 'transnational', i.e., both national and international, and act in both arenas to further their economic interests.

Notes

1   For a brief overview of these contributions see the introduction to this book.
2   See introduction to this book.
3   See Strange (1991), p. 34.
4   Strange (1991), p. 34.
5   Strange (1991), p. 35.
6   Strange (1991), pp. 38–9.
7   Strange (1998). See also Strange (1996) and Stopford and Strange (1991).
8   Strange (1991), pp. 38–9.
9   See Strange (1991).
10   See following paragraph.
11   Strange (1998).
12   See Börzel and Risse (2000). This paper is a part of contributions to the Jean Monnet Working Paper No. 7/00, Symposium: Responses to Joschka Fischer, and is available at http://www.jeanmonnetprogram.org/papers/00/00f0101.html.
13   For more details on this see Risse-Kappen (1995), Introduction.
14   See Risse-Kappen (1996).
15   See Risse-Kappen (1996), p. 57.
16   See Risse-Kappen (1996).
17   See Risse-Kappen (1996), pp. 64–5.
18   See Risse-Kappen (1996), p. 70.

19 See Risse-Kappen (1996), p. 70.
20 For some recent surveys of similar approaches to the study of European integration, see Bieler and Morton (2001) and also Bieling and Steinhilber (2000).
21 See van Apeldoorn, Overbeek and Ryner (2003).
22 See Cox (1987); Rupert (1995); van der Pijl, *The Making of an Atlantic Ruling Class* (1984, 1998).
23 Gramsci (1971), p. 77.
24 See van Apeldoorn, Overbeek and Ryner (2003).
25 See van Apeldoorn, Overbeek and Ryner (2003).
26 See Cocks (1991).
27 See Cocks (1991), p. 36.
28 See Cocks (1991), p. 37.
29 See Smith (2002).
30 See Marx (1978)
31 Smith (2002), p. 266.
32 See Börzel and Risse (2000). See also Risse, Green Cowles and Caporaso (2001).
33 See MacNamara (1998).
34 See Risse (1998).

References

Bieler, A. and Morton, A.D. (eds) (2001), *Social Forces in the Making of the New Europe. The Restructuring of European Social Relations in the Global Political Economy*, Houndmills: Palgrave.

Bieling, H.-J. and Steinhilber, J. (eds) (2000), *Die Konfiguration Europas. Dimensionen einer kritischen Integrationstheorie*, Münster: Westfälisches Dampfboot.

Börzel, T.A. and Risse, T. (2000), 'When Europe Hits Home: Europeanisation and Domestic Change, Robert Shuman Centre EUI Working Paper No. 2000/56, available at http://www.iue.it/RSCAS/WP-Texts/00_56.pdf.

Börzel, T.A. and Risse, T. (2000), 'Who is Afraid of a European Federation? How to Constitutionalise a Multi-level Governance System', Jean Monnet Working Paper No.7/00, Symposium: Responses to Joschka Fischer, available at http://www.jeanmonnetprogram. org/papers/00/00f0101.html.

Cocks, P. (1991), 'Towards a Marxist Theory of European Integration', in J.A. Frieden and D.A. Lake (1991), *International Political Economy: Perspectives on Global Power and Wealth*, 2nd edn, London: Unwin Hyman.

Cox, R.W. (1977), 'Labour and Hegemony', *International Organization*, Vol. 31, pp. 385–424.

Cox, R.W. (1981), 'Social Forces, States, and World Orders: Beyond International Relations Theory', *Millenium*, No. 10, pp. 127–55.

Cox, R.W. (1982), 'Production and Hegemony: Toward a Political Economy of World Order', in H.K. Jacobson and D. Sidjanski (eds), *The Emerging International Economic Order*, Beverley Hills, CA: Sage.

Cox, R.W. (1987), *Production, Power, and World Order: Social Forces in the Making of History*, New York: Columbia University Press.

Cox, R.W. (1991a), 'The Global Political Economy and Social Choice', in D. Drache and M.S. Gertler (eds), *The New Era of Global Competition*, Montreal: McGill-Queen's University Press.

Cox, R.W. (1991b), 'Real Socialism in Historical Perspective', in R. Miliband and L. Panitch (eds), *Communist Regimes: The Aftermath. The Socialist Register 1991*, London: Merlin Press.

Frieden, J. (1991), 'Invested Interests: The Politics of National Economic Policies in a World of Global Finance', *International Organization*, No. 45 (Autumn).

Frieden, J. (1994), *The Impact of Goods and Capital Market Integration on European Monetary Politics*, preliminary version, August.

Frieden, J. (1998), *The New Political Economy of EMU*, Oxford: Rowman and Littlefield.

Gill, S.R. (1991a), 'Gramsci, Historical Materialism and International Political Economy', in C.N. Murphy and R. Tooze (eds), *The New International Political Economy*, Boulder, CO: Lynne Rienner Publishers.

Gill, S.R. (1991b), 'Reflections on Global Order and Sociohistorical Time', *Alternatives*, No. 16, pp. 275–314.

Gill, S.R. (1992), 'The Emerging World Order and European Change', in R. Miliband and L. Panitch (eds), *Communist Regimes: The Aftermath. The Socialist Register 1991*, London: Merlin Press.

Gill, S.R. and Law, D. (1986), 'Power, Hegemony and International Theory: Recessions and Restructuring in the Global Political Economy', International Studies Association, Annual Congress, Anaheim, CA.

Gill, S.R. and Law, D. (1988), *The Global Political Economy: Perspectives, Problems and Policies*, Brighton: Wheatsheaf.

Gill, S.R. and Law, D. (1989), 'Global Hegemony and the Structural Power of Capital', *International Studies Quarterly*, No. 33, pp. 475–99.

Gramsci, A. (1971), *Selections from the Prisons' Notebook of Antonio Gramsci*, New York: International publishers.

Gramsci, A. (1975), *Quaderni dal carcere*, Torino: Einaudi.

Gramsci, A. (1977), *Selections from Political Writings 1910–1920*, New York: International Publishers.

Gramsci, A. (1978), *Selections from Political Writings 1921–1926*, New York: International Publishers.

MacNamara, K. (1998) *The Currency of Ideas: Monetary Politics in the European Union*, Ithaca, NY: Cornell University Press.

Marx, K. (1978), 'On the Jewish Question', in R.C. Tucker (ed.), *The Marx-Engels Reader*, 2nd edn, London: W.W. Norton.

Overbeek, H. (1987), 'Global Capitalism and Britain's Decline', PhD thesis, University of Amsterdam, Netherlands.

Overbeek, H. (1990), *Global Capitalism and National Decline: The Thatcher Decade in Perspective*, London: Routledge.

Overbeek, H. (1994), *Neoliberalism and Global Hegemony: Concepts of Control in the Global Political Economy*, London: Routledge.

Risse-Kappen, T. (1995), *Bringing Transnational Relations Back In: Non-state Actors, Domestic Structures and International Institutions*, Cambridge: Cambridge University Press.

Risse-Kappen, T. (1996), 'Exploring the Nature of the Beast: International Relations Theory and Comparative Policy Analysis Meet the European Union', *Journal of Common Market Studies*, Vol. 34, No. 1, March, p. 57.

Risse, T. (1998), 'To Euro or Not to Euro? The EMU and Identity Politics in the European Union', ARENA Working Papers WP 98/1, available at http://www.arena.uio.no/publications/wp98_1.htm.

Risse, T., Green Cowles, M. and Caporaso, J. (2001), 'Europeanization and Domestic Change: Introduction', in T. Risse, M. Green Cowles and J. Caporaso (eds), *Transforming Europe: Europeanization and Domestic Change*, Ithaca, NY: Cornell University Press.

Rupert, M. (1995), *Producing Hegemony*, Cambridge: Cambridge University Press.

Smith, H. (2002), 'The Politics of Regulated Capitalism: A Historical Materialist Approach to European integration', in M. Rupert and H. Smith (2002), *Historical Materialism and Globalization*, London: Routledge.

Stopford, J. and Strange, S. (1991), *Rival States, Rival Firms: Competition for World Market Shares*, Cambridge: Cambridge University Press.

Strange, S. (1991), 'An Eclectic Approach', in C.N. Murphy and R. Tooze (eds), *The new International Political Economy*, Boulder, CO: Lynne Rienner.

Strange, S. (1996), *The Retreat of the State*, Cambridge: Cambridge University Press.

Strange, S. (1998), 'Who are the EU? Ambiguities in the Concept of Competitiveness', *Journal of Common Market Studies*, Vol. 36 (1), March, pp. 101–13.

Van Apeldoorn, B., Overbeek, H. and Ryner, M. (2003), 'Theories of European Integration: a critique', in A. Cafruny and M. Ryner (eds), *A Ruined Fortress? Neoliberal Hegemony and Transformation in Europe*, Lanham: Rowman and Littlefield, pp. 17–46.

Van der Pijl, K. (1984), *The Making of an Atlantic Ruling Class*, London: Verso.

Van der Pijl, K. (1988), 'The Socialist International and the Internationalisation of Capital', *After the Crisis: Occasional Papers*, University of Amsterdam, Faculty of Political and Social Science.

Van der Pijl, K. (1989), 'Ruling Classes, Hegemony and the State System', *International Journal of Political Economy* (Fall), pp. 7–35.

Van der Pijl, K. (1998), *Transnational Classes and International Relations*, London: Routledge.

PART 2
PRACTICAL CONCERNS

Chapter 4

Political Economy Explanations of European Monetary Integration

4.1 Introduction

No debate in European integration theory has raised so many questions and has provoked so thriving an academic and intellectual literature as the one concerning European monetary integration. The establishment of a European currency union with the adoption of the Euro as the single currency for millions of EU citizens is arguably the single most important accomplishment of the EU. The monetary union has massive economic, political, and social consequences for the European and international political economy.

What this chapter will not even try to do is to provide a comprehensive historical account of the process leading to EMU, of its institutional setting and organisation, of its economic characteristics and of its socio-political implications. The aim of this contribution is rather more modest although theoretically challenging. It seeks to identify the underlying factors that made it possible to agree on such a complicated and controversial matter, to explain why EMU occurred within a particular time frame, and to identify the winners and losers that resulted from EMU.

The approaches to European political economy analysed in the previous chapters of this book establish the theoretical context within which to find answers to similar questions. Therefore the structure of this chapter will broadly follow the one of the first two chapters of the book. It will tackle first mainstream explanations of European monetary union, mainly neofunctionalist, intergovernmentalist, double game and domestic politics ones. Then it will move on to critical analysts, with special attention to neo-Gramscian and neoconstructivist accounts.

The objective is to report how both mainstream theorists and critical ones have attempted to clarify the 'who-gets-what' and 'who wins and who loses' questions typical of the international political economy approach to European economic integration in relation to the specific problems stemming from the process of European monetary integration.

4.2   Neofunctionalist Accounts of European Monetary Integration: The Need for Monetary Union

Chapter 1 of this book elaborated at length on the neofunctionalist approach to European integration which is based on the concept of spill-over and the existence of functional economic or political linkages between integration areas.

When applied to the issue of economic and monetary union, the spill-over proposition in its milder, political form implies that the 1992 single-market process increased the level of support among public opinion, interest groups and the EC governments for all those EC initiatives that could enhance the gains coming from the single-market programme, namely, the establishment of the single currency.

Moreover, in terms of economic spill-over, EMU was portrayed by the EC Commission, and by Jaques Delors in particular,[1] as functionally linked to the internal market process and necessary for its success.

The Commission's case[2] rests on the argument that complete capital liberalisation, undertaken in July 1990, and exchange rate stability, such as the one provided for by the European monetary system,[3] is incompatible with divergent national monetary policies. As Padoa-Schioppa argues,[4] the stability provided by the quasi-fixed exchange rate mechanism (ERM) of the EMS was viable only thanks to the existence of exchange rate controls. However, when, with the implementation of the Single European Act, exchange rate controls, together with the remaining non-tariff barriers in the trade of goods and services, were finally removed, the system was doomed to collapse unless European countries would agree to renounce autonomous monetary policies. In an environment of capital liberalisation with a single market for goods and services, in fact, there is a sort of trade-off between stable exchange rates and independent national monetary policies. In other words, a) free trade, b) capital mobility, c) fixed (or quasi-fixed) exchange rates and d) autonomous monetary policies form an 'inconsistent quartet'.[5]

The economic explanation for the existence of the 'inconsistent quartet' can be found in the Mundell-Fleming model. This macroeconomic model links the monetary economic equilibrium, that is, the equilibrium of monetarist variables that are given by the equilibrium between the money supply and demand and summarised in the so-called LM curve, and the real variables equilibrium, the equilibrium between investments and savings that is summarised by the so-called IS curve. The model also includes the equilibrium of the external economic relationships in the form of the balance of payments equilibrium, summarised in the so-called BP curve.

According to the Mundell-Fleming model, in a fixed exchange rate regime with full capital mobility, the BP would lie parallel to the 'x' axis, so that any monetary expansion would cause the interest rates to decrease and capital, given the assumption of its complete freedom of movement, would outflow till the interest rate reaches its original level without any rise in domestic demand. Capital outflow, however, would immediately put under strain the exchange rate eventually threatening its stability. Thus, any expansionary monetary policy would prove ineffective in stimulating national economy, while it would eventually undermine the stability of the exchange rate. In other words, there is a trade off between exchange rate stability and autonomous monetary policy-making.

As Figure 4.1 indicates, an increase of the money supply shifts the LM downwards to LM_1 bringing the interest rate from the equilibrium rate i_e to i_1 and the output from Y_e to Y_1. In a situation of perfect capital mobility, however, the decrease in the interest rate produces an immediate outflow of capital for exactly the same amount of money introduced in the economy with the expansionary monetary policy manoeuvre. As a consequence the LM bounces back to its previous position, and interest rate goes back to its equilibrium rate with no increase of the output level. Therefore, the country's independent adoption of an expansionary monetary stance proved ineffective in modifying the real economy. However, in the exchange rate market, the outflow of capital from the country in question, denominated in the national currency, increases

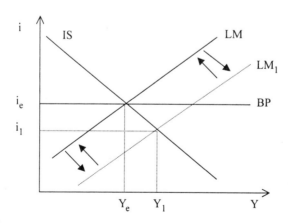

Figure 4.1   Mundell-Fleming model with full capital mobility

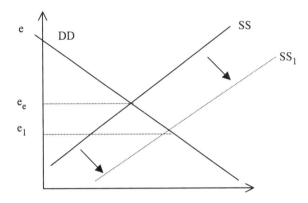

Figure 4.2   Exchange rate market after monetary expansion in full capital mobility

the supply of such a currency from SS to SS_1. Accordingly, if the currency were in a floating exchange rate regime, the equilibrium exchange rate would move from e_e to e_1. In a fixed or quasi-fixed exchange rate system, like the ERM of the EMS, the central bank of the currency considered will have to intervene to avoid devaluation. In the long run, however, such an intervention could prove difficult to sustain, eventually increasing the possibility for the system to enter a crisis and collapse. Concluding, according to this model, in a world of perfect capital mobility autonomous monetary policy is inconsistent with a system of fixed or quasi fixed exchange rates.

Returning to the issues relating to European integration, since the effective working of the internal market established with the Single European Act requires exchange rate stability, which brings about gains in efficiency and transaction costs' savings, the only viable solution is the pooling of national monetary policies in a monetary union. In other words there is a functional linkage between the Single European act and the establishment of EMU.

4.2.1 Critical Remarks

Thus formulated, the neofunctionalist argument appears, at first glance, to provide a compelling account for the development of EMU. However, the economic argument for the functional linkage between the internal market and the process of monetary union is not without problems, as demonstrated by the alternative proposals to EMU in the context of the internal market based on the notion of currency competition. Similar proposals were officially presented by the British government in the summer of 1990,[6] and later on developed into the Treasury's proposal of a thirteenth competitive European currency, the hard-ECU, issued and managed by a special monetary fund.[7]

The British case is particularly relevant. Although Britain did fully endorse and take part in the single market programme, it refused to accept the case for monetary union. The British stance thus challenged the assertion that for an internal market to work it is necessary to pool monetary policies in a currency union. Indeed, some services, like financial services, though perfectly integrated at the regional level, might still prefer to keep autonomous monetary policy decision-making at the national level. In particular, setting the interest rates at a higher level then the other financial centres might represent a relevant competitive advantage in attracting short- to very short-term capital. This, of course, is harmful for industrial activity. However, here the issue becomes one of power relations amongst domestic economic sectors/interest groups. In the context of globalisation, moreover, the issue is also influenced by the extent to which the industrial sector is actually relying on domestic production as opposed to production abroad.[8]

Finally, the timing of monetary union is not consistent with neofunctionalist expectations. The argument of spill-over assumes a learning period: once an integrative step has been taken, the actors discover that they must integrate further in order to realise fully its benefits. In the case of the EMU, however, this learning period did not evolve according to the theory. Capital liberalisation started in 1990 whereas the idea of a currency union had already been proposed in 1969 with the Werner Plan. Moreover the internal market became fully operative only on 31 December 1992 when the Treaty on European Union (TEU) had already been approved. This means that the will to integrate Europe in a currency Union cannot be considered an automatic outcome of the progress already achieved in terms of market integration and the establishment of the Single Market.

4.3   National Interests and EMU: Geopolitical Explanations vs Intergovernmentalist Political Economy

Because of the intergovernmental nature of the decision-making leading to the establishment of EMU, many scholars have stressed the central role played by the nation state and national interests in the evolution of European monetary integration. Both realists and intergovernmentalists, indeed, postulate that nation states dominate EC politics and that outcomes directly reflect the interests and relative power of the member states. Thus both of these related schools of thought analyse the EC as the result of strategies pursued by rational governments acting on the basis of their preferences and power. However, whereas realist scholars tend to identify the interests of the state in geopolitical terms,[9] intergovernmentalists assert the primacy of political economy considerations.

4.3.1 Mixing Geopolitical and Political Economy Motivations for EMU

David Andrews offers an exemplary mixed intergovernmentalist account of the negotiations over the EMU.[10] Having made clear from the outset that the analytical weight assigned to different explanatory factors must vary according to whether the analysis focuses on the negotiations, the ratification process, or the implementation phase, Andrews emphasises the issue of the success of the negotiations, leaving aside the issue of the problems associated with the ratification process and the prospects for implementation of the agreement.

Andrews' central argument is that the Maastricht Treaty resulted from the confluence of interests between the French and the German governments. On the one hand, Germany was particularly keen to secure European acquiescence to reunification. On the other hand, France acted on the basis of a mixture of political-economic and geopolitical considerations, aiming at both restoring some control over its monetary policy-making dominated by Germany within the EMS and, at the same time, at firmly securing a reunited Germany within the European sphere. Importantly, according to the author, the issue of Germany re-unification cannot be separated from geopolitical changes in the international system such as the collapse of the Soviet Union. This event opened, in the words of Andrews, 'a window of opportunity' for France and Germany to come to an agreement on the substance of the EMU. However, since the window of opportunity created by the diplomatic imperative for France of binding Germany to the community following German unification closed after 1992, the actual implementation of the EMU project was doomed to face increasing difficulties, as, indeed was the case.

Thus in contrast to neofunctionalists Andrews emphasises the national interests of the leading European powers in monetary union: French and German elites recognised a changing set of interests resulting from extraordinary developments in the global geopolitical order and political economy, and they reacted accordingly.

Critical remarks Whilst French and German foreign policy goals may have become congruent with monetary union, these goals do not in themselves explain the origins of the process, which predated both the fall of the collapse of Soviet Union and the fall of the Berlin Wall. Moreover, this approach cannot give account of the interest in EMU shown by smaller countries such as Belgium and Italy in 1988 and early 1989. Nor is it clear that the fear of German unification, in the absence of other motives, was sufficient to inspire the other EC states to overcome the difficulties involved in designing supranational institutions and transferring to them monetary sovereignty. Furthermore, this explanation does not account for the role played by political economy interests, namely interest groups pressures in promoting the goal of European Monetary Union. Thus the door is open for a more comprehensive and complete explanation which implies the analysis of structural economic interests and political economy considerations. As we will see in the following section, this need was addressed in the work of Andrew Moravcsik.[11]

4.3.2 A Purely Intergovernmentalist Perspective: The States as Rational Actors Maximising their Economic Interests

Andrew Moravcsik stresses the economic interests of strong and weak-currency countries, under conditions of capital mobility and macroeconomic convergence, within a typical intergovernmentalist framework.[12] As he writes,

> a combination of enduring economic interests, asymmetries of interdependence, and the desire to co-ordinate policy within a structure that assured more credible commitments best explains the conduct and outcome of the Maastricht negotiations.[13]

Of course, the leaders of the process were always France and Germany, who, by 1988 had already agreed on the goal of monetary unification and pressed to achieve it. The reasons underlying this decision were not, however, minimally related to geopolitical considerations, but were of a purely political economy nature, i.e., related to the economic interests of the actors involved.

In particular, as Moravcsik points out,[14] a political economy approach would explain why the position of Germany in the negotiations over EMU did not reflect the strong anti-inflationary position of the Bundesbank but rather a compromise between the Bundesbank's strict anti-inflationary stance and the preferences of the business sector for a devalued exchange rate and low interest rates. These two conflicting positions did indeed dominate the whole German domestic debate in the run-up to the Maastricht negotiations and agreement. Summing up, economic motivations are the only variables which can explain German demands in terms of the 'economic' definition of EMU at the intergovernmental conference, and, in particular its stress on the necessity for convergence criteria prior to unification, the implementation of capital mobility and the establishment of a completely independent European Central Bank. These demands reflected the domestic conflict between, on the one side, the business community and some sectors of the German government pushing for a competitive currency and a more relaxed macroeconomic and monetary approach, and, on the other side, the Bundesbank and the public opinion actively supporting a strict anti-inflationary policy.

On the French side, it is indisputable that the country's interest since 1984 was to increase the symmetry of the European monetary arrangements which, after the implementation of the ERM of the EMS, had clearly been dominated by Germany as the 'hegemon' of the system. However, according to Moravcsik what is important to verify are the reasons underlying this particular policy preference. Geopolitical factors, especially those related to the need to keep Germany firmly within Europe after its unification, are discounted on the grounds that the French policy preference did not change with the collapse of the Berlin Wall or with the unification of Germany, but rather remained steadily consistent from 1984 until the Maastricht negotiations. Indeed, political economy motivations ultimately explain French policies and actions. In fact the EMU was seen as perfectly consistent with the long-standing French international monetary goals. France had long since been committed to an anti-inflationary policy and had supported a strong Franc (the so-called *Franc fort* policy) and capital liberalisation since Mitterrand's macroeconomic policy shift in 1984. However, the European monetary arrangements established with the ERM of the EMS gave a structural advantage in terms of monetary policy-making to Germany. Therefore France had a clear interest in seeking to retain the same policy preference within a more symmetrical system like the one devised at Maastricht for the establishment of EMU. In this regard, a more symmetrical EMU offered more advantages than the asymmetrical EMS, including, as listed by Moravcsik, lower risk premia and exchange rate volatility, greater political legitimation and more symmetrical obligations *vis-à-vis* Germany which would translate into looser constraints on macroeconomic policy and therefore in a slightly more competitive European currency.[15] All these factors explain the very strong support given to EMU by the French business community.

Finally, the case of British opposition to EMU is particularly revealing in terms of showing the extent to which national preferences were formed on political economy considerations and not on geopolitical strategic ones. Whilst there is little evidence that Britain's rejection of EMU was based on 'antipathy' towards Germany, there is a great deal of evidence in favour of a political economy approach. Political economy theory, according to Moravcsik, correctly predicted that the British would accept only minor monetary or exchange rate commitments, mainly favoured by the British business elites for they were concerned on the one side by 'the slide in competitiveness that might result from any firm commitment to stable exchange rates'[16] and, on the other side, they 'would seek to avoid any permanent exclusion from monetary arrangements, for exclusion was perceived as undermining the global position of British industry and, above all, finance'.[17]

Table 4.1 summarises the positions of the three nations in the course of the negotiations leading to the establishment of EMU.

Critical remarks One of the most widespread criticisms of intergovernmentalist explanations is the difficulty of using concepts such as 'power' and 'coercion' to explain why minor countries should have accepted EMU. These concepts are in fact undeniably difficult to define analytically and measure empirically, particularly with respect to such a complex and multifaceted issue as the process of European monetary integration.[18] For Moravcsik, power is exerted by the major countries through the recourse to 'threats and promises', which, in turn, must be credible in order to be effective. However, Moravcsik does not specify precisely what factors render credible the threats and promises required for power to be exerted and he does not explain satisfactorily why an international agreement that does not maximise the smaller states' interests would be accepted.

Moreover, as Alesina and Grilli observe,[19] there are many circumstances under which pro-EMU countries would be better off keeping more reticent members out of a monetary union rather than forcing them to join. Even at the theoretical level, then, it is difficult to construct an explanation of the process leading to Economic and Monetary Union on the basis of an intergovernmental bargaining model without developing further analytical tools particularly in relation to domestic interest formation. Indeed, to be able to identify the interests of a State in the negotiations leading to international economic agreement like EMU it is important to identify the distributional effects of the agreement. To address this task the next section turns to the discussion of Frieden's account of the making of EMU.

Table 4.1   Economic and monetary union negotiations, 1988–92: preferences and outcomes

Elements of EMU	Germany	France	Britain	Commission	Outcome
Single currency (EMU)	Prefers EMU with no 'opt-out' but demands parliamentary vote to 'opt-in'	Prefers EMU with no 'opt-out'	Opposes EMU All countries have to 'opt-in' explicitly but cannot be excluded	French position	EMU with British and Danish 'opt-out' and unilateral German 'opt-in'
Strict convergence criteria ('two speed EMU')	Favours prior but flexible macroeconomic convergence criteria; prior autonomy of national central banks; and full capital liberalisation	None	Unclear	French position	German position prevails
Schedule and procedure for transition	Favours automatic movement in 1999, with qualified majority voting to decide which countries qualify. In the interim a weak EMI headed by a central banker	Favours rapid movement in 1997 or before by simple majority vote. Strong interim EMI starting in 1993, headed by an EU official	Favours maximal delay. Weak transitional EMI headed by a central banker	French position	Final transition in 1997 if a majority qualify, 1999 automatically, with QMV to determine membership. Weak interim EMI headed by a central banker

Elements of EMU	Germany	France	Britain	Commission	Outcome
ECB autonomy, mandate and voting procedure	Prefers autonomous bank, except for multilateral exchange-rate policy, firm anti-inflationary mandate, and simple majority decision-making	Favours political control, particularly over exchange rates, balanced mandate and decisions by simple majority	Opposes EMU but apparently argues that the ECB should be autonomous with a strong anti-inflationary mandate	French position plus ever stronger Commission role	German position prevails
Location of ECB and name of currency	Frankfurt; Euro	Paris, maybe Brussels, ECU	London, ECU	Brussels	Frankfurt, Euro (decision later)
Domestic budgetary controls with sanctions	Yes, by simple majority	No	No	No	Yes, decision by QMV (later)
Financial transfers	No bail-outs; no financial transfers	No financial transfers	No financial transfers	Fiscal federalism: large, permanent financial transfers	No bail-outs or federalism, but temporary increase in structural funds (decision later)

Source: Moravcsik (1998), p. 382.

4.3.3 Domestic Economic Sectors and EMU: Who Wins and Who Loses at the Domestic Level from the Establishment of EMU?

Jeffry Frieden makes a major contribution to the study of European political economy because he seeks to develop a model that specifies the interests of basic economic sectors with respect to the two interrelated dimensions of the degree of exchange rate flexibility and the level of the exchange rates.[20] The model makes it possible to explain and predict who wins and who loses at the domestic level from the establishment of EMU. We can also assume that the most motivated groups in supporting the establishment of EMU will be those economically most affected by monetary integration.

According to the rigorous analytical framework proposed by Frieden,[21] in relation to the exchange rate regime preferences, those groups heavily involved in cross-border economic activity will be more favourable to the establishment of EMU because it will reduce the costs of hedging and transactions. Moreover, especially if they are mainly involved in EU-wide economic relations, the loss of monetary policy autonomy would be a negligible sacrifice in exchange for the benefits stemming from the adoption of a single regional currency. The reverse is true for those socioeconomic groups mainly involved in national economic activities, including producers of non tradable goods and services who have nothing to win from the country's joining a currency union while they still attribute a high value to retaining autonomous monetary policy-making. Therefore, domestically oriented economic actors are assumed by Frieden to be rather indifferent if not opposed to the EMU project, while regionally or globally oriented economic actors are assumed to endorse it fully.

With respect to the second dimension of the model, namely groups' preferences *vis-à-vis* the level of the exchange rates, Frieden notes that fixing exchange rates can lead to a real appreciation of the currency, since national inflation rates are normally higher then those of the anchor country of the system.[22] This puts an evident strain on those traditional manufacturers competing with imports. It reduces the export competitiveness of nationally based manufacturers, mainly producing standardised goods for which price competition is extremely relevant, and primary producers of non-agricultural products, since the agricultural sector is covered by the arrangements of the CAP. The reaction of those groups to the real appreciation of their national currency following the government's commitment to EMU should be to ask for a devaluation while, however, still supporting the final goal of establishing a single currency given its advantages in terms of cost reduction for the manufacturing sector, especially if it is exposed to international competition.

Indeed, similar reactions were registered in the immediate aftermath of the Maastricht Treaty, when the manufacturing sectors of the countries with the weakest currencies, including Italy, Spain and Ireland, started voicing their discontent with the overvaluation of their national currencies triggering the ERM crisis of 1992 (and its *de facto* collapse) while at the same time overtly supporting the establishment of EMU.[23]

Summing up, the following assumptions as regards socioeconomic sectors' support from EMU might be derived from Frieden's model:

1   socioeconomic groups involved in cross-border economic activities, like internationally oriented banks and corporations, should support monetary union;
2   domestically oriented firms should be indifferent or hostile;
3   in case of a real appreciation of the currency, the manufacturing sector should push for a competitive devaluation.

According to Frieden, evidence on the positions adopted by the various interest groups in the different European countries involved in the process of European monetary integration seems to support the hypotheses highlighted above. As he writes,

> In most EU members, regionally or globally active firms and banks have been strongly supportive of monetary integration; this is true even in Germany, where the big international banks might be expected to share some of the Bundesbank's scepticism. By the same token, complaints from manufacturers and primary producers have certainly been important in those countries and instances in which a transitional real appreciation has threatened the national commitment to monetary integration.[24]

Critical remarks   Frieden's analytical model is indeed extremely useful in identifying the groups that might support the establishment of EMU in particular countries. Therefore, his approach helps to explain why smaller countries have in fact agreed to surrender part of their sovereignty to form a monetary union. Frieden's approach also allows us to define state interests on the basis of a systematic analysis of its domestic constituents' interests, thus avoiding the tendency to characterise state preferences in an idiographic way or to rely on a purely descriptive analyses of national interests, as, to a certain extent happens in Moravcsik's reconstruction of Maastricht negotiations.

The problem with Frieden's application, however, is that it fails to include within the model the reasons why the preferences of certain domestic groups should prevail over those of another group. The model fails to introduce the notion of power relations. As we will see further on, some EPE contributors have tried to address precisely this shortcoming in Frieden's analysis by proposing an analytical framework able to account also for the existence of power and power relations amongst societal groups. However, before turning to the discussion of this issue, the following paragraph will present an overview of the various attempts made in the discipline to carry out a synthesis between neofunctionalist, intergovernmentalist and domestic politics explanations of European monetary integration.

4.4 Attempts to Effect a Synthesis of Mainstream Traditional Approaches to EMU

4.4.1 The Two-level Game Approach and its Application to the Establishment of EMU

Robert Putnam's integrated domestic-international politics model has been applied by many scholars as the analytical framework within which to interpret the process leading to the establishment of EMU.

Some applications of the two-level game approach focus on the institutional implications of bargaining links. These applications contend that it is important to view the debate over EMU as embedded in an institutional pattern of inter-state cooperation on many levels. For example, Lisa Martin[25] examines the way in which formal institutions and decision-making procedures have shaped negotiations on monetary union. She argues that the institutional structure of the EU has both created and facilitated demands for cross-issue linkages and that these linkages characterise the successful bargaining on the EMU. However, domestic ratification procedures, such as referenda or parliamentary ratifications, and changes in the context of linkage also posed challenges for the implementation and enforcement of the Maastricht arrangements. These challenges were intensified by domestic concerns about the democratic accountability of legislative behaviour of the EC institutions. This domestic-international institutional dynamics is then used to explain the slow-down of the process of European integration and the EMS crisis of 1992.

While Martin focuses on bargaining linkages, Geoffrey Garrett identifies the Bundesbank as the key institutional actor of the process of European monetary integration in all its phases. Garrett argues that the Bundesbank's policy was crucial for the economic fortune of the other EC members, the stability of the EMS and ultimately the prospects for EMU. Thus Garrett adopts an institutionalist approach at the national level and an intergovernmentalist one at the international level.[26]

A more strictly intergovernmentalist application of the integrated international-domestic politics approach to the process of European monetary integration was proposed by Jeoffrey Woolley[27] with reference to the specific case of Germany. Woolley focuses in greater detail on the domestic politics of EMU. Like Garrett, he regards the German strategy as closely related to the changed environment created by German unification. However, he highlights the foreign policy impact of German domestic politics, arguing that German Chancellor, Helmut Kohl, may have had little choice in domestic political terms but to make German support to EMU conditional upon agreement about European political union. His argument rests upon the hypothesis, empirically tested, that the linkage between economic and monetary unification and political unification was accomplished as a result of German policy. Indeed, he argues that the insertion of the issue of European Political Union (EPU) in the Maastricht agenda was a function of Kohl's need to make compatible international and domestic interests by, on the one hand, giving to the EC partners German commitment to the EMU in exchange for their consent to German unification. On the other hand, it was necessary to assure domestic constituents of the commitment to EPU in order to have their consensus to the EMU in the implementation phase. However, Woolley concludes that it was precisely this decision that provoked the substantial slowing of the progress toward EMU after the signing of the Maastricht agreement. The domestic actors that Woolley deems most significant are the German governing coalition partner, the Free Democratic Party (FDP), the opposition party, the Social Democratic Party (SPD), the Bundesbank and the Lander. Woolley pays much less attention to the role of the private sector in shaping attitudes towards Economic and Monetary Union as linked to the European political union.

4.4.2 A Compromise Solution: Sandholtz's Eclectic Perspective

An attempt to assemble the three main theoretical approaches to the process of European monetary integration, namely the intergovernamental approach, the institutional approach and the domestic politics one, has been effected by Wayne Sandholtz in his article 'Choosing Union: monetary politics and Maastricht'.[28] Because his principal goal is to explain why different governments came to define their national interests in ways that included monetary integration, Sandholtz develops five propositions aimed to answer this question.

At the outset Sandholtz assumes that states preferences are endogenous and require explanation, that is, he recognises the need to analyse domestic politics in order to account for international events, but the explanatory propositions he uses are taken from different approaches with the aim of being able to assign a relative weight to each of them to justify conclusions about which factors are more important in explaining outcomes. Thus, institutionalist explanations of the Maastricht agreement can be combined with traditional intergovernmental ones and with new domestic politics considerations to provide a comprehensive account of the overall phenomenon.

The institutional propositions taken by Sandholtz range from the thesis according to which the spill-overs from the 1992 single market process increased the level of support among public and leaders for EC level initiatives; to the hypothesis that the drive for EMU came largely from France and states that wanted a greater voice in EC monetary policy-making; to the view that a number of governments favoured EMU because it would provide the higher possible level of counter inflationary policy credibility by once and for all 'tying their hands'.[29]

From the intergovernmental point of view the main traditional claim is that the Maastricht agreement reflected Germany's desire to gain EC partners' support for the process of German unification. Finally, the domestic politics approach comprises two arguments: the first highlights the distributional effects of economic policies while the second turns to the constraints set by the weight of the opinion in the electorate.[30]

In the integrated approach by Sandholtz, only if taken together are these different propositions sufficient to explain why there was space for an international agreement on monetary union among the various national preferences.

Moreover Sandholtz's analysis introduces a neoconstructivist element by rooting the discussion of the Maastricht Treaty in the conversion to neoliberal monetary discipline in several European countries during the 1980s. The convergence to low inflation rates that occurred in the EMS during this period was in fact not due to any EMS change that rendered it more effective. Rather the success of the EMS derived from the new inclination of a number of EC countries, particularly the weakest ones, to commit themselves to low inflation policies.

4.5   The Role of Identities and Ideas in the Making of EMU: Neoconstructivist Explanations

Neoconstructivist explanations of the establishment of EMU can be divided into two basic groups:

1   identity oriented constructivists;
2   economic ideas oriented constructivists.

The first group of scholars[31] is, to a certain extent, more radical in the adoption of neoconstructivist assumptions in that they believe that the process of monetary integration, and, in particular, the establishment of EMU can be explained within the context of identity politics. Their effort is therefore mainly oriented to verifying the 'symbolic' nature of the 'Euro' in relation to the national collective identity and symbols. Importantly, these authors discard as contradictory economic motivations for EMU and attribute explanatory value only to non-economic political constructions

The second groups of authors,[32] particularly Kathleen McNamara, on the contrary, still attribute importance to economic factors to explain EMU, but stress the role of economic ideas as opposed to economic interests. In their view, EMU became a necessity in the context of the establishment of a new economic consensus, the neoliberal 'consensus of competitive liberalism' amongst the political elites of all EC member states.

4.5.1   Collective Identity as the Explanatory Variable of States' Stances over EMU

The main argument of identity-based neoconstructivist 'reconstruction' of the making of EMU is based on the following propositions:

1   the establishment of EMU is mainly a political event. Indeed, from a purely economic point of view the endeavour would not have even been attempted since its economic benefits are controversial and difficult to define; .
2   the political meaning of EMU is given by the 'visions' about the European order prevailing in the different member states;
3   similar 'visions' need to be understood within the framework of identity politics. This means that the different stances over EMU adopted by the different EU member states can be explained with reference to different national identities.

The reason why national identities are so relevant in the analysis of European monetary union is that 'money' is a 'political' notion intimately related to the symbolic process of state and nation building. Because the national currency is a symbol of the national identity the renunciation of such a symbol must be interpreted within the context of a changing national identity and the development of the European identity as constructed within the national one. To a certain extent, the Euro is the symbol of the new European identity, which, however, is perceived differently in various EU member states.[33]

For example, because French and German political elites of all political orientations have incorporated the European identity into the national identity, the debate in these two countries was not about whether to join EMU but when and why. In Britain, on the other hand, Europe remains outside and, to some extent, contrary to the collective definition of the British identity. Hence political elites continue to resist joining EMU.

This general line of argument is developed by Thomas Risse. In France, according to Risse, 20 years ago the French political elite would not have agreed to EMU for:

1   the prevalence of Keynesian monetarist policies incompatible with the monetarist outlook of EMU;
2   an intergovernmentalist vision of the European political order based on the idea of 'a Europe of nations' incompatible with such a huge transfer of sovereignty as that implied in EMU.

During the 1990s, however, there was a major change in French ideology underpinning economic and monetary policy and, more generally, towards the European order. These changes, moreover, occurred across the political spectrum. On the one hand, French socialists re-oriented towards neoliberal economics and a federal Europe. As a result, for the French Left, the French identity is transformed and Europeanised, but only to the extent to which the new idea of Europe could resonate with previous visions of the state. Europe was thus seen as a projection of France in a period of globalisation. Hence, at Maastricht the socialist government of François Mitterrand defended a version of EMU that was consistent with French state interventionism. Indeed, the French proposed during the negotiations that monetary policy should be co-decided by the Council of Ministers and the ECB and that the ECB had to realise the community goals of economic growth and employment. Although EMU eventually looked rather different from the French ideas about the

European economic order, the socialist government continued to support it as part of its 'political' vision of Europe.

Similar changes in the prevailing visions of the European order combined with reconstructions of French national identity took place in the French Right. However, ideas of grandeur and independence still resonated with the French Right.

Summing up, support and opposition for EMU in the French debate have centred around competing conceptions of national sovereignty and French identity.

The reconstructions of the French national identities were triggered by two identity crises: first, the failure of the socialist programme in the 1980s, and second the end of the Cold War which brought to a re-united Germany and a more marginalised France. The way out for both those crises was Europe and the Euro.

In the case of Germany, the reason for the stubbornness of the German elite in favour of Europe, despite its economic disadvantages for the country, must again be found in identity politics. General support for the single currency is based on Euro-patriotism, a significant aspect of German collective identity developed in response to its nationalist and militarist past. Moreover, the consensus prevailing amongst all political parties for a federalist political order in Europe, further strengthened the case for EMU which was seen as a step towards political integration. On the other hand, opposition to the Euro also originated in the so-called DM patriotism. This explains the German government's insistence on the rigid implementation of the Maastricht criteria: the desire to make the Euro as strong as the DM, and the insistence on shaping the European Central Bank on the model of the German Bundesbank.

Therefore, to the extent that there has been a German debate on the Euro, this was set in terms of Euro patriotism vs DM patriotism. However, the former construction is much stronger than the latter, and this explains why Germany was so keen to enter EMU.

Finally, British Euro-scepticism is grounded on collective understandings of English national identity. Within the United Kingdom 'visions' of the European political order have ranged from those opposing further Europeanisation in all political parties to a minority of 'federalists' in the Labour and Liberal Democratic parties who support the idea of a 'Europe of nations.'

This collective identity of Britain *vis-à-vis* Europe is reflected in the attitude towards EMU. Both the Labour and the Conservative parties advocate a 'wait and see' policy and both are committed to hold a referendum before entering. The general public opposes the introduction of the Euro and the official position of the government at Maastricht was to bargain for an 'opt-out' clause. Indeed, the collective identification with national symbols, national history, and national institutions is far greater in the British political discourse than a potential identification with European symbols, history and institutions. The social construction of Englishness as the core of British national identity 'comprises the meanings attached to institutions, historical memories and symbols',[34] as a consequence, the vision of Europe cannot transcend the narrow confines of intergovernmentalism.

Summing up, the first neoconstructivist argument why Britain does not enter EMU is that the pound sterling is one of the most powerful symbols of Britain's great past as a world power. In the words of Risse: 'This symbolism is directly related to notions of sovereignty – an English exceptionalism distinguishing Britain from the European Continent.'[35]

The second argument is that the Euro and EMU are steps towards a political union, which is against British sovereignty. The Euro would lead to a more politically integrated Europe, therefore to reduced British sovereignty.

Concluding, in this neoconstructivist analysis, British rejection of EMU is understandable only by making reference to constructions of national identity.

Critical remarks In so far as constructivism highlights the cultural terrain on which debates on European union are generally framed, it has a certain appeal. However, the approach is problematic because it is based on a tautology: every single step in the process of European integration, including EMU, can be referred to a particular aspect of the collective perception of national *vis-à-vis* European identity. Thus constructivist approaches to EMU face the same problem as all idealist explanations in the social sciences: the analysis takes the existence of ideas as given rather than seeking to explain how and why ideas originated and changed as a result of political and economic factors. Moreover, the definition itself of national/European identity is not straightforward as Risse seems to believe and might be the object of even more controversies than the author claims is the case in relation to the definition of the economic interests involved in the establishment of EMU. Indeed, the author seems to discard too easily and in too simplistic a way the economic case for the single currency.

Therefore, in the following section attention is turned to how neoconstructivists inserted economics and economic ideas into their analyses.

4.5.2 McNamara and the Changing of the Prevailing Economic
Ideological Paradigm

The central role attributed to economic ideas and ideological paradigms is the basis of Kathleen McNamara's contribution to the explanation of monetary integration.[36] In her seminal work on the subject McNamara claims that the explanation for European monetary cooperation, and, in particular, of the success of the ERM of the EMS, lies in the new 'neoliberal policy consensus'[37] about the objectives and tools of monetary policy spreading in Europe from the mid-1970s. This consensus, in turn, was the consequence of a shift in the dominant beliefs about macroeconomic policy – from the Keynesian paradigm to the neoliberal one – that occurred within the framework of increasing international interdependence.

The focus of the analysis, thus, shifts to the 'reconstruction' of the 'national elites' ideas about the nature of the domestic economy and the 'goals and instruments' of monetary policy and how those directly informed decision-makers' positions on European monetary integration.

As McNamara writes:

> Ideas are critical in the monetary realm because of continuing uncertainty over the basic workings of the macro economy, the difficulty of collecting and interpreting signals from macroeconomic data about the effects of policy, and the lack of agreement over what constitutes 'correct' macroeconomic policy.[38]

In other words, the uncertainties surrounding the actual working of the macroeconomic sphere, especially regarding monetary policy, brings about the necessity for policy-makers to rely on shared beliefs which provide them with strategies to implement policies. These shared beliefs, however, belong to different ideological paradigms. Competing paradigms specify radically different policy outcomes. Indeed, the policy prescriptions contained in similar paradigms are not neutral. Why, then, did policy-makers adopt the strict anti-inflationary stance implied in the establishment first of the ERM of the EMS and then of EMU?

For McNamara, the reason is that in the period preceding the creation of the EMS, the majority of European states had abandoned the Keynesian approach to monetary policy in favour of neoliberalism. The rejection of Keynesianism gave credibility to the EMS endeavour, despite the decision to liberalise capital movements, and represented the basis for the agreement on EMU.

In fact, the neoliberal consensus is based on the pursuit of strict anti-inflationary policies and centres around the following beliefs: first, that expansionary macroeconomic or monetary policies are ineffective in improving the performance of real economic variables, namely the level of output and unemployment, while producing inflationary pressures. Moreover, similar policies weaken exchange rates, further increasing inflation and creating balance of payment's problems. The second belief which is at the core of the neoliberal consensus is that the trade off between higher inflation and less unemployment predicted by the Phillips curve is untenable in the medium to long-term. Instead the only way to increase the level of employment and output is to maintain stable inflation rates. At the same time, the achievement of price stability is put at risk by the government's tendency to cheat on anti-inflationary policies to achieve higher growth rates especially during elections. Therefore, the neoliberal approach discourages state's intervention in the economy to further the credibility of anti-inflationary measures. Once the policy-makers of the EC member states became convinced of the appropriateness of similar claims, they started implementing them, first at the national level, and then in the EMS as an anti-inflationary strait-jacket.

The reasons why this policy consensus could be achieved are represented, according to the author, by the following ones:

1   the perceived failure of Keynesianism in the face of the first oil crisis;
2   the existence of an alternative policy paradigm, monetarism, to frame and legitimise the new macroeconomic policy;
3   Germany's success with restrictive, monetarist policies.[39]

The Maastricht Treaty also reflected the neoliberal 'consensus of competitive liberalism' that emerged in Europe after the first oil crisis.[40] As noted above, the neoliberal paradigm denied the role of expansionary monetary policies as a tool to improve the performance of the real economy. Once the Single European Act was fully implemented, with complete capital liberalisation, the states found themselves having to choose between exchange rate stability and independent monetary policy. The existence of a consensus on a neoliberal approach made the choice to pool monetary policies in a monetary union unavoidable. That all EC policy-makers were convinced about such a choice is then proved by the fact that the Commission justified the adoption of EMU using the theory of the 'inconsistent quartet' by Padoa-Schioppa, thus explicitly recognising the existence of a trade-off between stable exchange

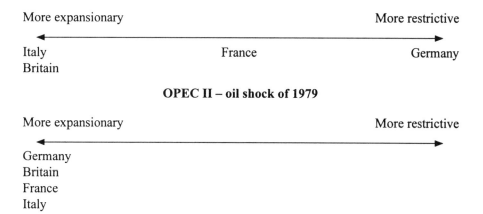

OPEC I – oil shock of 1973

More expansionary   More restrictive

Italy   France   Germany
Britain

OPEC II – oil shock of 1979

More expansionary   More restrictive

Germany
Britain
France
Italy

Figure 4.3   Macroeconomic policy in Europe: responses to OPEC I and II

Source: McNamara (1998), p. 64.

rates and autonomous monetary policies and endorsing the sacrifice of the latter on the basis of a clear neoliberal reasoning.

Thus McNamara concludes that the existence of a neoliberal consensus amongst the EU governments on a low-inflation German model style EMU allowed for the reaching of an agreement at Maastricht.

Critical remarks Clearly, the change in the prevailing ideological paradigm from the mid-1970s onwards is one side of the spread of the new credo in macroeconomic policy, a credo emphasising strict monetary and fiscal policy in the context of exchange rate stability. However, what is lacking from this interpretation of monetary integration is the reasons why this shift happened in that particular historical moment. The solution to this dilemma is to be found in a more comprehensive analysis of the economic interests underpinning this ideological shift and of the related socioeconomic groups taking advantage from it in the context of the change in the power relations taking place in the socioeconomic arena within a particular historical conjuncture. Some answers to these questions are provided by neo-Gramscian explanations of EMU.

4.6   Power Relations and Socioeconomic Interest Groups in the Neo-Gramscian Perspective

As with neoconstructivism, so also within the neo-Gramscian tradition it is possible to recognise two different approaches to EMU. The first stresses the role of the transnational hegemonic bloc in institutionalising, through the establishment of the neoliberal project of EMU, its priorities and interests at the regional level.

An alternative reading of the making of EMU from the neo-Gramscian perspective still considers the national dimension as the most relevant one in the process of European monetary integration and tries to define the interests of the leading (or 'hegemonic') socioeconomic groups through a systematic analytical framework.

Let us have a closer look at these perspectives.

4.6.1   EMU as the Constitutionalisation of the Structural Power of a Transnational Socioeconomic Bloc

From the neo-Gramscian standpoint, European restructuring, i.e., the process of European integration in the last years, from the establishment of the Single Market to the process of European monetary integration, resulted from the emergence of a 'transnational historical bloc of forces' creating a new neoliberal political order designed to represent the interests of the transnational capitalist class.

In other words, the struggle at both the national and regional level over the institutional nature and content of EMU reflects the struggle between opposed transnational socioeconomic groups for the implementation of different political economy projects. The one which has prevailed at Maastricht, is the neoliberal political economy project of the hegemonic bloc formed by the transnational capitalist class. At the European level, this project implied the constitutionalisation of the liberalisation of capital markets, the creation of the single market, and the particular form of EMU based on tight monetary and fiscal policies and on central bank independence.

Why did such a project prevail over the other alternatives?

The reasons are both structural and social. From the structural point of view, the substitution of the previous model of European integration, based on the notion of state intervention in the national economy and liberalisation of cross-border relations, the so-called model of the 'embedded liberalism' or 'compensatory liberalism', entered a crisis because of the pressures exercised on the one side, by a persistent fiscal crisis, and, on the other side, by the new global patterns of capital accumulation. This led to a significant reshaping of the form of state.

From the social point of view, the neoliberal project could prevail thanks to the consensus of a strong socioeconomic coalition, or bloc, composed, according to Stephen Gill, a leading neo-Gramscian, by '... both affluent workers, as well as broader sections of the middle classes, as well as interests of *haute finance* and international mobile capital'.[41] The term more easily describing the conception of EMU in this neo-Gramscian perspective is 'new constitutionalism'.[42] Such a term indicates the process of institutionalisation of forms of governance at the European level, like the particular forms of EMU agreed at Maastricht, that serve to perpetuate the hegemony of the transnational capitalist bloc.

Gill identifies at least four main features of new constitutionalism.[43] First, the so-called 'bond vigilants', i.e., broadly speaking, the international financial institutions, and the EC for that matter, enforce upon the states the neoclassical rule that, to achieve low inflation, monetary policy must be separated from pressures of domestic politics and, hence, accountability. This is normally ensured through the creation of independent central banks, which institutionalises (or 'constitutionalises') both the goal of low inflation and the separation of monetary policy and domestic politics. The establishment of EMU responded perfectly to this element of new-constitutionalism, since it implied the creation of an independent European central bank, unaccountable to domestic politics and pursuing the only goal of price stability. Of course, however, there is no economic necessity that low inflation should be the only goal of monetary policy. Low inflation is a 'political judgement' that clearly favours the interests of particular socioeconomic groups over others.

The second element of new constitutionalism is a fiscal one, and requires that budget deficits must be sustainable. This is clearly spelled in the Maastricht criteria on fiscal convergence and reiterated in the growth and stability pact. The sanction for those governments not following the rule of sustainable deficits is that they face 'rising risk premiums', i.e., *ceteris paribus*, they risk having to adopt higher interest rates to be able to sell their debt (bonds) to international investors. Of course, international investors belong to the transnational capitalist class, and they have a vested interest in smaller budgets which allow for a higher degree of privatisation of public assets. Also in this case, then, the 'constitutionalised' rule serves the interests of a very specific interest bloc.

The third element is transparency and market based surveillance. This is reflected in the adoption of rules which make monetary and fiscal policy-making by central governments accountable only to the markets. This renders the markets, and, consequently, the social group of transnational investors and capitalists, the sole judges of the appropriateness of similar policies. Moreover, the transparency requirement facilitates the flow of information to market operators and international regulators about the conduct of economic policy, thus increasing their power and control over the states. 'These "new constitutionalist" initiatives will have the effect of lessening short-run political pressures on the formulation of economic policy.'[44] In other words, thanks to new constitutionalism, of which EMU is a clear example, the democratically elected national government lose the power to control economic policy. This power is instead attributed to technocrats or civil servants.

Summing up, for Gill,[45] the effects of this neoliberal restructuring in Europe are:

1   to shift the general form of state in the direction of a more disciplinary neoliberal framework;
2   to increase the size of the private sector relative to the public sector in economic activity;
3   to therefore increase the ration of money that is in private hands relative to that in the hands of the public sector;
4   to attenuate democracy through providing more autonomy for non-elected, unaccountable bodies;
5   Maastricht has therefore been conceived to sustain a hospitable investment climate and, together with the Single European Act, to facilitate the maximisation of the structural power of capital in Europe.

In broader terms, this European restructuring is just a moment of a more global restructuring process, producing consequences not only at the level of inter-state relations, but on social relations, on culture and on institutions.[46] In particular, the outcomes of this global neoliberal restructuring are:

1   from the political economy point of view, the prevalence of the private sector over the public;
2   from the socio-cultural point of view, the spread and deepening of market values and of possessive individualism;
3   from the sociological point of view, the commodification of social relations, by this meaning the insertion of social and personal relation within the market sphere, under the rule of the demand, supply and price;

4   from the point of view of values, the tendency for efficiency to prevail over equity;
5   from the psychological standpoint, the erosion of social solidarity is translated into the increase of personal insecurity and uncertainty.

Critical remarks Apart from the traditional mainstream criticisms to critical theories, which will not be dealt with here, what might be noted in this neo-Gramscian approach is that it risks being too generic in the use of the notion of 'neoliberalism' to explain the specific issue of EMU. 'Neoliberalism' is, after all, a general articulating principle which is commensurate to a wide range of concrete policy options. It is therefore ill-suited to explain differences in policy choices across countries or across time.

Also the notion of a transnational capitalist class able to enforce its preferences in all EU states through the 'new-constitutionalist process' does not allow for differences in the behaviour and in the interest definition of the different capitalist classes still existing in the different member states. For example, it is not necessarily true that the interests of the British financial elite coincide with the interest of the German bourgeoisie or with those of the Italian small and medium entrepreneurs. Indeed, the European capitalist class does not appear, at a closer analysis, as cohesive and monolithic as the transnationalist version of neo-Gramscianism assumes.

The following section will, therefore, try to elucidate the differences still existing amongst the interests of the different ruling (or 'hegemonic') blocs in the different European countries proposing an analytical framework able to trace and explain them.

4.6.2 An Alternative Neo-Gramscian Analytical Framework and its Application to the Attitudes of Italy and the UK in the Process of European Monetary Integration

The critical political economy approach to the credibility of exchange rate proposed here[47] challenges the mainstream theory belief that markets, in general, and financial markets in particular stand aside of history and society and behave independently from social and political considerations. This approach grounds financial markets behaviour in the underlying political economy structure of capitalist economies subordinating their expectations to the interests of the hegemonic (in the Gramscian sense) socioeconomic groups.[48] It challenges the assumption of the infallibility of the markets and of their independent 'inner rationality' and proposes an alternative political economy rationality, which embeds markets' expectations into a given socioeconomic structure.

This political economy approach to the credibility of exchange rate commitments and of the rationality of financial market behaviour transcends the ahistorical and abstract explanations provided by mainstream accounts without falling into the trap of historical or cultural relativism. It also provides the theoretical underpinnings for a rigorous analytical framework consisting of different levels of explanations structured in a clear-cut hierarchy. By introducing the crucial assumption that power relations are, eventually, the main heuristic tools in any attempts to explain socioeconomic events, it inserts the notions of power and power struggles into the analysis. These power struggles are not, however, assumed to be confined to the state, but rather extend to the socioeconomic groups which define the particular capitalist structure of a given nation state. Purely economic explanations or purely political ones are not, of course discarded, but are rooted into the analysis of the underlying political economy structure.

The political economy approach adopted in this chapter is based on three different levels of analysis, which correspond to three different levels of explanation. The first level of analysis, which might be called the 'political economy analysis', is represented by an analysis of the domestic structure of capital and of power relations between the various socioeconomic actors as historically developed. It represents the limits within which further developments must necessarily take place. This first level of analysis, then, allows for the identification of what Gramsci called the 'historic bloc', the power relations among the social forces under consideration within a given mode of production and historical conjuncture. It also provides a basis for comparison with different sets of power relations in different countries.

However, these kinds of structural considerations cannot account for the whole history of Italian and British stances in the process of European monetary integration. Nor can they provide the basis for reliable predictions of future behaviour. Therefore, it is necessary to connect this first level of analysis with the more conjunctural analysis of the second and the third levels, in order to obtain a dynamic picture of the phenomenon under consideration. The second level of analysis, 'purely economic analysis', separates out the first level of Gramsci's relations of force and focuses on the identification of the concrete interest groups' preferences in a short-term time-scale. It focuses on the concrete struggle for economic power, and particularly on the competition amongst interest groups to obtain favourable economic policies. It is at this level that classifications of socioeconomic preferences towards exchange rate levels and regimes may be tested empirically.[49]

Finally, the third level, 'purely political analysis', focuses on the day to day political struggles or the specific means by which economic interests become policies after having been processed through the political and institutional system. It is here that the political bargaining process, the role of political parties and leaders, and the incentive/disincentive mechanism are taken into consideration. This conjunctural analysis, then, follows conceptually the formal separation between the 'economy' and 'state' in capitalism. Ultimately, however, it has to be connected to the integral and organic political economy analysis, where the mediation of fundamental class conflict and hegemony is considered.

A comprehensive explanatory model requires a synthesis of each of these levels in order to provide the most reliable possible picture of the phenomenon under analysis. This reflects the fact that in the real world there are overlapping relationships of mutual reciprocity between the economic structure, the economic interests promoted by socioeconomic groups, and the political and institutional life. Thus, for example, the Italian decision to enter the ERM can be analysed as a political decision in the framework of the day-to-day political life. However, it has also much deeper roots in the underlying struggle for power among the different Italian economic interest groups, mainly trade unions and the employers' organisations. On the other hand, the British decision to enter the ERM was primarily a function of day-to-day political life and the need to gain political consensus on the eve of a general election.

This analytical framework makes it possible to derive a 'phenomenology of credibility' of the international economic commitments and, in particular of exchange rate commitments. Credibility is not based on pure economic expectations, but rather on a much more complex set of political economy considerations. In particular, it is possible to hypothesise that the more foreign economic commitments in general, and exchange rate policies in particular, are rooted in the interests of a given hegemonic bloc, the more these commitments are credible. That is, in the case of fixed exchange rates or target zone commitments, the more they can count in the 'consensus' of the most powerful sections of society, the less likely they are to be challenged by the markets. Indeed, there is a dialectic relation between interests and expectations; expectations of the markets are deeply influenced by the interests and preferences of the leading socioeconomic sectors of the country under consideration. Market expectations, and thus also markets' behaviour, are crucially affected by considerations about something 'more fundamental than the fundamentals': the economic structure and the way in which it is reflected in economic and political life. This definition is perfectly consistent with the political scientists' view that exchange rate commitments are international agreements and therefore need to be based on the existence of a domestic 'consensus' rooted in the 'interests' of domestic actors.

From the economists' standpoint, this approach to the credibility of exchange rate pegs could help reconciling the two opposing theories on speculative attacks. The contemporary debate in exchange rate economics is in fact characterised by the opposition between 'fundamentalists', i.e., supporters of the thesis that real exchange rate fluctuations largely reflect changes in macroeconomic fundamentals,[50] and those who believe that:

> Foreign exchange markets behave more like the unstable and irrational asset markets described by Keynes than the efficient markets described by modern finance theory.[51]

The latter approach assumes that speculative attacks are self-fulfilling, or that in a multiple equilibriums environment, the markets produce their own exchange rate expectations without any intelligible connection with fundamentals.[52] In turn, these expectations produce speculative attacks, which ultimately compel governments to abandon the exchange rate peg and to adopt *ex-post* softer monetary stances. A compromise approach has been proposed which allows for multiple equilibriums only within a certain range of fundamentals' performance.[53] Alternatively, economists tend to overcome the problem by lifting the assumption of market participants' complete information on the performance of economic fundamentals.[54]

This chapter argues, however, that the failure of the fundamentals to explain speculative attacks does not necessarily imply that exchange rate markets act 'irrationally' or 'inefficiently' or that they are constrained by the lack of information. It can also mean that the markets, in deciding which of the multiple equilibriums is more likely to be adopted by the government after a speculative attack, evaluate a wide range of events, including socio-political and structural ones. Thus the credibility of an exchange rate commitment is crucially dependent on the behaviour and interests of socioeconomic actors in a particular historical moment.

Adopting a similar political economy definition of credibility, the Italian commitment to the ERM can be considered very credible. Indeed, it was rooted not only in the pure economic interests of the socioeconomic hegemonic group, but also in their political need to shift the balance of power from the national to the European level in order to maintain their leading position. When the consensus faded, the only obvious conclusion that the markets could draw was to attack the lira in the ERM. However, that the consensus had faded only at the second level of analysis, that is, at the level of pure economic considerations and not of structural ones, is demonstrated by the fact that Italian commitment to the realisation of Economic and Monetary Union (EMU) did not disappear despite the ERM crisis. On the other hand, the British decision to enter the ERM was far less credible because it was in contrast with the more structural interests of its leading fraction, which were then re-affirmed in the British government's opposition to EMU.

Of course, this model is not static and changes may occur at each level of analysis. At the first level of analysis, changes are certainly long-term ones and are represented by substantial transformation of the underlying structure of power. Italy, for example, experienced a decline of the power of trade unions and strengthening in the power of the industrial and banking organisations from the second half of the 1980s onwards. In Britain, a change in power relationship among economic interest groups occurred after 1931 when the City surrendered its power to the industrial sector and did not fully recover until the 1960s.[55]

At the second level of analysis, the preferences of the socioeconomic groups considered may vary from time to time and from country to country. Indeed, in 1979 neither of the British economic sectors showed an overwhelming enthusiasm for the making of the European Monetary System (EMS). However, by 1985 the British industrial sector, as represented by the Confederation of British Industry (CBI) started to push for British entry in the ERM, while from the late 1980s the British Trade Unions have (with some exceptions) supported entry into the monetary union. Similarly, the Italian CGIL, once one of the most convinced opponent of the European monetary integration process, eventually endorsed the EMU as envisioned at Maastricht.

Finally, at the third level, changes are linked to the decline of the leadership of given political parties or leaders. The end of the Thatcher era and the '*tangentopoli*' revolution in Italy are clear examples of changes at the third level of analysis. Their importance, however, must not be overestimated since, in the lack of more structural changes, their consequences appear rather superficial.[56]

Critical remarks The critical political economy approach to the credibility of exchange rate proposed challenges the mainstream theory belief that markets, in general, and financial markets in particular stand aside of history and society and behave independently from any social or political considerations. On the contrary, the approach proposed here explains the behaviour of financial markets in terms of the underlying political economy structure of capitalist economies. The assumption of the infallibility of the markets and of their independent 'inner rationality' is rejected in favour of a political economic rationality, which embeds markets' expectations into a given socioeconomic structure within a given historical conjuncture.

A political economic approach to the credibility of exchange rate commitments and of the rationality of financial market behaviour helps to transcend the limitations inherent in the debate between neorealist and institutionalist accounts of European monetary integration without falling in the trap of historical or cultural relativism. It provides a systematic and rigorous analytical framework consisting of different levels of explanations structured in a clear-cut hierarchy. It also introduces the crucial assumption that power relations constitute the main heuristic tools in any attempts to explain socioeconomic events. It thus inserts the notion of power and, in particular, of power struggles into the analysis without confining them to the state, but rather extending it to the socioeconomic groups defining the capitalist structure of a country. Purely economic explanations or purely political ones are not, of course discarded, but they are inserted into the structured analytical framework.

Given the nature of the questions posed in this chapter, this analysis has been limited to the power struggles within the borders of the nation state and between domestic socioeconomic groups. However, in principle it is possible to apply the theoretical framework to the power struggles between transnational socioeconomic groups to the extent that the decision-making level shifts from the national to the regional or to the international level. This is indeed the most likely scenario in case the process of EMU results in more political integration at the European level.

Concluding, this political economic approach to monetary policy-makes it possible to account for phenomena that would, otherwise, appear rather obscure. In particular, it is possible to explain why, even if usual economic measures of credibility did not show evident signs of any financial markets' loss of faith in the British commitment to the ERM, the pound sterling was driven out of the ERM by speculators. Indeed, the credibility of the sterling exchange rate peg was undermined by the lack of a structural consensus about its permanence in the ERM, a lack of consensus which was easily detected by the financial markets.

On the basis of similar considerations, this approach helps to explain why two different countries, with two completely different positions within the ERM were compelled to take the same decision at the same moment. In fact, both countries experienced the same loss of socioeconomic consensus to pegged exchange rates at the same time, though this loss was of a more structural nature in the case of the UK. Finally, the approach in question allows the analysis to be extended to the making of the EMU, and to the position adopted by the two countries *vis-à-vis* the establishment of the European single currency area. As already noted, in the UK the loss of consensus was structural and was rooted in the consideration that further steps in the process of European monetary integration substantially endangered the interests of the British dominant socioeconomic groups.

This gives account of the subsequent hostility of the UK towards EMU and its refusal to enter it. By contrast, in Italy the loss of consensus was of a more contingent nature, and did not underline any substantial opposition to the establishment of the single currency alongside the lines decided upon at Maastricht. Hence, an enthusiastic adherence to the project from all the major political economy players with all that it implied in terms of adoption of strict macroeconomic policies.

Notes

1   See the Report on Economic and Monetary Union (1989), where the case is put for the need of a parallel approach to the process of economic and monetary integration; See also CEC (1990), p. 17: 'The economic advantages of the Single Market are certainly not fully achievable without a single currency'.

2   See CEC (1990), p. 17 :'If the move to EMU were not to take place, given 1992, it is quite likely that either the EMS would become a less stable arrangement or capital market liberalisation would not be fully achieved or maintained'.

3   This is not the place to give a thorough account of the European Monetary System. Just for general information, see Fratianni, von Hagen and Waller (1992). See also Cobham and Zis (1999).

4   See Padoa-Schioppa (1994), p. 121.

5   For further analysis of the economic mechanism, see Padoa-Schioppa (1988).

6   See HM Treasury (1990a).

7   See HM Treasury (1990b). The economic argument in favour of a greater currency competition is based on the early works by Hayek (1970, 1976, 1979); for further reading on the subject see De Cecco (1992) and Currie (1989).

8   For an elaboration on these issues see Talani (2000).

9   For a realist interpretation of the process leading to EMU see Baun (1996). See also Middlemas (1995).

10 See Andrews (1993). See also Andrews (1994).

11   See Moravcsik (1998), ch. 6.
12   See Moravcsik (1998), p. 381.
13   See Moravcsik (1998), p. 386.
14   See Moravcsik (1998), p. 387.
15   See Moravcsik (1998), p. 411
16   See Moravcsik (1998), p. 417
17   See Moravcsik (1998), p. 417. For a different interpretation of the political economy
     motivations lying at the roots of the British decision not to enter EMU see Talani (2000).
18   See Eichengreen and Frieden (1994) and Sandholtz (1993).
19   See Alesina and Grilli (1993).
20   See Chapter 1 in this book.
21   See Frieden and Jones (1998).
22   See Frieden and Jones (1998), p. 178.
23   For a very detailed account of these events in Italy and the UK see Talani (2000).
24   See Frieden and Jones (1998), p. 179.
25   See Martin (1993).
26   See Garret (1993), Woolley (1993), Sandholtz, W. (1993) and Andrews (1993).
27   See Woolley (1993).
28   See Sandholtz (1993).
29   See Giavazzi and Pagano (1988).
30   For further details on the role of public opinion and electorate in the process of European
     integration see Eichenberg and Dalton (1993).
31   See below for references.
32   See below for references.
33   For more details about this interpretations see Risse (1998). See also Engelmann, Knopf,
     Roscher and Risse (1997).
34   See Risse (1998), p. 13.
35   See Risse (1998), p. 13.
36   See McNamara (1998).
37   See McNamara (1998), p. 43.
38   Source: McNamara (1998), p. 64.
39   See McNamara (1998), p. 64.
40   McNamara (1998), p. 166.
41   See Gill (1997), p. 210.
42   See Gill (1997).
43   See Gill (1997), p. 218.
44   See Gill (1997), p. 222.
45   See Gill (1997), p. 223.
46   For a more detailed analysis of this process see Chapter 8.
47   See Talani (2003).
48   See Gill (1991).
49   See, for example, Frieden (1991, 1994).
50   For more details see De Grauwe (1996), p. 71.
51   See Krugman (1989).
52   For a detailed account of the approach see De Grauwe (1996), p. 75.
53   See Flood and Marion (1996).
54   For an application of this approach to the 1987 crash see Romer (1993).
55   See Ingham (1984).

56 For more details on the positions of Italy and the UK in the ERM of the EMS and on the EMU see Talani (2003).

References

Alesina, A. and Grilli, V. (1993), 'On the Feasibility of a One-speed or Multi-speed European Monetary Union', *Economics and Politics*, Vol. 5 (2), July.

Andrews, D.M. (1993), 'The Global Origins of the Maastricht Treaty on EMU: Closing the Window of Opportunity', in A. Cafruny and G.G. Rosenthal (eds), *The State of the European Community: The Maastricht Debate and Beyond*, Boulder, CO: Lynne Rienner Publishers.

Andrews, D.M. (1994), 'Capital Mobility and State Autonomy: Toward a Structural Theory of International Monetary Relations', *International Studies Quarterly*, No. 38, pp. 193–218.

Baun, M.J. (1996), *An Imperfect Union: The Maastricht Treaty and the New Politics of European Integration*, Boulder, CO: Westview Press.

Cobham, D. and Zis, G. (1999), *From EMS to EMU – 1979 to 1999 and Beyond*, Basingstoke: Macmillan and New York: St Martin's Press.

Commission of European Communities (1990), *One Market, One Money*, Economic Papers, No. 44.

Currie, D. (1989), 'European Monetary Union or Competing Currencies: Which Way for Monetary Integration in Europe?', *Economic Viewpoint*, September.

De Cecco, M. (1992), *Monete in concorrenza*, Bologna: Il Mulino.

De Grauwe, P. (1996), *International Money*, Oxford: Oxford University Press.

Eichenberg, R.C. and Dalton, R.J. (1993), 'The Europeans and European Community: The Dynamics of Public Support for European Integration', *International Organization*, Vol. 47, pp. 507–34.

Eichengreen, B. and Frieden, J. (1994), *The Political Economy of European Monetary Union*, Boulder, CO: Westview Press.

Engelmann, D., Knopf, H.J., Roscher, K. and Risse, T. (1997), 'Identity Politics in the European Union: The Case of Economic and Monetary Union', in P. Minkkinen and H. Potomaki (eds), *The Politics of Economic and Monetary Union*, Amsterdam: Kluwer Academic Publishers.

Fratianni, M., von Hagen, J. and Waller, C. (1992), *From EMS to EMU*, London: Centre for Economic Policy Research.

Frieden, J. (1991), 'Invested Interests: The Politics of National Economic Policies in a World of Global Finance', *International Organization*, No. 45, Autumn.

Frieden, J. (1994), *The Impact of Goods and Capital Market Integration on European Monetary Politics*, preliminary version, August.

Frieden, J. (1998), *The New Political Economy of EMU*, Oxford: Rowman and Littlefield.

Frieden, J. and Jones, E. (1998), 'The Political Economy of European Monetary Union: A Conceptual Overview', in J. Frieden, D. Gros and E. Jones (eds), *The New Political Economy of EMU*, Oxford: Rowman and Littlefield.

Flood, R.P. and Marion, N.P. (1996), 'Speculative Attacks: Fundamentals and Self-fulfilling Prophecies', *National Bureau of Economic Research*, Working Paper 5789, Cambridge, MA: NEBR.

Garret, G. (1993), 'The Politics of the Maastricht Treaty', *Economics and Politics*, Vol. 5 (2).

Giavazzi, F. and Pagano, M. (1988), 'The Advantage of Tying One's Hands: EMS Discipline and Central Bank Credibility', *European Monetary Review*, Vol. 32, pp. 1055–75.

Gill, S. (1991), 'Historical Materialism, Gramsci and International Political Economy', in C.N. Murphy and R. Tooze (1991), *The New International Political Economy*, Boulder, CO: Lynne Rienner Publishers.

Gill, S. (1997), 'An EMU or an Ostrich?: EMU and Neoliberal Globalisation; Limits and Alternatives', in P. Minkkinen and H. Potomaki (1997), *The Politics of Economic and Monetary Union*, Amsterdam: Kluwer Academic Publishers.

Hayek, F.A. (1970), 'Denationalisation of Money', *Hobart Paper Special*, No. 70, October, London: IEA.

Hayek, F.A. (1976), 'Choice in Currency: A Way to Stop Inflation', *IEA Occasional Papers*, No. 48.

Hayek, F.A. (1979), 'Toward a Free Market Monetary System', *Journal of Libertarian Studies*, Vol. 3 (1).

HM Treasury (1990a), 'Economic and Monetary Union', *Treasury Bulletin*, Summer, London: HMSO.

HM Treasury (1990b), 'The UK Proposal for a EMF and a Hard ECU', *Treasury Bulletin*, Autumn, London: HMSO.

Krugman, P. (1989), 'The Case for Stabilising Exchange Rates', *Oxford Review of Economic Policy*, No. 5, pp. 61–72.

Ingham, G. (1984), *Capitalism Divided? The City and Industry in British Social Development*, London: Macmillan Education.

Martin, L. (1993), 'International and Domestic Institutions in the EMU process', *Economics and Politics*, Vol. 5 (2).

McNamara, K. (1998), *The Currency of Ideas: Monetary Politics in the European Union*, Ithaca, NY: Cornell University Press.

Middlemas, K. (1995), *Orchestrating Europe*, New York: Fontana Press.

Moravcsik, A. (1998), *The Choice for Europe*, Ithaca, NY: Cornell University Press.

Padoa-Schioppa, T. (1988), 'The European Monetary System: A Long Term View', in F. Giavazzi, S. Micossi and M. Miller (1988), *The European Monetary System*, Cambridge: Cambridge University Press.

Padoa-Schioppa, T. (1994), *The Road to Monetary Union in Europe: The Emperor, the Kings and the Genies*, Oxford: Clarendon Press.

Risse, T. (1998), 'To Euro or not to Euro? The EMU and Identity Politics in the European Union', Arena Working Papers, WP 98/1, available at http://www.arena.uio.no/publications/wp98_1.htm.

Romer, D. (1993), 'Rational Asset-Price Movements without News', *The American Economic Review*, Vol. 83 (5).

Sandholtz, W. (1993), 'Choosing Union: Monetary Politics and Maastricht', *International Organization*, Vol. 47.

Talani, L. (2000), *Betting For and Against EMU*, Aldershot: Ashgate Publishing.

Talani, L.S. (2003), 'The Political Economy of Exchange Rate Commitments: Italy, the UK and the Process of European Monetary Integration', in A. Cafruny and M. Ryner (eds), *A Ruined Fortress?. Neoliberal Hegemony and Transformation in Europe*, London: Rowman and Littlefield.

Woolley, J.T. (1993), 'Linking Political and Monetary Union: The Maastricht Agenda and German Domestic Politics', *Economics and Politics*, Vol. 5 (2).

Chapter 5

The ECB Monetary Performance in its First Years: National Interests and Economic Sectors' Preferences Assessed

5.1 Introduction

Who wins and who loses from the implementation of monetary policy in Europe? This chapter will address these questions by identifying the national interests and economic sectors which gained more from the monetary performance of the ECB in its first years of activity.

The chapter is divided into three sections. The first reviews the economic outlook of European economy at the beginning of EMU. The second addresses the analysis of European monetary policy in light of the developments of the real economy. The third one elaborates on the national and economic sectors' preferences in terms of monetary policy in order to identify the actual winners and losers from such a policy.

5.2 Economic Background at the Beginning of EMU

On 1 January 1999, the official birth date of the Euro, the international economic environment was characterised by the persistence of unusually high levels of growth in the US (what made some talk about the end of the business cycle) and the growing concerns for the Asian financial crisis. The EU was experiencing one of the highest aggregate unemployment rate since the 1930s alongside a slowing GDP, especially in Italy and Germany.

No wonder that the attention of many, within both the academic and the political circles, was focusing on the pro-cyclical effects of the monetary constraints imposed by both the Maastricht Treaty and the Growth and Stability Pact while the European institutions sought to devise an appropriate employment strategy (or, at least rhetoric).[1] Indeed, as a result of the many cooperation agreements signed by the trade unions, particularly in the

Table 5.1   GDP growth and unemployment in the Euro-zone, 1998–99

| | Unemployment rate (%) | | GDP growth rate (%) | | |
	1998	1999	1998	1999 – Q1	1999 – Q2
Austria	4.7	4.3	3.3	1.7	1.7
Belgium	9.5	9.0	2.9	1.7	1.7
Finland	11.4	10.0	5.6	3.4	3.3
France	11.7	11.0	3.4	2.4	2.1
Germany	9.4	9.1	2.0	0.6	0.6
Ireland	7.8	6.7	8.9		
Italy	11.9	11.4	1.3	0.8	0.8
Netherlands	4.0	3.2	3.2	3.1	3.1
Portugal	5.1	4.8	3.5		
Spain	18.8	15.6	4.0	3.2	3.6

Source: Eurostat.

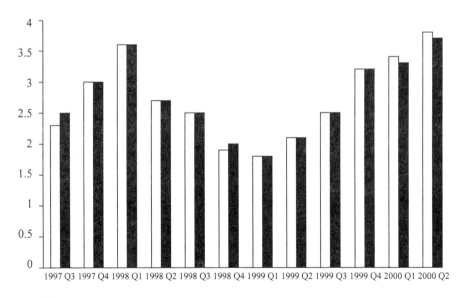

☐   GDP growth rate (constant prices 1995 in ECU) Euro-zone

■   GDP growth rate (constant prices 1995 in ECU) EU 15

Figure 5.1   EU 15 and Euro 11 growth rates

Source: Eurostat.

traditionally inflationary/club-med countries (notably Italy and Spain), the level of inflation, i.e., the main statutory concern of the ECB, was keeping a very low profile recording an unprecedented 0.8 per cent and making some worry about the possibility of negative inflation.

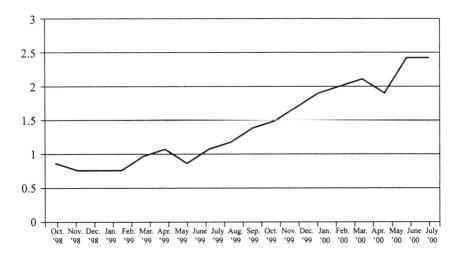

Figure 5.2   HICP in Euro-area (% changes)

Source: ECB.

How did the ECB react to the growing worries over the performance of real economy variables?

At the outset it is worth noting that the ECB is the most independent of all central banks.[2] Indeed, its independence is guaranteed by statute in order to underwrite the central goal of monetary stability, defined as a level of inflation rates below 2 per cent. Although independence from national and supranational political constraints has created further preoccupation over the democratic deficit of the European institutional setting, it has allowed central bankers to concentrate theoretically only on monetary variables, leaving aside the performance of the real economic indicators, namely growth and employment rates.

The reality of the first years of implementation of a single monetary policy in the Euro-area, however, demonstrates that monetary policy considerations have not been separated from the performance of real economy.

To this analysis we turn in the next section.

5.3 The Performance of the ECB from its Establishment: Flexibility vs Transparency

There were many concerns about the performance of the ECB at the eve of its establishment, given the unprecedented nature of its tasks as responsible for the implementation of a European common monetary policy and the management of a European common currency in the lack of full political integration. These concerns ranged from the lack of credibility of the ECB monetary stances, to its lack of flexibility, from the need to increase its democratic accountability, to that of ensuring its independence from the governments of the member states.

According to the CEPR,[3] from its inception, the ECB displayed more flexibility than expected regarding asymmetries within the Euro-zone. This result was possible thanks to the adoption of a so-called 'two pillar monetary strategy' at the expenses of transparency. Given the goal of price stability, defined as HIPC inflation between 0 and 2 per cent, the two pillars of monetary policy are on the one hand, a money growth reference target and, on the other hand, a number of unspecified indicators including the exchange rates and asset prices. In a period in which the majority of central banks abandon monetary targeting to replace it with the much more transparent and accountable (expected) inflation targeting, this strategy has been judged rather obscure.[4]

One might argue that in the trade-off between transparency and flexibility, the balance should not necessarily incline in favour of the former. Indeed, if the ECB were to make public regularly its (expected) inflation targets, this could even weaken its credibility *vis-à-vis* financial markets, in case the target could not be reached, leaving less scope of manoeuvre to harmonise monetary policy with the performance of the Euro-zone in real terms. However, the issue is far from being uncontroversial. Critics underline that the reduction of transparency following from the multiplication of targets and indicators leads to surprises which unsettle financial markets while uncertainty might result in higher borrowing costs.[5]

Leaving the debate over the trade-off between transparency and flexibility to the experts[6] and turning to the concrete monetary policy performance of the ECB during its first years of activity the picture does not get much clearer.

The first issue to address is the importance attributed by the ECB to output growth in Euro-land (and in some member countries in particular) relative to inflation.

Since the establishment of EMU, in 1999, the economic outlook recorded a marked slow-down in all OECD countries for the first time since the 1970s.

Whereas the Japanese economy had been in recession for some years, in the year 2001 the US economy experienced the first substantial fall of the business cycle in a decade. The Euro-zone, with a lag of some months with respect to the US, also slowed significantly in the year 2001.

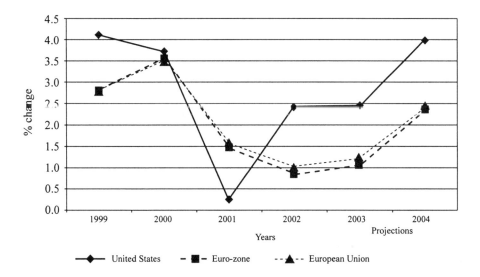

Figure 5.3   Real GDP % changes, 1999–2004

Source: OECD.

This chapter does not attempt to analyse the underlying causes of such a global decline,[7] though it is important to notice that this had a major impact especially on the most important European economies, namely Italy, France and Germany (see Figure 5.4 and Table 5.2).

Theoretically, as underlined in many speeches and documents,[8] the ECB would pay little attention to the short-run output developments so as not to lose credibility in its anti-inflationary stances with financial markets.

Despite this, already at a superficial analysis it is easy to notice that the 30 point cut of interest rates to 3 per cent on 1 January 1999 was associated with deflationary risks in the wake of the Asian crisis. Furthermore, the April 1999 cut to 2.50 per cent coincided with declining output in important Euro-land members (notably Germany). Finally, the cut of 17 September 2001 in the minimum bid rate on the Eurosystem's main refinancing operation by 50 points to 3.75 clearly matches a similar decision taken by the US Federal

European Political Economy

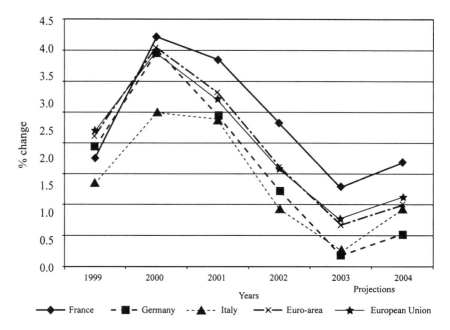

Figure 5.4   Output gaps

Source: OECD.

Reserve in the aftermath of the terrorist attacks of 11 September and their recessive consequences.

More sophisticated analyses clearly show that the ECB monetary policy, and, in particular, the timing and frequency of interest rate changes reflected the desire to engage in some output stabilisation and not only to control prices, even if leading central bank personalities constantly deny it.[9]

If the output level was never officially recognised as a point of reference in the monetary policy-making of the ECB, but was certainly taken into consideration, the opposite happened with monetary targets. Indeed, the 'two pillar strategy' theoretically rests on the prominence of the target for M3 growth as the main official indicator for ECB monetary policy decisions. However, on many occasions, when the target has been overshot, the ECB has not reacted accordingly. For example, despite the fact that the target had been publicly set at 4.5 per cent for 1999, no measures were taken by the ECB when it became clear that the target would not be achieved by the end of the year. On the contrary, the ECB cut the interest rates and engaged in sophisticated explanations over the reasons why the departure from the

Table 5.2   Real GDP per country

Percentage change from previous period	1999	2000	2001	2002	Projections 2003	2004
Austria	2.7	3.5	0.7	1.0	1.1	2.0
Belgium	3.2	3.7	0.8	0.7	1.3	2.3
Denmark	2.6	2.8	1.4	1.6	1.6	2.6
Finland	3.4	5.5	0.6	1.6	2.2	3.4
France	3.2	4.2	1.8	1.2	1.2	2.6
Germany	2.0	2.9	0.6	0.2	0.3	1.7
Greece	3.6	4.2	4.1	4.0	3.6	3.9
Ireland	11.1	10.0	6.0	6.0	3.2	4.2
Italy	1.7	3.1	1.8	0.4	1.0	2.4
Netherlands	4.0	3.3	1.3	0.3	0.7	1.9
Portugal	3.8	3.7	1.6	0.5	0.3	2.3
Spain	4.2	4.2	2.7	2.0	2.1	3.1
Sweden	4.6	4.4	1.1	1.9	1.5	2.8
United Kingdom	2.4	3.1	2.1	1.8	2.1	2.6
United States	4.1	3.8	0.3	2.4	2.5	4.0
Euro area	2.8	3.6	1.5	0.9	1.0	2.4
European Union	2.8	3.5	1.6	1.0	1.2	2.4

Source: OECD.

reference M3 growth rate did not represent any rupture with the 'two pillar' monetary strategy.

As the outlook for inflation turned upward by the end of 1999, the ECB promptly intervened by increasing the interest rate by 50 basis points. Of course, given the parallel increase in the M3 growth, this seemed to be consistent with the monetary strategy declared by the ECB, while the final divorce between the ECB changes in the interest rates and the M3 growth rate appears justified by the necessity to keep the HICP within the 2 per cent limit.

In any case, the suspicion that the M3 target was never really given the importance implicit in the adoption of the 'two pillar strategy' and was often subordinated to pragmatic considerations about the level of output, never abandoned the experts. Indeed, reacting to the many criticisms towards the first pillar, the ECB effected some modifications of the M3 series, by first removing non-resident holdings of money market funds from the definition of Euro zone M3 and then purging non-resident holdings of liquid money, market paper and securities.

Table 5.3   ECB main refinancing operations

Date[1]	Deposit facility	Main refinancing operations		Marginal lending facility
		Fixed rate tenders	Variable rate tenders	
		Fixed rate	Minimum bid rate	
With effect from	*Level*	*Level*	*Level*	*Level*
2003 6 June	1.00	–	2.00	3.00
7 March	1.50	–	2.50	3.50
2002 6 December	1.75	–	2.75	3.75
2001 9 November	2.25	–	3.25	4.25
18 September	2.75	–	3.75	4.75
31 August	3.25	–	4.25	5.25
11 May	3.50	–	4.50	5.50
2000 6 October	3.75	–	4.75	5.75
1 September	3.50	–	4.50	5.50
28 June[2]	3.25	–	4.25	5.25
9 June	3.25	4.25	–	5.25
28 April	2.75	3.75	–	4.75
17 March	2.50	3.50	–	4.50
4 February	2.25	3.25	–	4.25
1999 5 November	2.00	3.00	–	4.00
9 April	1.50	2.50	–	3.50
22 January	2.00	3.00	–	4.50
4 January[3]	2.75	3.00	–	3.25
1 January	2.00	3.00	–	4.50

Notes

1   The date refers to the deposit and marginal lending facilities. For main refinancing operations, unless otherwise indicated, changes in the rate are effective from the first operation following the date indicated. Dates of settlement and amounts are shown in Table 1.3 of the ECB *Monthly Bulletin*.
2   On 8 June 2000 the ECB announced that, starting from the operation to be settled on 28 June 2000, the main refinancing operations of the Eurosystem would be conducted as variable rate tenders. The minimum bid rate refers to the minimum interest rate at which counterparties may place their bids.
3   On 22 December 1998 the ECB announced that, as an exceptional measure between 4 and 21 January 1999, a narrow corridor of 50 basis points would be applied between the interest rates for the marginal lending facility and the deposit facility, aimed at facilitating the transition to the new regime by market participants.

Source: ECB.

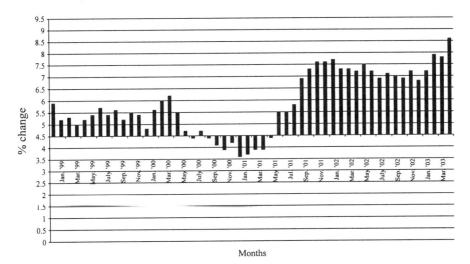

Figure 5.5   Adjusted M3 percentage changes per month

Source: ECB.

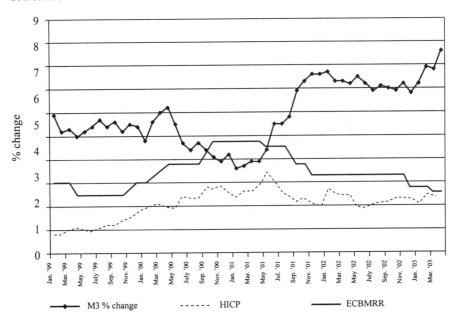

Figure 5.6   M3, HICP and ECB main refinancing rate % changes, 1999–2003

Source: ECB.

However this adjustment is no more than a cosmetic change and does not improve the reliability of the monetary pillar. If anything, the figure below shows that M3 percentage changes and interest rate decisions by the ECB go in opposite directions. Contradictory actions clearly limited the transparency and credibility of the ECB monetary policy-making.

Even more obscure is the role attributed by the ECB to the exchange rates within the two-pillar monetary strategy.[10] Indeed, the second pillar of the strategy makes explicit reference to a series of indicators influencing the ECB monetary decisions amongst which the Euro exchange rates.

However, looking at the performance of the newly born currency in the first months of its existence it raises spontaneously the suspicion that the Bank had adopted an attitude of 'benign neglect' *vis-à-vis* the exchange rate of the Euro.[11]

Indeed, the Euro lost around 15 per cent of its value *vis-à-vis* the dollar between August 1999 and August 2000 while the parity with the dollar was already lost in January 2000. Also the effective nominal and real exchange rate of the Euro experienced a marked decrease (–11.3 and –10.1 respectively between August 1999 and August 2000).

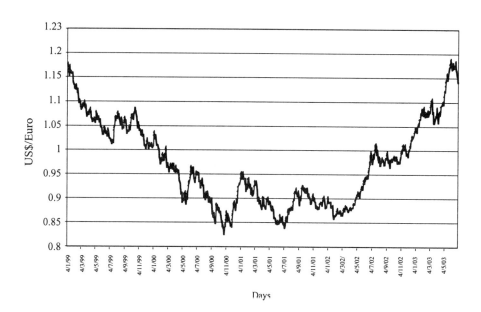

Figure 5.7   **USD/Euro exchange rates, 1999–2003**

Source: ECB.

Of course the ECB has always asserted that the performance of a currency must be assessed in the long run. And indeed in the long run the Euro/dollar exchange rate has witnessed a reversal of its pervious performance with a marked appreciation of the Euro, though it might be better to talk about a strong depreciation of the dollar.

However, the substantial lack of concerns on the fall of the Euro on the side of the European monetary authorities provoked further doubts about the real scope of the two-pillar strategy.[12] In the last section, attention is focused on the distributional effects of such a monetary policy to investigate on the political economy dimension of the ECB interventions.

5.4 National Interests and Economic Sectors' Exchange Rate Preferences

In framing an analysis of the ECB monetary and exchange rate stances within a typical intergovernmentalist framework it is worth recalling some of the institutional characteristics of the decision-making bodies of the ECB.

Although the ECB is of course formally independent from any possible intrusion in its decision-making process by the governments of the Euro-zone member countries and the 'no-bail out clause' eliminates any possibility for the ECB to intervene to support any member states fiscal position, some of its institutional characteristics retain intergovernmentalist elements. In particular, the composition of the Governing Council, which includes the governors of the national central banks and the members of the executive board, strongly reflect national differences.[13]

In itself, this does not demonstrate that the ECB monetary policy is geared towards the interest of the largest countries. It does, however, allow for the legitimate suspicion that national central bankers may indeed at least reproduce national expectations and demands in the formal meetings of the Governing Council of the ECB. Moreover, the lack of publicity of the minutes of the discussions going on in the course of the meetings of the Governing Council and of the Executive Board adds to the difficulty in identifying to what extent national interests count in the decision-making process, though, as noticed by many, the publication of similar minutes would not necessarily eliminate the possibility of shifting the real discussion to more informal settings.[14]

With respect to national preferences formation, and, therefore, to the identification of the set of national interests that are more likely to reverberate on the ECB policy-making, it is worth recalling Frieden's model on economic sectors' preferences *vis-à-vis* the exchange rate level and regime.[15] It is indeed true that similar preferences cannot be expressed any more with respect to national currencies, but it is not implausible to hypothesise that national economic sectors have a vested interest in the performance and international status of the Euro.[16]

In particular, following Frieden, it is possible to claim that the export oriented manufacturing sectors would gain the most from a devalued currency. Therefore, the countries heavily relying on the performance of the export oriented manufacturing sector, like Italy, Germany and France to a lesser extent, should have a vested interest in adopting a policy of *laissez-faire* with respect to the depreciation of the Euro.

Though the subject would need a much more thorough analysis than what is possible to effect in this context, it is difficult to deny that the weakness of the Euro favourably influenced the performance of European exports, particularly in certain countries.

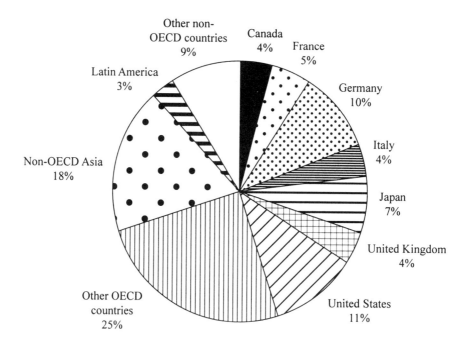

Figure 5.8   Export-orientation of OECD countries – % shares of world exports

Source: OECD.

Table 5.4 Euro 11 trade balance, 1999–2000

Main trading partners – Eur 11 (€bn)	Eur 11 exports to partners			Eur 11 imports from partners			Trade balance	
	Jan.–June 2000	Jan.–June 1999	Growth	Jan.–June 2000	Jan.–June 1999	Growth	Jan.–June 2000	Jan.–June 1999
UK	89.5	75.9	18%	74.9	60.9	23%	14.6	15
USA	74.1	62.8	18%	63.2	55.8	13%	10.9	7
Switzerland	30.6	27	13%	23.5	21	12%	7.1	6
Japan	16	12.4	28%	32	25.9	24%	–16	–13.4
Sweden	18.8	16	18%	18.4	15.8	17%	0.4	0.2
China	8.7	7.5	15%	23	16.2	43%	–14.3	–8.6
Russia	7.3	5.3	38%	18	9.7	86%	–10.7	–4.4
Poland	14	11.7	20%	9.3	7.2	28%	4.7	4.5
Denmark	11.1	10.3	8%	10.2	8.5	19%	0.9	1.8
Hungary	10.2	8.2	25%	9.4	7.6	24%	0.8	0.6

Source: Eurostat.

Indeed, in the period between Jan-July 1999 and Jan-July 2000, the Euro 11 exports to the USA and Japan increased respectively by 18 per cent and 28 per cent, while extra Euro 11 exports overall grew by 20 per cent. Consequently, EU trade-balance with the US improved visibly in the year 1999-2000, recording a steady surplus trend for the whole year 2000.

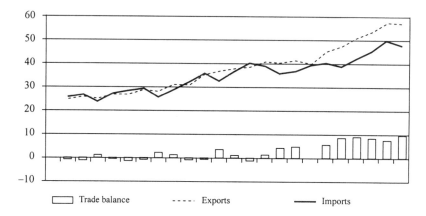

Figure 5.9   EU-USA quarterly trade balances, 1995–2000 (€bn)

Source: Eurostat, *Statistics in Focus, External Trade*, Theme 6–2/2001.

In 1999–2000, positive trade balances were experienced particularly in countries like Germany and Italy whose output growth heavily relies on the performance of the export oriented manufacturing sector. France, Italy and Germany reported also a substantial increase in their trade balances with the US.

That similar results were related to the performance of Euro-zone exports of manufactured goods is demonstrated by their dramatic increase in the period between January/March 2001 and January/March 2002. Such a performance is particularly meaningful because on the one hand, it happened when the global and, in particular, the US economy were at the apex of the recession,[17] and therefore it cannot be explained in terms of increase in the aggregate demand of countries outside the Euro-zone.

On the other hand, also European countries were in the middle of the slowdown and it is consequently difficult to relate it to an increase of Euro-zone supply.[18] The only plausible explanation for such an upsurge in the export of manufactured goods from the Euro-zone to the rest of the world in the period considered is represented by the weakness of the Euro that clearly

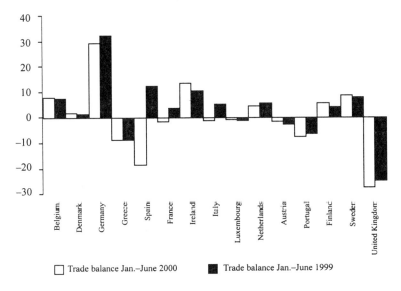

Figure 5.10   EU 15 trade balance 1999–2000

Source: Eurostat.

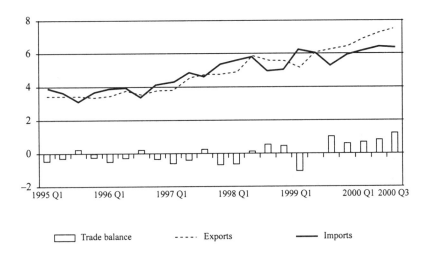

Figure 5.11   Quarterly trade between France and USA (€bn), 1995–2000

Source: Eurostat, *Statistics in Focus, External Trade*, Theme 6–2/2001.

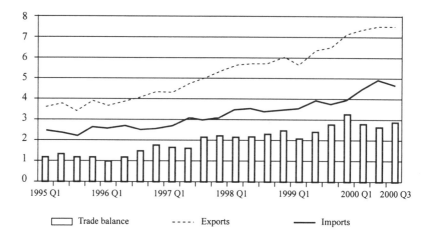

Figure 5.12   Quarterly trade between Germany and USA (€bn), 1995–2000

Source: Eurostat, *Statistics in Focus, External Trade*, Theme 6–2/2001.

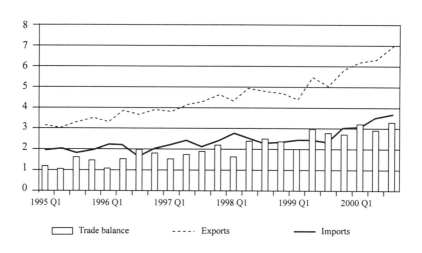

Figure 5.13   Quarterly trade between Italy and USA (€bn), 1995–2000

Source: Eurostat, *Statistics in Focus, External Trade*, Theme 6–2/2001.

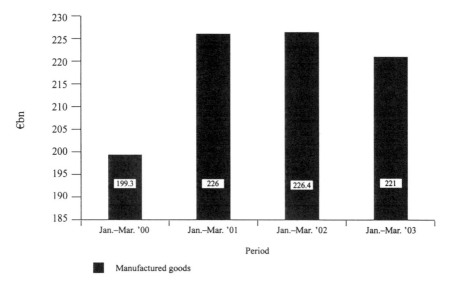

Figure 5.14   Euro-zone exports manufactured goods (€bn)

Source: Eurostat.

compensated both the slowdown in the Euro-zone industrial production and the reduction of the external aggregate demand. In this respect it is worth noting that the Euro kept well below the parity with the dollar for the whole period between April 2000 and July 2002, giving the first signs of an appreciation only in April 2002.[19]

Moreover, those countries that are more heavily relying on the export of manufactured goods for their output growth, are also those which benefited most from the weakness of the Euro. For example, Italy's balance of trade in manufactured goods with the US shows a very positive trend until 2002 when the Euro started appreciating again.

Finally, the relation between the performance of manufactured export in the biggest Euro-zone countries, and the exchange rate level of the Euro (in particular, *vis-à-vis* the dollar) is further proved by the fact that as the Euro started appreciating, the export performance of those countries started to worsen. For example, German export performance was at its apex in the year 2001, when the Euro was very depreciated *vis-à-vis* the dollar, whereas its outlook for the years 2003 and 2004 is fairly bleak. The situation is very similar in the case of Italy and France, while exactly the opposite happens to the export performance of the UK and the US.

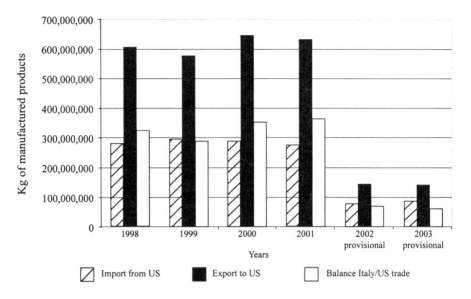

Figure 5.15   Italian manufactured goods trade with US, 1999–2003, kg

Source: Istat.

Indeed, the outlook for the trade balance of the whole Euro-zone is not particularly encouraging for the years 2002 and 2003.

5.5   Conclusions

Concluding it is not an easy task to assess the effectiveness of the ECB monetary policy-making and even to clearly identify its strategy. Indeed, many questions remain open. What is the importance attributed by the ECB to output performance in the Euro area relative to inflation? Do considerations about single member states matter, or is it the outlook of the Euro-zone as a whole which defines the Bank's choices? What is the attitude of the highest European monetary authority towards the exchange rates? Is it possible to speak about the existence of a European exchange rate strategy or do the developments of the Euro reflect only the will of the markets?

This contribution tried to answer some of these questions suggesting an intergovernmental interpretation of the first years of the ECB monetary policy. Regarding this, the institutional independence of the ECB, and the lack of publicity of its meetings' minutes, does not allow to draw any conclusions on

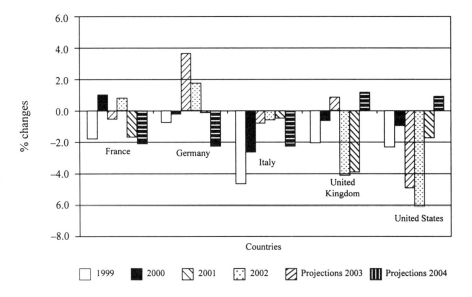

Figure 5.16   Export performance in selected OECD countries

Note: Export performance is the ratio between export volumes and export markets for total goods. The export volume concept employed is the sum of the exports of non-manufactured goods and manufactures. The calculation of export markets is based on a weighted average of import volumes in each exporting country's markets, with weights based on trade flows in 1995. The export markets for total goods facing each country is calculated as the weighted sum of the individual export markets for non-manufactured goods and manufactures, where the weights correspond to the commodity export structure of the exporting country in 1995.

Source: OECD.

the intergovernmental nature of its formal decision-making process. However, the consequences of the monetary policy actions or non-actions of the ECB on some leading member states and, within them, on their most relevant economic sectors, hint to the existence of some relation between the interests of the biggest nation states and the preferences of their leading economic sectors and the policy choices of the central bankers.

In particular, the emphasis on the performance of the monetary aggregates (M3) as the first pillar of the ECB monetary strategy, seems to conceal the desire by the Central Bank to trade-off some of the transparency that the adoption of an alternative monetary strategy would imply (like targeting the inflation rate, for example), in exchange for more flexibility. In turn, this flexibility has

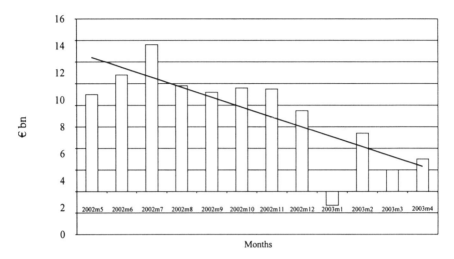

Figure 5.17   Euro-zone trade balance April 2002–2003 % changes

Source: Eurostat.

been used to pursue output objectives that would not be acceptable otherwise within the strict anti-inflationary mandate of the ECB.[20]

Similarly, the attitude of the ECB towards the performance of the exchange rate, particularly in the first two years of its activity, an attitude that the economists fail to fully understand,[21] acquires a completely different meaning in the light of the analysis of the manufacturing export performance of the Euro-zone, and, in particular of some of the Euro-zone countries.

This does not mean, however, that this is the only possible one. Indeed, other explanations may be proposed to explain the same phenomenon, namely, the monetary policy of the ECB in its first years of performance, though this contribution limited the analysis to the intergovernmentalist case.

Notes

1   See previous chapter.
2   For a similar interpretation see Berger, de Haan and Eijffinger (2000). See also Cukierman, Webb and Neyapti (1992).
3   See CEPR (2000).
4   For a structured criticism of this monetary pillar, see CEPR (2002).
5   See CEPR (2000).
6   See, for example, Artis (2003).

7   For more information see ECB (2002).
8   For some quotations see CEPR (2002).
9   See CEPR (2002).
10   See CEPR (2000), for a similar interpretation.
11   Intervention of the central banks in favour of the Euro in the summer 2000.
12   Doubts on the behaviour of the Euro exchange rates have been expressed by many economists. See, for example, Artis (2003); Koen (2000).
13   This point is taken from Artis (2003).
14   See Artis (2003).
15   See previous chapter.
16   See previous chapter.
17   See Figure 5.4.
18   See Figure 5.4.
19   See Figure 5.6.
20   About the effective mandate of the ECB there is a huge debate within the academic community. See, for example, CEPR (2002).
21   See Artis (2003).

References

Artis, M. (1998), 'The Unemployment Problem', *Oxford Review of Economic Policy*, Vol.14 (3).

Artis, M. (2003), 'EMU: Four Years On', EUI: unpublished.

Artis and Winkler, B. (1997), 'The Stability Pact: Safeguarding the Credibility of the European Central Bank', CEPR Discussion Paper No. 1688.

Berger, H., de Haan, J. and Eijffinger, S. (2000), 'Central Bank Independence and Update of Theory and Evidence', CEPR DP No. 2353, London: CEPR.

Blanchard, O.J. (1998), 'Discussion to "Regional Non-adjustment and Fiscal Policy"', *Economic Policy*, No. 26, April, p. 249.

Buti, M., Franco, D. and Ongena, H. (1997), 'Budgetary Policies during Recessions: Retrospective Application of the Stability and Growth Pact to the Post-war Period', Economic Paper No 121, European Commission, Brussels.

Cameron, D. (1997), 'Economic and Monetary Union: Underlying Imperatives and Third-stage Dilemmas', *Journal of European Public Policy*, No. 4, pp. 455–85

Cameron, D. (1998), 'EMU after 1999: The Implications and Dilemmas of the Third Stage', *Columbia Journal of European Law*, No. 4, pp. 425–46.

Cameron, D. (1999), 'Unemployment in the New Europe: The Contours of the Problem', EUI Working Papers, RSC No. 99/35.

CEPR (2000), *One Money, Many Countries: Monitoring the European Central Bank 2*, London: CEPR.

CEPR (2002), *Surviving the Slow-down, Monitoring the European Central Bank 4*, London: CEPR.

Crouch, C. (2000), *After the Euro*, Oxford: Oxford University Press.

Cukierman, A., Webb, S.B. and Neyapti, B. (1992), 'Measuring the Independence of Central Banks and its Effects on Policy Outcomes', *The World Bank Review*, No. 6, pp. 353–98.

Duff, A. (1997), *The Treaty of Amsterdam*, London: Sweet and Maxwell.

Eichengreen, B. and Frieden, J. (1998), *Forging an Integrated Europe*, Ann Arbor: University of Michigan Press.

Eichengreen, B. and Wyplosz, C. (1998), 'The Stability Pact: More than a Minor Nuisance?', *Economic Policy*, No. 26, April.

European Commission (1993), 'White Paper on Growth, Competitiveness, and Employment: The Challenges and Ways Forward into the 21st Century', COM(93) 700 final, Brussels, 5 December 1993, http://www.europa.eu.int/en/record/white/c93700/contents.html.

European Council meeting on 9 and 10 December I Essen-Presidency Conclusions, http://ue.eu.int/newsroom.

European Council meeting on 9 and 10 December I Essen-Presidency Conclusions, http://ue.eu.int/newsroom.

European Council (1996), Florence-Presidency Conclusions, 21–22 June, http://ue.eu.int/newsroom.

Featherstone, K. (1999), *The Road to Maastricht*, Oxford: Oxford University Press.

Frieden, J. (1998), *The New Political Economy of EMU*, Oxford: Rowman and Littlefield.

Grauwe, Paul de (1997), *The Economics of Monetary Integration*, 3rd rev. edn, Oxford: Oxford University Press.

Gros, D. and Thygesen, N. (1998), *European Monetary Integration*, London: Longman.

Koen, V. (2000), 'EMU: One Year On', *OECD Observer*, March, Paris: OECD.

Nickell, S. (1997), 'Unemployment and labour Market Rigidities: Europe vs North America', *Journal of Economic Perspectives*, No. 11, pp. 55–74.

Obstfeld, M. and Peri, G. (1998), 'Regional Non-adjustment and Fiscal Policy', *Economic Policy*, No. 26, April.

Talani, L.S. (1999), *Betting For and Against EMU: Who Wins and Who Loses in Italy and in the UK from the Process of European Monetary Integration*, Aldershot: Ashgate Publishing.

Tsoukalis, L. (1997), *The New European Economy Revisited*, Oxford: Oxford University Press.

Chapter 6

European Monetary Union and the European Employment Strategy: The Neofunctionalist and the Neo-Gramscian Cases Confronted

6.1 Introduction

Though unemployment in Europe has been steadily increasing since the 1970s (see Figure 6.1), the recognition of unemployment as one of the most important problems of the European Union is a very recent one.

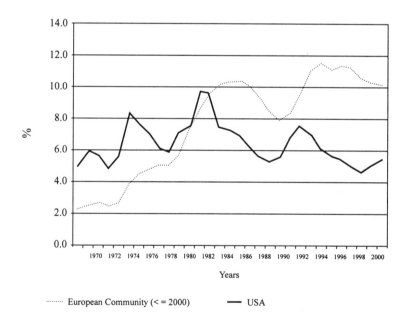

Figure 6.1   Unemployment rates, 1970–2000

Source: Eurostat.

The adoption of a common approach to the problem is even more recent, dating back to the white paper on unemployment of 1993, the same year that the Maastricht Treaty was finally ratified by the EU member states. No doubt there is a strong relation between the establishment of EMU and the so-called European Employment Strategy (EES), a relation which has been underlined on many occasions by the Commission itself to justify the peculiar stress of the EES on the flexibility of the labour markets.

However, the debate on the impact of EMU on European countries' growth and unemployment rates can also be understood with reference to the neo-Gramscian approach, which emphasises the consequences for policy of the balance of power between the key socioeconomic actors. In fact, the path to EMU, as defined by the Maastricht Treaty and by the subsequent agreement on the Stability Pact, directly and substantially affects the powers and prerogatives of trade unions in their traditional policy realms. In particular, the statutory ECB goal of a low and stable inflation rate has undeniable consequences for trade union bargaining. Moreover, the implementation of monetary policy by the ECB through establishing the level of European interest rates, undoubtedly affects investment decisions and, consequently, the level of unemployment. Finally, the rigid limitations on the conduct of national fiscal policy imposed by the Maastricht Treaty for the transition to EMU and by the Stability Pact in its aftermath, have greatly influenced the terms of the debate over the survival of the welfare state in all its components. Therefore, the trade unions' position towards further progress on the way to monetary union must be read in terms of reaction to this process of institutionalisation and of the attempt to regain the terrain lost since the beginning of the process of monetary integration.

This chapter examines critically the neofunctional case for the implementation of the EES and the empirical evidence of its impact on the bargaining powers of the European trade unions, with special attention to the case of Italy. The chapter is divided into two sections. The first deals with the economic literature on the labour markets and employment consequences of the Maastricht way to EMU. The problem here will be to see how it is possible to build a neofunctionalist case to justify the adoption of labour market flexibility as the only way to solve the problem of unemployment in Europe within the macroeconomic institutional framework defined by the establishment of EMU. In the second part, the analysis shifts to the neo-Gramscian approach with the aim to verify to what extent the implementation of EMU is the result of and/or has contributed to change the existing balance of power between the different socioeconomic actors. Attention is focused on Southern Europe in general, and Italy in particular. Here, after giving a general introduction on the characteristics of the so-called 'southern cluster' or 'Mediterranean regime', the analysis moves to the relationship between EMU, changes in the labour market structures, and the power position of the trade unions.

6.2 The Neofunctionalist Case for the EES: Labour Market Flexibility as a Consequence of EMU?

6.2.1 EMU and Unemployment

The establishment of EMU is a major institutional undertaking whose economic outcomes are not only constrained, but also defined by its institutional framework. This is to say that the economic consequences of EMU are specific to the way in which this particular currency union has been devised and this, in turn, is the product of a unique historical process. Therefore the purpose of this chapter is not to analyse the economic impact on unemployment of currency unions in general. The focus of this analysis is on a particular type of currency union: the one defined by the Maastricht agreement on EMU in 1991 and refined by the adoption of the Stability and Growth Pact by the European heads of state and government in 1997. It will not however discuss why EMU has this particular institutional configuration because, though it is an issue of major importance, it has been addressed widely in the literature.[1]

From an institutional point of view, the Maastricht Treaty and its protocols resolved the long-lasting controversy between the 'monetarist' and the 'economist'[2] approaches to monetary union. This was possible on the one hand by establishing a rigid institutional framework with a clear-cut economic objective (that of pursuing price stability) and a three-stage timetable to achieve EMU (cf. Gros and Thygesen, 1998), and on the other hand by devising a set of convergence requirements that applying member states had to respect before entering. These requirements included permanence in the 'new' ERM (within 15 per cent bands) for at least two years; inflation rates no more than 1.5 per cent higher than the average of the three most virtuous member states; interest rates no more than 2 per cent higher than the average of the three most virtuous member states; a debt-to-GDP ratio not exceeding 60 per cent, subject to conditions; and, most importantly a deficit to GDP ratio not exceeding 3 per cent (TEU art. 104(c) and art. 109 (j)).

The economic viability and the political (or political economy) rationale of the Maastricht criteria has been the subject of a number of studies from a variety of theoretical perspectives, which is why the issue will not be tackled here (see note 2). What is important to underline is, however, that their strict anti-inflationary aim was even strengthened by the adoption of the Growth and Stability Pact in 1997 (Eichengreen and Wyplosz, 1998, p. 71). The pact confirms the objective of a deficit to GDP ratio not exceeding 3 per cent and commits EMU member states to a medium term budgetary stance close to balance or in surplus. It also defines the terms and sanctions of the excessive deficit procedure. Exemption from respecting this fiscal criterion within EMU is allowed only in case of a decline in GDP of 2 per cent or more and of a temporary and small excess deficit. With a GDP declining by between 0.75 and 2 per cent, the decision on exemption from sanctions is left to the Council of Ministers. With lower decreases in GDP, the excessive deficit procedure will be implemented in any case, and countries obliged to keep up to 0.5 per cent of their GDP in non-interest-bearing mandatory deposits with the ECB until excess deficit is re-absorbed. If this does not happen within two years, deposits are transformed into outright transfers (Gros and Thygesen, 1998, p. 341).

The major question to answer at this point is how, if at all, the implementation of this particular kind of currency union will influence EMU member states' performances in terms of unemployment. There are two ways of tackling the issue. The first is to assess to what extent this particular form of currency union contains a recessive bias, thus reducing the level of output *ceteris paribus*. The other way is to see how the establishment of EMU has been linked in theory and, in the following section, in practice, to the flexibility of labour markets. These two streams of reasoning might have opposite outcomes. Indeed, while the former would point to an increase in the level of unemployment, the second could lead to its decrease. However, the tricky part lies in the fact that the first way of reasoning might be used to further the second, thus adding to its economic rationale and reinforcing its political feasibility.

The first stream of economic reasoning assesses the overall recessive effects of the implementation of the Maastricht fiscal criteria and/or of the GSP. Some authors have argued that the effort brought about by the implementation of the Maastricht criteria, and in particular of the fiscal ones, as well as the determination to stick to the ERM in a period of high interest rate policy, can explain the upsurge of European unemployment in the 1990s (Artis, 1998). Of course, economic analyses are far from reaching an agreement on the issue. Indeed, the counter-arguments tend to underline the necessity of fiscal consolidation and anti-inflationary policies. Others point out that the time period over which unemployment as been growing in Europe is too long to be easily explained in macroeconomic terms (Nickell, 1997). However, deflationary policies implicit in the implementation of the Maastricht way to EMU seem to have eventually increased the level of European unemployment, at least by increasing the equilibrium rate of unemployment (a phenomenon called hysteresis in the literature; e.g., Artis, 1998; Cameron, 1997, 1998, 1999).

Moreover, some econometric simulations show that the implementation of the Stability Pact from 1974 until 1995 in four European countries (notably, Italy, France, Germany and the UK) would have limited economic growth by reducing the annual growth rate. This would have led to cumulated output losses of around 5 per cent in France and the UK, and of 9 per cent in Italy. The theoretical implication of these results is, of course, that the GSP constraints would limit (and will limit, in the future) the use of automatic stabilisers to counter recessive waves, thus increasing the severity of recessions. This, however, will happen only if member states are not able to achieve a balanced or surplus budgetary position allowing them to use automatic stabilisers during mild recessive periods in the appropriate way without breaching the Maastricht/GSP threshold (cf. Eichengreen and Wyplosz, 1998, p. 93).

There is, to be sure, a counter-argument that the growth and stability pact gives credibility to the ECB anti-inflationary stances, thus reducing the level of interest rates required to maintain the inflation rate below 2 per cent and boosting economic output and employment. Finally, even if the recessive bias of the fiscal criteria and the GSP were proved, this would not necessarily lead to a higher unemployment level (Artis and Winkler, 1997; also Buti, Franco and Ongena, 1997).

However, there is another way in which the Maastricht criteria and the Stability Pact might affect unemployment, a more indirect way, which is the basis to justify a neofunctionalist automatic spill over leading from EMU to labour market flexibility. This is related to how member states should react to possibly arising asymmetric shocks. By definition, autonomous monetary policy and exchange rate policies are not available to react to idiosyncratic shocks in a currency union. At the same time, common monetary and exchange rate policies should be used with caution since they can have mixed results if the other members of the Union are simultaneously experiencing an opposite business cycle situation. Thus, economic theory leaves few options: fiscal policy, labour mobility, and relative price flexibility.

Indeed, a country could react to an asymmetric shock by using national fiscal policy, both as a counter-cyclical tool, through the action of automatic stabilisers, and in the form of fiscal transfers to solve more long-term economic disparities (as in the case of Italian Mezzogiorno). However, in the special kind of monetary union analysed in this chapter, the Maastricht criteria and, to an even greater extent, the requirements of the Stability Pact constrain substantially the ability of member states to resort to national fiscal policy to tackle asymmetric shocks.

Alternatively, some authors suggest the redistributive and stabilising functions of fiscal policy be performed at the European level. Regarding this, the proposals range from the increase in the size of the European budget, to the pooling of national fiscal policies, to the establishment of a Common fiscal body, which would act as a counterbalance to the ECB (e.g., Obstfeld and Peri, 1998). The feasibility of similar proposals looks at least dubious in the light of the difficulties EU Member states encounter in finding some agreement on the much less challenging task of tax harmonisation (Overbeek, 2000). Moreover, the discussion of fiscal policy inevitably raises more general concerns about the loss of national sovereignty. Overall, the EU member states are unable either to reach an agreement on the creation of a common fiscal policy or to find some way to increase the size of the EU budget as to introduce a stabilisation function.

Given the difficulties in using national fiscal policy to tackle asymmetric shocks, and the lack of any substantial fiscal power at the European level, economists suggest the option of greater labour mobility. The EU does indeed provide an institutional framework in which labour mobility can be enhanced. The Treaty's articles regarding the free movement of workers, the Single Market programme, and recent provisions in the Third Pillar are all directed toward this objective. However, economic analyses show little evidence of mass migration in response to asymmetric shocks in the EU (unlike in some respects the US) (Obstfeld and Peri, 1998). Indeed, few European policy-makers would seriously endorse temporary mass migration as a credible way to react to national economic strains, for obvious political as well as social considerations.

Thus, there remains only one policy option for national policy-makers to tackle the problems arising from asymmetric shocks: increasing the flexibility of labour markets so that 'regions or states affected by adverse shocks can recover by cutting wages, reducing relative prices and taking market shares from the others' (Blanchard, 1998, p. 249). Not only this. Since reform of the labour market is clearly a structural intervention, it will help eliminating also the structural component of unemployment, apart from the cyclical one, if it is still possible to distinguish between the two (Artis, 1998).

Indeed, the employment rhetoric and strategy officially adopted by EU institutions in the last few years shows clearly that the European Union has chosen to give priority to labour flexibility as 'the' means to tackle the problem of unemployment in Europe. To this attention is turned in the next section.

6.2.2 The EU Strategy and Rhetoric on Unemployment and the EES

That the European Union chose to tackle the problem of unemployment by acting on the labour flexibility side is shown clearly by the employment rhetoric and strategy officially adopted by EU institutions in the last few years.

The 'White Paper on Growth, Competitiveness, and Employment' of 1993 made no mystery of the fact that the way to increase employment passed through structural changes in the European labour markets:

> Increasing the rate of growth which the economy of the Community can sustain for many years and boosting the employment content of growth requires a strategy based on three inseparable elements:
> 1. The creation and the maintenance of a macroeconomic framework which, instead of constraining market forces, as often happened in the recent past, supports them;
> 2. Determined actions in the structural area aimed at increasing the competitiveness of European industry and removing the rigidities which are curbing its dynamism and preventing it from reaping the full benefits of the internal market; an adequate framework for developing new market opportunities should be created;
> 3. Active policies and structural changes in the labour markets and in the regulations limiting the expansion of certain sectors (notably the service sector) which will make it easier to employ people and will therefore increase the employment content of growth.[3]

More precisely, the White Paper specified that structural action should be taken in three main areas:

1   greater flexibility should be introduced in the economy as a whole. In particular the regulatory framework should become more enterprise friendly;
2   strategies should be developed to create an efficient labour market able to respond to new competitive situations;
3   the international environment must be kept open to allow the Community to participate fully in the development of those areas of the world where the greater potential of unsatisfied demand presently exists and which are likely to experience the highest rates of growth over the next decade.

The Maastricht path to economic and monetary union was then generally recognised as the appropriate framework in which to address structural problems. In particular, an essential element of a budgetary restraint policy was represented by the adoption of measures to 'improve the financial situation of the social security system',[4] which, translated from the EU institutional language, meant to reduce the level of social expenditure and, thus, protection.

Of course this would be possible only on the basis of a broad social consensus, or, in the words of the White Paper:

> Attacking the sources of present unemployment problems requires therefore a clean break with the past. This will be possible only if a large consensus on the necessary course of action to be followed can be achieved both within each country, between management and the labour force in industry and among members of the European Community.[5]

Calls for a full support of structural changes by the social partners at both the national and the European level were then reiterated in the conclusions of the European Council meeting at Essen in December 1994. On this occasion a European employment strategy was adopted which impinged on five key areas amongst which work flexibility played a major role.[6] The Essen summit insisted on increasing the employment-intensiveness of growth, in particular by adopting:

1　a more flexible organisation of work in a way which fulfils both the wishes of employees and the requirements of competition;
2　a wage policy which encourages job-creating investments and in the present situation requires moderate wage agreements below increases in productivity;
3　the promotion of initiatives, particularly at regional and local level, that create jobs which take account of new requirements, e.g., in the environmental and social services spheres.

Much emphasis was put also on reducing non-wage labour costs extensively enough to ensure that there is a noticeable effect on decisions concerning the taking on of employees and in particular of unqualified employees.[7]

Drawing on the strategy agreed in Essen and on the White Paper, the European Council meeting in Florence on June 1996 held a detailed discussion on the subject of growth and employment.[8]

Again, the institutions of the EU, governments and regional and local authorities, as well as the social partners were all asked to support, at their own level of responsibility, the speeding up of the labour market reforms in the context of the budgetary constraints provided for by the Maastricht way to EMU.

To this end, the European Council called on the member states to step up their efforts at budgetary consolidation, taking account of the general principles laid down in the TEU, and in particular the desirability of reducing expenditure rather than increasing revenue. In this context, the European Council also called on the social partners to continue to promote a wages policy favourable to employment and competitiveness. In particular, member states and, where appropriate, the social partners were asked to examine social security systems in relation to job creation.[9]

The very important step in the definition of the EU policy towards employment was, however, represented by the insertion of a brand new title on employment by the EC Amsterdam Treaty.[10] Indeed, in the opinion of commentators[11] Amsterdam marks the final shift towards the liberal approach to employment that had taken place since the White Paper and the Essen European Council decisions.

The EU Treaty's new Title on Employment aimed to put in place a comprehensive strategy to achieve the objective of a 'high'[12] level of employment with the participation of both national governments and societal actors. The emphasis again was on reaching a similar objective through an 'adaptable workforce' and 'labour markets responsive to economic change'.[13] In terms of procedures, art. 125 of the EC Treaty states that the member states and the Community will work together towards developing a co-ordinated strategy for employment. Art. 126 deals with the contribution of member states and the coordination of their action. According to art. 127 the Community will contribute to this action by incorporating employment issues into its policies and activities. Art. 128 details further the process of coordination mentioned in art. 126 and highlights the work to be done at the Community level on a yearly basis, particularly by the Council and the Commission, entailing a joint report, guidelines on employment and recommendations to the member states where appropriate. Under art. 129 the Council may adopt incentive measures to encourage cooperation between member states and support their action in the field of employment. Finally art. 130 provides for the creation of an employment committee with advisory status to promote coordination between member states' policies in the area of employment and the labour market.

Importantly, the Community strategy for employment was to be closely tied to the provisions on economic and monetary policy.[14] This aspect was emphasised by the European Council of Vienna (11–12 December 1998) where the European Heads of State and Government called for more coordination between employment and the broad economic policy guidelines. On this occasion, the European Council also asked for the development of a European Pact for Employment. A report on the development of this Pact was drawn up by the Cologne European Council, which also endorsed it.

The main innovation of the Pact is the provision for a dialogue between those responsible for budgetary, monetary, wage and structural policies, by this meaning the effective subordination of wage and labour markets policies to the budgetary constraints imposed by the TEU and the stability pact. Indeed, the essential elements of the Pact are:

1   coordination of economic policy and improvement of mutually supportive interaction between wage developments and monetary, budget and fiscal policy through macroeconomic dialogue aimed at preserving non-inflationary growth dynamic, so-called Cologne process;
2   further development and better implementation of the coordinated strategy to improve the efficiency of the labour markets by improving employability, entrepreneurship, adaptability of businesses and their employees, and equal opportunities for men and women in finding gainful employment (Luxembourg process);
3   comprehensive structural reform and modernisation to improve the innovative capacity and the efficiency of the markets in goods, services and capital (Cardiff process).[15]

Of course, one should not overestimate the impact that the EU recommendations, initiatives or proposals have in terms of effective policy-making. Indeed, despite the many declarations of intent, the responsibility for the implementation of labour policies still lies in the hands of the member states, leaving the ECB as the only truly common European institution for macroeconomic policy-making.

But what does labour flexibility mean? How has it been implemented at the national level? What kind of changes does it imply? Does it really help in solving unemployment? How did the relevant socioeconomic actors react in the different European countries? Who wins and who loses from the implementation of a similar policy? An attempt to answer these questions will be provided in the following sections with special attention to the case of Italy.

6.3 A Neo-Gramscian Perspective: Socioeconomic Groups and the Power Consequences of the EES

6.3.1 Flexibility vs Exclusion: The Anglo-Saxon Model as opposed to the Mediterranean Model

The expression 'flexibility of labour markets' as used by the scholars of industrial relations (e.g., Rhodes, 1997) refers to three forms of flexibility:

1. internal (or functional) flexibility in the work place;
2. external (or numerical) flexibility *vis-à-vis* the wider labour market;
3. greater pay flexibility at local levels.

Categorising the level of flexibility/rigidity of European labour markets along the dimensions of internal and external flexibility, we can distinguish what in the literature is referred to as the 'southern cluster' (Rhodes, 1997, pp. 10–11). This is characterised by a remarkable shift, from very low levels of both external and internal flexibility of the 'legal' or 'licit' labour markets in the 1970s to a much higher level of flexibility in the 1990s. Contemporaneously these economies (first and foremost Italy and Spain) saw the growth of 'illicit' labour markets and a shift from labour exporting to labour importing (cf. OECD, 1987).

This process took place amid heated struggles between socioeconomic groups that inevitably changed the balance of power between them. In this context, the issue of European integration in general and EMU in particular provided the excuse to shift the power battle from the national to the European level. However, despite the rhetorical appeal of 'Europe' this shift was by no means politically neutral. In the move from the national to the international level, some groups acquired more strength and cohesion. Others lost a great deal of their bargaining power for reasons ranging from a decreased organisational or representative capacity to a structural bias of the EU institutional setting in favour of certain societal interests (cf. Holman, 1996). The game of transnationalisation is indeed much easier played by the employers' organisations than by the unions, given the many cleavages within the European working class reflected in the cumbersome functioning of the European Trade Unions Confederation (ETUC) (see Talani, 2000 for an overview; see also the contribution by Ryner and Schulten in Overbeek, 2003). This contribution will underline how, by shifting the struggle around labour flexibility in Italy between employers and employees from the national to the European level, also the relative power positions between the two groups changed which made it easier to introduce neoliberal labour market reforms.

Whether these labour reforms represent the solution to the problem of unemployment in Mediterranean countries is indeed a different issue. As Esping-Andersen (1999) reminds us there exists a considerable gap between the widely accepted theoretical claim that deregulation will create jobs and the evidence that rigidities seem to matter only selectively. This is particularly true for Mediterranean countries like Italy, where institutional rigidities have often been offset by informal flexibilities including self-employment and the black market.

Moreover, similar labour rigidities must be understood in the context of the societal structure of Mediterranean countries. The so-called Mediterranean model is often characterised as a *familial* one, i.e., one based on the assumption that the family male is the only breadwinner. This would explain that the exceedingly high levels of female and youth unemployment are not inconsistent with a high level of labour protection and a low level of social protection. The family is the locus of social protection, and wife and children remain dependent on the income of the father up to a very late age. The protection of the job of the latter thus becomes of fundamental importance for the entire society. This model differs substantially from the liberal model prevailing in Anglo-Saxon countries, wherein the trade-off between flexibility and exclusion there is a tendency towards the former with all that it implies in terms of decrease in equality. And indeed in Anglo-Saxon countries a high degree of labour market flexibility produces high levels of employment at the expense of a growing wage polarisation between unskilled and skilled workers (see the contributions by Jessop and by Becker in Overbeek, 2003).

Many claim that in the era of globalisation the Anglo-Saxon model is the only viable one in view of the competitive pressures stemming from lower labour costs in less-developed countries. And indeed that is the basic argument used by the supporters of flexibility, particularly within employers' organisations. But apart from the fact that the impact of globalisation on employment is far from clear (see the contribution by Overbeek in Overbeek, 2003) the price in terms of increase in inequality might not be worth paying in countries where the societal setting is opposed to the Anglo-Saxon one. This, however, is not the place to address the many complex issues influencing the future of employment in a globalising world. Therefore we now turn to the analysis of the Italian case.

6.3.2   Italy and the Process of European Monetary Integration: Shifting the Level of Governance

In Italy, European issues and in particular those related to the process of European monetary integration were consistently used by the leading socioeconomic groups (particularly big industry) to reduce the level of labour protection and increase the flexibility of labour markets (cf. Talani, 2000).

To analyse this in more detail this section will first deal with the decrease in labour protection legislation in relation to Italian entry in the ERM of the EMS. Subsequently it addresses labour market flexibility as a consequence of EMU.

The struggle over the 'Scala Mobile' It is generally agreed that the first relaxation in Italian labour protection legislation was represented by the abolition of the so-called *Scala Mobile*, the Italian wage indexation mechanism. This was made possible by commitment to the EMS, with all that it implied in terms of strict anti-inflationary policies. The abolition of the *Scala Mobile* was a consequence of the new dominant position of Italian capitalist groups and also served to enhance their position.

The 'hot autumn' of 1969 marked the beginning of the 'era of union centrality' (cf. Lange, Ross and Vanicelli, 1982, p. 97; see also Giugni, 1981, p. 341; Regini, 1981). This was an era in which Italian economic policy was characterised by prevailing concerns for the maintenance of the purchasing power of wages, the institutionalisation of workers' rights and the leading role played by the trade unions and their political counterparts in Italian socioeconomic policy-making. The growing strength of trade unions during this period is reflected clearly in the ascending slope of its membership parabola whose density rates increased constantly from 1969 onwards reaching their peak in 1978 (with 49 per cent of total employed, an 18.2 per cent increase with respect to the 1969 figure) (see Figure 6.2).

The era of union centrality reached its political apex in 1975, with the signing of an agreement between the union confederations and Confindustria to upgrade the *Scala Mobile*, a system protecting workers' wages against inflation. The agreement provided for a three months payment of a fixed amount for each unit increase in the inflation rate, the so-called *punto di contingenza*.[16] The main features of the agreement, which was the product of collective bargaining and not the result of a parliamentary process,[17] were the relatively high and immediate degree of inflation protection paying equal amounts to all workers, and thus reducing wage differentials, and the automatic character of the system.

Figure 6.2   Density of union membership in Italy, 1969–85

Source: Centro Studi Economici Sociali e Sindacali (CESOS), *Le relazioni sindacali in Italia: Reports*, various issues.

The agreement represented a major victory for the union movement. However, the defence of this victory proved to be very problematic and eventually led, with the beginning of the economic crisis of the late 1970s–early 1980s, to major conflicts not only between the unions and their social and political referents, but also within the unions themselves.

In the face of the growing economic problems, particularly unemployment, the Italian Union Federation[18] in 1978 adopted a new strategic orientation, the so-called EUR strategy. This was based on a trade-off between fewer guarantees to the workers and more participation in investment decisions, and it was aimed at increasing employment through the new instrument of tripartite negotiations with the government and employer representatives. Given the increasing involvement of the Italian Communist Party in the governmental area, thanks to the pacification process between the PCI and the DC (the so-called 'historic compromise'), this 'new course' of Italian unions appeared to secure their participation in the official sites of Italian economic policies decision-making. On the contrary, following the tragic end of 'national solidarity', the EUR strategy marked the beginning of a descending parabola of union bargaining power and political influence (Accornero 1994). The historic compromise suffered a serious blow with the 1978 kidnapping and subsequent murder of DC leader Aldo Moro.

As already noted, the dismantling of the *Scala Mobile*, or, at least, the substantial reform of its mechanisms, together with the reduction of state intervention in the economy, constituted the main issues at stake in the domestic debate over the establishment of the European Monetary System. Indeed, it was precisely in the course of this debate that the differences within the governmental majority and within the union federations over the future of the *Scala Mobile* became unbridgeable. Within the union movement itself, the 'automatic' increases of the *Scala Mobile* were increasingly attacked. This is true especially for the UIL, which in this period was beginning to be controlled by the new PSI of Craxi (see Merkel, 1987 for a detailed account), and for the CISL, traditionally linked to the catholic interests and to the DC. By 1982, for instance, both Pierre Carniti, Secretary General of the CISL and Giorgio Benvenuto, Secretary General of UIL, were favourable to a major reform of the wage indexation mechanism within the context of tripartite negotiations. On the other hand, the Communist component of the CGIL was far less ready than the others to modify the system. The inconsistencies in the positions of the different unions eventually led to the first major blow to the *Scala Mobile* represented by the accord of 22 January 1983 (see Lange, 1986, p. 30). With this accord, for the first time since 1975, the unions accepted the reduction of the automatic inflation-indexed payments coupled with an 18-month freeze of wage bargaining in the private corporate sector. This constituted a major defeat the significance of which should not be underestimated, even if the government agreed to protect the real purchasing power of workers by cutting taxes, limiting the rise of government controlled prices and changing the family allowance system.

Given the compromise nature of the 1983 accord and the fact that the balance of power between unions and employers was still shifting towards the latter, in late 1983 the unions agreed to pursue a possible revision of the 1983 accord. The issues at stake were still wages and job flexibility and, above all the *Scala Mobile*, but this time Confindustria was taking a much tougher position and the unions reached the negotiating table without having achieved a joint position. The CISL and the UIL were favourable to further reduction in the *Scala Mobile*, while the CGIL made the reform of the system conditional on a government's commitment not to distribute the costs of further economic growth and employment exclusively among the working class. The situation was further complicated by the governmental leadership of Bettino Craxi, who sought to enhance the power of the executive in taking hard economic policy decisions (*decisionismo*) and by an even stronger opposition to the communist party. The atmosphere was so heated that in early February 1984, the communist and the socialist factions of the CGIL split, assuming different positions on the *Scala Mobile* and on the need to consult the workers before signing any agreement. This step slowed, if not prevented, CGIL participation in any compromise.

On 12 February the Minister of Labour Gianni De Michelis presented a draft accord that maintained the trade-off nature of the 1983 accord. It proposed a limitation of the number of units to be paid every three months during 1984, but it also promised that, in case of higher inflation rates, the following year fiscal interventions would compensate any unforeseen losses. The CISL and the UIL promptly declared their willingness to conclude negotiations, while the CGIL, after a moment of hesitation, declared its unwillingness to accept it, thus joining the PCI in its negative assessment of the manoeuvre. Open conflict broke out between the government on one side, and the PCI and the communist component of the CGIL on the other side, when Craxi translated the basic terms of the 14 February protocol in a decree to be converted in law. Despite the campaign of the communists and their parliamentary allies, especially the deputies of the *Democrazia Proletaria*, and despite the massive popular demonstrations throughout Italy, this eventually happened on 12 June 1984. In June the PCI decided to pursue a referendum on art. 3 of the decree that concerned the cuts to the *Scala Mobile*. By late September more than the required number of signatures had been submitted. On 7 December 1984 the Central Office of the *Corte di Cassazione* declared the referendum constitutional. On 9 and 10 June 1985, after a long and bitter referendum campaign further complicated by the administrative elections of 12 May 1985, Italian voters finally defeated the PCI effort to overturn art. 3 when 54. 3 per cent voted 'no' and only 46.7 per cent voted 'yes'.

The long battle over the *Scala Mobile* made it manifestly clear that the era of Italian political economy characterised by the market and political power of the union movement and by the PCI's ability to act as a political 'guarantor' of union cooperation with government policy had come to an end. The battle over the *Scala Mobile*, transcending its economic meaning, became a struggle over the balance of power within the different Italian socio-political and economic actors. The issue at stake was the control over the pattern of growth and distribution in the Italian political economy. With its conclusion, the basic contours of the political economy had fundamentally changed and the era of union centrality had ended with the labour movement and the PCI as net losers.

What were the reasons for such a change? Analysts of industrial relations in Italy identify some tendencies in the union organisation development during the late 1970s and early 1980s which might help to explain this phenomenon.[19] On the one hand there was a renewed dependency of Italian industrial relations on the party system, after their relative autonomy during the early 1970s (cf. Lange and Regini, 1989). This is demonstrated by the shift from the centralised political negotiations of the 1960s and early 1970s to the new tripartite agreements of the late 1970s and 1980s in which the political parties and the government played a much more important and active role. On the other hand, unions found it increasingly difficult to perceive which interests to represent. A deeper crisis of representation occurred during this period and this, together with the new linkages to the political parties, led to a growing division within the union movement and to a progressive decline of their political and bargaining power (see Regini, 1981, ch. 7).

These factors, however, are not enough to explain the change in power allocation, and greater attention must be paid to the fact that the phenomena under analysis took place in a period of deep economic changes and crises (see Vannicelli, 1984, p. 404).

After the recession of 1970–71, Italy experienced a moderate recovery led by the depreciation of the lira after the abandonment of the European stake in the spring of 1973. This, however, proved to be only a palliative measure, to the extent that in late 1974, early 1975, a full-blown economic crisis developed (Salvati, 1984). Italian unemployment started to grow almost constantly from 1974 onwards reaching a double digit figure, 10.2 per cent, in 1984. Real GDP succeeded in recovering only slightly from the 1975 slump of –3.6 per cent with the devaluation of the lira in 1976. However, at the beginning of the 1980s it was again registering negative levels.

The Italian industrial and banking sectors tended to single out the unsustainable labour costs as a fundamental cause of the country's industrial sector crisis. They consequently identified elimination of the wage indexation system, so strenuously defended by the trade unions and the left political parties, as the only viable solution to the Italian economic crisis.

The prolonged recessive phase, by weakening the pressures on the labour market, limited substantially the workers' bargaining power, and encouraged the entrepreneurial and the financial sector to try to abolish those rules or institutions which limited their autonomy. However, the decrease of the union bargaining power was not uniform across all sectors of labour. Certain strata of workers enjoyed greater protection under existing laws or by their crucial position in the productive process.[20] Thus, while the recession generally undermined the power bases of the union movement, it particularly reduced its capacity to represent the aggregate interests of the workers, that is, to act as a pre-mediator among a set of different interests. This is the role that enables a union movement to maintain a common position during negotiations.

Furthermore, structural interventions in industry, technological innovation, the growing importance of services, the spread of small companies, the increasing reliance on foreign labour and the rise of the 'invisible' or 'black' economy are all phenomena that served to increase industrial productivity and competitiveness. However, each of these factors also contributed to the fragmentation and loss of power of the trade union movement.

Thus the *Scala Mobile* was abolished in the context of a historic loss of power for Italian labour characterised not only by the crisis of representation but also by the increasing difficulty in aggregating different interests and simultaneous loss of capacity to obtain favourable measures in exchange for their consensus to stricter economic policies. These developments are related to the underlying transformation of accumulation structures in Italy towards post-Fordist patterns (see Jessop, ch. 2, in Overbeek, 2003).

Corresponding to the decline of the unions' capacity to influence socioeconomic development is the opposite phenomenon of the rise of private company power. This has been an international and structurally determined phenomenon connected with the aforementioned transformation of the global economy. This structural development has also, at the same time, been dialectically interrelated with the political agency of big capital. Transnational corporations, being usually less affected by national regulations, called for deregulation in the domestic corporate sector and exported, mainly through the American channel, the Japanese conception of the 'firm as a community' giving rise to the development of a 'corporate identity'. This undermined previous social achievements in many European countries, in Italy in the form of the eventual abolition of the *Scala Mobile*, in which process the disciplinary effects of European economic and monetary integration proved very important.

Italy, EMU and labour market flexibility The tendency of the Confindustria to approach the problems of labour costs through the mechanisms by which they are determined, starting from indexation, was confirmed by the following round of the battle over the *Scala Mobile* which led to its definitive abolishment with the 1993 agreement.

After a long controversy between the CGIL, CISL, UIL, Confindustria and the government, the latter had, with the law No. 191 (13 July 1990) prorogued the *Scala Mobile* for the whole year 1991. However, from January 1992, the mechanism was again under the bargaining autonomy of the social partners. At the expiration of the deadline, the government confirmed, with the *Protocollo* of December 1991, its firm decision not to allow any other prorogation by law of the *Scala Mobile*. It indeed stated that all the problems relating to a new general system of bargaining and to the structure of retribution should be tackled by 1 June 1992. The battle was likely to be extremely hard unless there was some external factor pressing the trade unions, or better the CGIL, to accept the agreement on wage policy as the only possible alternative to the abyss. This external factor was represented by the threat of speculative attacks on the lira.

To cite these speculative attacks as a decisive external factor is not to imply that the Italian economic elite self-consciously provoked them. However, the Italian employers' class certainly acted within the limits of the possible by constantly voicing the unsustainability of the currency peg. This clearly signalled the markets the likelihood of a depreciation of the lira in case of attacks. However, also the timing of the attacks was important. It all had to happen after the trade unions, scared by the instability of the markets, had agreed to finally curb wage indexation. This was the only way for the employers to be able to gather fully the benefits of a much wanted currency devaluation.

Indeed, the Protocol signed on 31 July 1992, just a month before the speculative attacks against the lira, represented a major victory for the employers. The trade unions had agreed to the almost complete elimination of the *Scala Mobile* and had accepted the block of wage bargaining at plant level for the whole of 1993 in exchange for a forfeit sum of L20.000 ($\pm$ $8) a month for all workers.

The question of the structure of wage bargaining, not tackled in the Protocol, was left to further negotiations, leading to the agreement of 1993. The latter institutionalised the new balance of power between Italian social partners by introducing two levels of collective bargaining: the national and the plant levels. Moreover, it provided the take-off platform for future changes of the social protection legislation, particularly reform of the pension system (cf. Regini and Regalia, 1997). Finally it increased the level of flexibility of the Italian labour markets by improving the Italian training system (boosting internal flexibility) and legalising temporary work agencies (improving external flexibility) (see Rhodes, 1997, p. 14).

In the context of the decreasing bargaining power of the trade unions, some steps towards the deregulation of employment conditions had already been taken with the Law 223/91 which modified the procedures of placement by introducing the so-called 'nominative call' in place of the 'compulsory call'. It also recognised collective dismissals as a possible solution for firms' crises, a measure which, together with the introduction of the new instrument of mobility insurance (a longer form of early retirement), was meant to guarantee Italian companies freedom to 'fire' in case of necessity (see Gualmini, 1998). Coming to the 'hire' side of liberalising policies, Law 221 abolished the obligation for firms to choose workers from the so-called *liste di disoccupazione* (compulsory hiring lists) and introduced the principle of free choice.

In terms of job creation and labour market flexibility, a number of further initiatives were taken later on, particularly by the Berlusconi governments, on whose effectiveness, however, it is still not possible to draw conclusions.

The first Berlusconi government introduced, with the Law 451/94, the so-called 'public utility works'[21] which seemed to many yet another form of badly concealed *assistenzialismo* whose only outcome was to postpone the problem of unemployment for a very limited number of people. Moreover the Berlusconi government launched some fiscal incentives for young employers starting new enterprises and a law on ad-interim jobs.

However, it was the second Berlusconi government, elected in May 2001, to be the most active on the side of labour market flexibility.

On 3 October 2001, the then minister of Labour, Roberto Maroni, presented the so-called 'Libro Bianco sul mercato del lavoro' (white book on the labour market) containing a number of measures to render the Italian labour market more flexible.[22] On 15 November 2001, the government proposed a draft law (the so-called 'Disegno di legge delega Ddl 848) to delegate to the government the power to legislate on all the issues relating to employment and labour market.

After a long period of social struggle amongst the Italian socioeconomic groups, and after the murder of the father of the labour market reform, Prof. Marco Biagi, the government and 39 employers' and employees' associations signed, on 5 July 2002, the so-called 'Patto per l'Italia' (Pact for Italy), declaring the necessity to adopt the law as soon as possible.[23] On 5 February 2003 the Italian parliament finally approved the Ddl 848 which became the Law no. 30 of 14 February 2003, also known as the Biagi law. The latter came into force on 13 March 2003. From that day onwards, the government has the power to pass any law regarding the reform of the labour market without having to go through the parliamentary procedure.

The content of the reform is clearly oriented towards a marked increase of the degree of liberalisation and flexibility of the labour market. It is indeed too early to judge the impact of similar measures on the Italian labour market. It is however important to note that the overall rate of unemployment is not the major problem to be faced by Italian labour. More serious challenges arise from the pervasiveness of the black market and the great differences in terms of region, age and gender.[24]

6.4 Conclusions

Summing up, the neofunctionalist case automatically linking the establishment of EMU to the flexibilisation of labour markets seems to conceal a number of power struggles amongst the different socioeconomic groups at both the national and the transnational level.

Indeed, as the case of Italy demonstrates, the implementation of an EU employment strategy relying significantly on labour market flexibility, whose rationale is often neofunctionally linked to the establishment of EMU, is by no means neutral in its political economy impact and substantially modifies the existing balance of power between employers' organisations and trade unions. Furthermore, as this chapter shows, the implementation itself of flexible labour market policies was made possible by the strengthening of the bargaining power of the employers' organisations enshrined in the institutionalisation at the European level of the neoliberal economic paradigm focusing on the implementation of strict monetary and fiscal policies.

If the process of globalisation does modify the role of the nation state from the welfare model to the Anglo-Saxon model or 'competition state' (see Cerny in Buelens, 1999), it might be argued that the process of regionalisation allows for a simplification of this process by strengthening the institutional power of transnational capitalist elites *vis-à-vis* organised labour in the shift from the national to the European level of governance. This game of transnationalisation is indeed much easier played by the employers' organisations than by the unions, given the many cleavages within the labour interest representation groups and the disaggregating tendencies embedded in the present globalised capitalist structure.

Whether, then, this process of transnationalisation is the outcome of the pro-active role of organised transnational actors (see van Apeldoorn in Overbeek 2003), or is the inevitable result of the restructuring of the world economy in the context of globalisation, is a subject for further analysis.

As far as this contribution is concerned, it seems clear that this redefinition of the power relations amongst socioeconomic groups is well advanced and was clearly favoured by the role played by the process of European monetary integration.

Notes

1   See, for example, Crouch (2000), Dyson and Featherstone (1999), Eichengreen and Frieden (1998), Frieden (1998), de Grauwe (1997), and also Talani (2000).
2   The distinction between 'monetarists' and 'economists' emerged in the course of the discussions over the Werner Plan and referred to the strategy to be adopted during the transitional period. The 'monetarists' stressed the importance of achieving exchange rate stability through European institutional arrangements, while the 'economists' pointed out the necessity of policy co-ordination and, ultimately, convergence before agreeing on the adoption of a European fixed exchange rate regime or a currency union. For more details see Tsoukalis (1997).
3   European Commission (1993).
4   European Commission (1993).
5   European Commission (1993).
6   See European Council meeting on 9 and 10 December I Essen-Presidency Conclusions, http://ue.eu.int/newsroom.
7   Ibid.
8   The bases for the discussion were represented by: the Commission communication entitled 'Action for Employment in Europe: A Confidence Pact', the joint interim report on employment as well as the other documents before it, including the conclusions drawn from the Tripartite Conference on Growth and Employment held in Rome on 14–15 June 1996 and the French Memorandum on a European social model. See Florence European Council, 21–22 June 1996-Presidency Conclusions, http://ue.eu.int/newsroom.
9   See Florence European Council, 21–22 June 1996-Presidency Conclusions, http://ue.eu.int/newsroom.
10 See Title VIII, articles 125–130 of the EC Treaty as modified by the Amsterdam Treaty.
11 See, for example, Duff (1997).
12 A long controversial went on in the course of the IGC on whether the objective of 'full' employment was to be inserted in the new title, as suggested by the new French socialist government. Eventually, however, the prevailing opinion was to substitute 'full' employment with 'high' employment. See Duff (1997).
13 Duff (1997).
14 See art. 126 (1) and art. 128 (2).
15 See http://www.europa.eu.int.
16 It is important to note that in the same year, 1975, the Bank of Italy committed itself to buy all unsold Treasury Bills.
17 Art. 39 of the Italian Constitution indicates the requisites for a collective agreement to achieve the force of law, but this article has never been implemented.
18 The Italian UIL (a federation of CGIL and CISL) was established in 1972 and lasted until 1984 when, during the heated debate over the *Scala Mobile*, it was dismantled.
19 For a thorough analysis of the Italian trade union organisation literature until the early 1980s see Giugni (1981, p. 324); for a more theoretical review of the relationship between industrial relations and political science see Gourevitch, Lange and Martin (1981, p. 401).
20 In the analysis carried out by Vannicelli, it is possible to identify four distinct groups of workers:
    a)   the 'core' of the workforce consisting of industrial workers usually active in the union movement who were affected by the economic crisis to a lesser extent;

b)   an expanding group of precarious workers who were pushed by the recession into a condition of permanent, State subsidised unemployment;
c)   women and young people with little hope to find employment;
d)   a group of 'unofficially' employed people recruited by the 'invisible' or even 'black' economy.
   See Vannicelli (1984, p. 404).
21   The law allowed public administrations and some private organisations to promote projects for works of public interest and to use long-term unemployed selected from the *liste di disoccupazione* for a limited period of time.
22   For more information see the website of the Italian Labour Ministry at http://www.welfare. gov.it.
23   For all the information relating to the pact and for the text see http://www.welfare.gov.it/ NR/rdonlyres/ebuv5tvajrasify2koysjz3z7zola7h2zfbzogaiekkuoevsx2zavq22sftghelciyud q3m4vljpylt/20020905pattoitalia.pdf.
24   For the related data see the Italian Statistical Institute (ISTAT) website at the following address http://www.istat.it/.

References

Accornero, A. (1994), *La parabola del sindacato*, Bologna: Il Mulino.
Artis, M. (1998), 'The Unemployment Problem', *Oxford Review of Economic Policy*, Vol. 14, 3.
Artis and Winkler, B. (1997), 'The Stability Pact: Safeguarding the Credibility of the European Central Bank', CEPR Discussion Paper No. 1688.
Blanchard, O.J. (1998), 'Discussion to "Regional Non-adjustment and Fiscal Policy"', *Economic Policy*, No. 26, April, p. 249.
Buelens, F. (ed.) (1999), *Globalisation and the Nation State*, Aldershot: Edward Elgar.
Buti, M., Franco, D. and Ongena, H. (1997), 'Budgetary Policies during Recessions: Retrospective Application of the Stability and Growth Pact to the Post-war Period', *Economic Paper* No. 121, Brussels: European Commission.
Cameron, D. (1997), 'Economic and Monetary Union: Underlying Imperatives and Third-stage Dilemmas', *Journal of European Public Policy*, 4, pp. 455–85.
Cameron, D. (1998), 'EMU after 1999: The Implications and Dilemmas of the Third Stage', *Columbia Journal of European Law*, No. 4, pp. 425–46.
Cameron, D. (1999), 'Unemployment in the New Europe: The Contours of the Problem', *EUI Working Papers*, RSC No. 99/35.
Crouch, C. (2000), *After the Euro*, Oxford: Oxford University Press.
Duff, A. (1997), *The Treaty of Amsterdam*, London: Sweet and Maxwell.
Dyson, K. and Featherstone, K. (1999), *The Road to Maastricht*, Oxford: Oxford University Press.
Eichengreen, B. and Frieden, J. (1998), *Forging an Integrated Europe*, Ann Arbor: University of Michigan Press.
Eichengreen, B. and Wyplosz, C. (1998), 'The Stability Pact: More than a Minor Nuisance?', *Economic Policy*, No. 26, April.
Esping-Anderson, G. (1999), *Social Foundations of Post-industrial Economies*, Oxford: Oxford University Press.

European Commission (1993), 'White Paper on Growth, Competitiveness, and Employment: The Challenges and Ways Forward into the 21st Century', COM(93) 700 final, Brussels, 5 December 1993, http://www.europa.eu.int/en/record/white/c93700/contents.html.

Frieden, J. (1998), *The New Political Economy of EMU*, Oxford: Rowman and Littlefield.

Giugni, G. (1981), 'The Italian System of Industrial Relations', in P.B. Doeringer (ed.), *Industrial Relations in International Perspective: Essays on Research and Policy*, London: Macmillan.

Grauwe, Paul de (1997), *The Economics of Monetary Integration*, 3rd rev. edn, Oxford: Oxford University Press.

Gros, D. and Thygesen, N. (1998), *European Monetary Integration*, London: Longman.

Lange, P., Ross, G. and Vannicelli, M. (1982), *Unions, Change and Crisis: French and Italian Union Strategy and the Political Economy*, London: Allen and Unwin.

Gourevitch, P., Lange, P. and Martin, A. (1981), 'Industrial Relations and Politics: Some Reflections', in P.B. Doeringer (ed.), *Industrial Relations in International Perspective: Essays on Research and Policy*, London: Macmillan.

Gualmini, E. (1998), 'Italy', in H. Compston (ed.), *The New Politics of Unemployment*, London: Routledge.

Merkel, W. (1987), *Prima e dopo Craxi: le trasformazioni del PSI*, Padova: Liviana Editrice.

Nickell, S. (1997), 'Unemployment and Labour Market Rigidities: Europe vs North America', *Journal of Economic Perspectives*, No. 11, pp. 55–74.

Obstfeld, M. and Peri, G. (1998), 'Regional Non-adjustment and Fiscal Policy', *Economic Policy*, No. 26, April.

Overbeek, H. (ed.) (2003), *The Political Economy of European Unemployment*, London: Routledge.

Regini, M. (1981), *I dilemmi del sindacato*, Bologna: Il Mulino.

Regini, M. and Regalia, I. (1997), 'Employers, Unions and the State: the resurgence of Concertation in Italy', *West European Politics*, Vol. 25 (1), pp. 210–30.

Rhodes, M. (1997), 'Globalisation, Labour Markets and Welfare States: A Future of "Competitive corporatism?"', *EUI Working Papers*, No. 97/36.

Salvati, M. (1984), *Economia e politica in Italia dal dopoguerra ad oggi*, Milano: Garzanti.

Talani, L.S. (2000), *Betting For and Against EMU*, Aldershot: Ashgate Publishing.

Tsoukalis, L. (1997), *The New European Economy Revisited*, Oxford: Oxford University Press.

Vannicelli, M. (1984), 'A Labor Movement in Search of a Role: The Evolution of the Strategy of the Italian Unions since 1943', PhD thesis, Harvard University.

Chapter 7

The Progress of the Social Dimension in Europe: Spill-overs or Organised Interests?

7.1 Introduction

Assessing the progress of the European Social dimension is like watching a bottle filled only by half: for some people the bottle is half empty, for others it is half full.

Indeed scholarly analyses of the development of European social policy tend to be polarised between those who underline its success and those who cannot help but notice its limits particularly as compared to the bright success of the Union in terms of economic integration.

Needless to say that the former view is mainly taken by late or revised or concealed neofunctionalists[1] while the latter is often to be ascribed to intergovernmentalists.[2]

However there are also some authors that, instead of focusing on whether the bottle is half empty or half full, decided to investigate the reasons why there is only a certain quantity of liquid in the bottle (whichever it is). Amongst the various interpretations, the one stressing the role of organised national and transnational interests is particularly promising and will be adopted in this contribution to study the case of the agreement on the Social Protocol at Maastricht, with particular attention to the Italian and British organised interests.[3]

Indeed, as this chapter will show, much of the liquid was put in the bottle of EU social policy in the course of the negotiations between the European Social Partners going on in parallel to the IGC on the establishment of EMU. Therefore, this chapter will explain the linkages between the process of European monetary integration and the achievements of the European trade unions in terms of social integration at the European level. The main question is: How is the process of European monetary integration related to the progress in the social dimension of European integration?

The objective is to analyse the behaviour of the European trade unions, both at the national and at the European level of organisation, and the development of their requests in the realm of social and political integration as related to the evolution of the process leading to EMU. The main underlying hypothesis is that there is indeed a linkage between the development of European social policy and the progress towards EMU. Thus, the main empirical and theoretical questions are related to the nature of this linkage.

The final aim is to verify to what extent the outcomes of the negotiations over the establishment of a social dimension in Europe may be explained in terms of a neofunctionalist 'spill-over' in the development of the process of European integration as a whole, or as partial and convenient 'side-payments' national organised interests pushing for EMU were willing to grant to national employees' organisations in exchange for their consensus to the institutionalisation (or constitutionalisation[4]) of the desired set of macroeconomic policies.

Empirically, the analysis will be conducted at different levels: the level of European institutions and European interest groups, with particular attention to the action of the ETUC, and the national level focusing on the cases of Italy and of the UK.

The first part of the chapter is devoted to the analysis of the progress of the European social dimension.

7.2 The Development of European Social Policy: Waiting for Spill-overs to Come

The core thesis of the neofunctionalist explanation of the development of European social policy is expressed in the following words of Leibfried and Pierson:

> Although extensive barriers to EU action have prevented any true federalisation of European Social Policy, the dynamics of creating a single market have made it increasingly difficult to exclude social issues from the EU agenda. The emergence of a multitiered structure is less the result of attempts by Eurocrats to build a welfare state than it is a consequence from the initiative to build a single market. By spillover we mean the process through which the completion of the internal market produces growing pressures for the EU to invade the domain of social policy.[5]

The analysis of the actual social policy-making at the European level, however, brings the same authors to conclude that the efforts of the EU to produce an activist social policy have been rather feeble. Nonetheless, they assert that the neofunctionalist case would be proved by the fact that the process of building the single market, including the establishment of a single currency area in Europe, 'not only touches on welfare-state sovereignty, but also significantly erodes the autonomy of welfare state regimes'.[6]

Such a conclusion is far from proving the actual realisation of a 'spill-over' from the creation of the single market to the adoption of a common European social policy which, *de facto*, is very limited, as the authors themselves do recognise. It does certainly prove the 'necessity' of the adoption of such a policy particularly given the fact that previous guarantees at the national level are being dismantled without being substituted by anything at the regional level. There is indeed some confusion between a 'descriptive' conclusion, and a 'prescriptive' one. The descriptive statement from the neofunctionalists reads as follows: the process of economic integration will lead to further integration in the EU social sphere by means of institutional, economic or political 'spill-overs'. The institutional spill-over would imply that markets, in general and labour markets in particular 'need' market correcting political integration. Therefore, the creation of the internal market will lead, by definition, to the creation of an integrated European Social Dimension. The economic spill-over underlines that European markets will be more competitive if the EU provides high-level social services, like education, vocational training etc. Finally the political argument for the inevitability of a common EU social policy is that European unity is grounded on European identity and that it is embedded in the DNA of European identity the need for redistributive policies and a welfare state, because this is what distinguishes the European system from the rest of the world.[7]

However we are still waiting for any of these spill-overs to come. Indeed, the analysis of the developments of a common European social policy, even, as we have pointed out above, as carried out by neofunctionalist authors, only brings to the prescriptive conclusions that there 'should' be a common approach to social policy in Europe because the national level one has eroded the bases of the national welfare state systems.[8] Indeed, for some, and perhaps even the majority of observers, the latter is a good outcome, but these same people would not like to see any reconstruction of the social dimension at the European level, so they would not like any spill-over to produce further integration in the social policy realm.

Moreover, as underlined by many,[9] such a situation is not neutral in terms of power relations. On the contrary, it clearly favours those who have more to win from the disintegration of the welfare states at the national level as well as from the lack of integration of social issues at the European level, over those who have to lose from both processes, namely organised labour and the trade unions.

This is why the development of European social policy cannot be disentangled from the underlying analysis of organised interests' gains and losses as well as positions in the process of European social integration.

The definition of European social policy is by itself a terrain over which to fight the battle over its existence and its level of integration amongst the different approaches. Indeed, neofunctionalists tend to adopt a broad definition of social policy, based on T.H. Marshall's famous contribution, according to which social policy is:

> the use of political power to supersede, supplement or modify operations of the economic system in order to achieve results which the economic system would not achieve of its own ... guided by values other then those determined by open market forces ...[10]

Within the rather broad scope of this definition, it is possible to include a rather broad range of issues such as the Common Agricultural Policy, European regional policy, European transport policy and the environmental policy.

The notion of the social dimension adopted here, however, is narrower and embraces two basic pillars. The first is the legislative pillar, comprising substantive and procedural developments involving EU legislative acts and treaty arrangements. The second is the social dialogue pillar, which relates to the role and power of the so-called social partners.[11]

There is a strong consensus among the scholars that the progress of the European social dimension has not been particularly outstanding.[12]

The early stages of European integration coincided with the rapid expansion of the role of the state in the social policy field. However, not much was achieved in terms of social policy at the European level. The Treaty of Rome included mainly references to those aspects of social action relating to the status of the workers. Art. 48–51 referred to the free movement of workers, and art. 52–8 to the freedom of establishment. Art. 117–128 referred specifically to social policy including references to the improvement of working conditions, equal pay for equal work between men and women, and paid holidays, but without providing for any implementing procedure. Finally there were specific provisions for the role of the European Social Fund (art. 123), whose main task was that of rendering the employment of workers easier and of increasing their geographical and occupational mobility.[13]

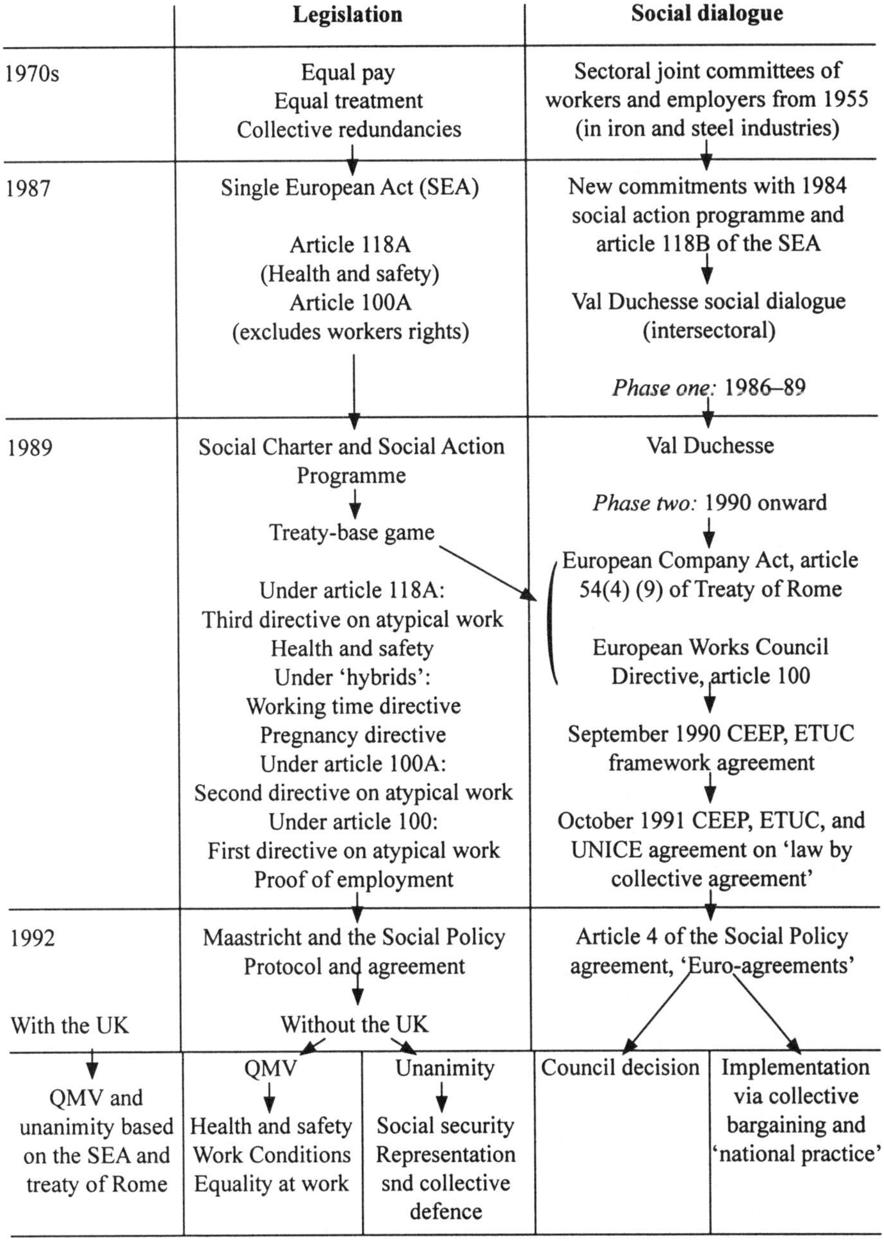

	Legislation	Social dialogue
1970s	Equal pay Equal treatment Collective redundancies ↓	Sectoral joint committees of workers and employers from 1955 (in iron and steel industries) ↓
1987	Single European Act (SEA) Article 118A (Health and safety) Article 100A (excludes workers rights) ↓	New commitments with 1984 social action programme and article 118B of the SEA ↓ Val Duchesse social dialogue (intersectoral) *Phase one:* 1986–89
1989	Social Charter and Social Action Programme ↓ Treaty-base game Under article 118A: Third directive on atypical work Health and safety Under 'hybrids': Working time directive Pregnancy directive Under article 100A: Second directive on atypical work Under article 100: First directive on atypical work Proof of employment ↓	Val Duchesse *Phase two:* 1990 onward ↓ European Company Act, article 54(4) (9) of Treaty of Rome European Works Council Directive, article 100 ↓ September 1990 CEEP, ETUC, framework agreement ↓ October 1991 CEEP, ETUC, and UNICE agreement on 'law by collective agreement' ↓
1992	Maastricht and the Social Policy Protocol and agreement	Article 4 of the Social Policy agreement, 'Euro-agreements'

With the UK	Without the UK		Council decision	Implementation
↓ QMV and unanimity based on the SEA and treaty of Rome	QMV ↓ Health and safety Work Conditions Equality at work	Unanimity ↓ Social security Representation snd collective defence		via collective bargaining and 'national practice'

**Figure 7.1   The evolution of the twin pillars of the social dimension
up to the Maastricht Treaty**

Source: Reproduced from Rhodes (1995), p. 81.

With the advent of economic recession in the 1970s, and the rise in unemployment, member states showed a more positive attitude towards a common European social policy and the Council of Ministers adopted the first Social Action Programme in 1974. This Programme contained measures relating to four main areas: achievement of full employment, improvement of living and working conditions, closer participation of Social Partners in the EC decision-making, involvement of workers in management decisions. However, since the EEC Treaty did not require a social programme and the Community did not have direct powers of intervention, action could be taken only at the political level, and its implementation did not go very far.[14]

By the end of the 1970s, the political and social scene at the national level changed dramatically, and attention rapidly turned to labour-market rigidities and the alleged excesses of the welfare state. Coupled with the so-called 'Euro-sclerosis', meaning the stalemate in the European social and political integration process, the early 1980s saw the launching of supply-side economics and of the deregulation at the national level. This was accompanied by the steady weakening of trade union power.[15] Indeed, the revival of the European integration process in the mid-1980s was closely related to the desire of big business to eliminate the remaining barriers to the creation of a single market in Europe, and to the shift in the balance of political power which saw the trade unions as the net losers. At the level of European social policy this was reflected in a shift of emphasis from regulation and distribution, to market and competition. The internal market programme was born in this political context and social policies hardly figured at all in the early stages of the 1992 process.[16]

Such a situation could not last for long. The European integration process has had significant consequences in terms of distribution and redefinition of winners and losers and therefore it has required some forms of side payments for the losers.

Similar pressures led to the approval in 1989 of the 'Social Charter of workers' rights', aimed at obtaining social consensus to the liberalisation process implied by the 1992 programme. The Charter included statements calling for minimum wages, paternity leave and protection of atypical employment, but it was not binding and depended on action plans to be implemented.

Therefore, social policy became one of the most controversial issues in the intergovernmental conferences which led to the treaty revisions agreed at Maastricht in December 1991.

7.3 Organised Interests in the Maastricht Social Protocol

The path to economic monetary union, as defined by the Maastricht Treaty and by the following agreement on the Stability Pact, directly and substantially affects the powers and prerogatives of trade unions in their traditional policy realms.[17]

In particular, the statutory ECB goal of a low and stable inflation rate has undeniable consequences on the limits within which trade unions will be able to conduct wage policies. Moreover, the implementation of monetary policy by the ECB, through the decisions over the level of European interest rates, greatly influences investment decisions and, consequently, the level of unemployment. Finally, the rigid limitations on the conduct of national fiscal policy imposed by the Maastricht Treaty for the transition to EMU and by the Stability Pact for its aftermath, deeply modify the terms of the debate over the survival of the welfare state in all its components.

Therefore, the trade unions' position towards further progress on the way to monetary union must be read in terms of reaction to this process of institutionalisation and of the attempt to regain the terrain lost since the beginning of the process of monetary integration.

The trade unions entered the debate over the making of EMU from a position of weakness. They perceived the decision-making process on EMU going on in the 1991 IGC as something outside their reach. It was not possible to modify it but it was necessary to react to it by asking for a more effective and far reaching social policy and of the social dialogue in the European context in exchange for its acceptance.[18]

The next sections will analyse in detail the behaviour of the Italian, British and European social partners during the intergovernmental conference establishing EMU.

7.3.1 Italy and EMU: A Widespread Socioeconomic Consensus

The strategy of Italian capital, particularly industrial, in the process of European integration *tout court* – and much more in the process of European monetary integration – has always been guided by the desire to shift to the European level the decision on a set of politically sensitive macroeconomic policies.[19]

This strategy, far from being abandoned with the failure of the ERM, has been institutionalised throughout the adoption of the Maastricht way to EMU as well as the approval of the Stability Pact, with evident consequences for the trade unions, whose only option was to shift the struggle to the social policy realm.

Indeed, as further elaborated below, this claim is not only true for Italian trade unions, or for British ones, but is true for European trade unionism as a whole or, at least, as represented by the ETUC.[20] Consequently, Italian trade unions' interventions in the debate over the establishment of EMU should be seen as both adding and taking stimulus from the broader debate going on within the ETUC.

From the very beginning of the discussions over the Delors Plan for the establishment of a single currency area in Europe, the Italian trade unions did not reject the goal of EMU. However, they tended to insert it into the broader debate of furthering the social and political dimension of European integration.

This inclination appears clearly in the proposals of the CGIL-CIS-UIL for the 1990 Italian semester of Presidency of the Council of Ministers in which it was claimed:

> At the moment, the tendency which seems to prevail in the European institutions is to attribute to the establishment of European Monetary Union a spill-over value with respect to all the other policies which are believed to be induced exactly by the implementing of EMU. This propensity, if it leads to considering monetary policy as the only integration policy, reproduces at a higher level the imbalances, which characterised the whole process of European integration. ... Instead it is necessary to guarantee policies of management of the economy aimed at ensuring economic and social cohesion, supported by instruments of democratic accountability and of social consensus able to integrate and balance the mere monetary-economic goal of the integration process.[21]

The goal of monetary union, by itself, was not questioned. However, it was underlined that this goal had to be accompanied by a set of decisions aimed at giving some substance to the social dimension of European integration which, on the contrary, had been, up to that point, set aside or treated with ambiguity. Indeed, the steps towards the achievement of the same status for the economic and the social dimensions of the European development taken in the summit of Hanover (27/28 June 1988),[22] of Rodi (2/3 December 1988)[23] or Madrid (26/27 June 1989)[24] had been somehow frustrated by the contents of the Social Charter[25] and by the delays in the implementation of the Social Action Programme.

In particular, for the CISL, to achieve a socially integrated Europe it was necessary to act in different directions. First, in the labour market area, with some harmonisation of working conditions within Europe to allow for labour mobility and with the strengthening of vocational training. Second, in the area of collective wage bargaining, perhaps starting from some kind of experiment at the transnational level. Third, in the area of the harmonisation of individual rights, with the implementation of the Social Charter. Finally, in the area of welfare state with the decision of which model to choose for the European Community.[26]

Emilio Gabaglio, then Confederal Secretary of the CISL, also insisted on some conditions that it was necessary to fulfil to give some substance to the social dimension of Europe. Commenting on the poor performance of the first meeting of the IGC in Rome on 13 and 14 December in terms of social debate, he asserted that the building of the economic/monetary dimension of Europe must be accompanied at least by the definition of a Community-level instrument allowing for the consultation, information and participation of the workers inserted in a trans-European productive structure. The second requirement was the definition on the basis of experiments within the EU and agreements with the other European trade unions of a collective bargaining instrument. The third was the strengthening of the role of the social partners at the European level, also through the strengthening of the ETUC.[27]

The position of the UIL was rather similar to that of the CISL, apart from the stronger emphasis put on the political dimension of Europe[28] and on the need to pursue the goal of a European Federation, for which the realisation of EMU could represent an important element since: 'The currency could represent the lever of the European Federation. The currency will help as it will help the management of the economy at the European level.'[29]

Thus, the UIL did not reject the goal of monetary union. On the contrary its General Secretary, Giorgio Benvenuto, on the eve of the first gathering of the 1990 IGC requested the 'determination of clear guidelines and deadlines for EMU which will be a strong factor to hasten the path of integration'.[30] However, also from the UIL point of view, these developments had to be accompanied by further movement in the social sphere. In the words of Benvenuto:

> It would be extremely serious if, once again, the social issues remained outside the door, excluded from the big issues under discussion. We ask that they fully enter the debate, with the same status of the economic-monetary issues.[31]

Even the CGIL, which had been opposed to the process of European monetary integration and to the establishment of the European Monetary System in 1978, had adopted, by the beginning of the 1990s, a much more positive stance towards the issue.

In his speech at the ETUC Luxembourg Congress, Bruno Trentin, General Secretary of the CGIL, completely endorsed the Delors' project of European integration founded on the Single Market, the establishment of EMU and the revision of the Treaty of Rome. However, he answered to the challenges arising from it by calling for the transformation of the ETUC into an advocate of European integration.[32] To achieve this aim it was necessary to act both internally and externally. Internally, it was necessary to continue the process of structural reform started with the Luxemburg Congress[33] and by increasing the representativeness of the ETUC. Externally it was necessary to put pressure on the national governments at both the national and the European level to enhance the effective role and power of the European workers' organisation. This meant clearly defining the proposal and bargaining powers of the ETUC with respect both to the EU institutions and to the national and multinational companies as well as their national and European interests' associations.

In particular, the attention of the CGIL focused on three areas of action. First, the area of organisation through the building of a truly European trade unions confederation able to speak and to act in the name of all European workers overcoming national borders and, thus, also overcoming the need to coordinate different sovereign organisations. Second came the area of rights by elaborating, starting from the Social Charter, the bases of a truly European labour, trade union and social regulation and law. Third there was the area of the role of the social partners through the deepening of the Social Dialogue and the identification of a European level of bargaining.[34]

Summing up, it is possible to claim that there was a common line of the Italian trade unions towards the developments going on in the monetary realm. This was to counterbalance them by asking for further developments in the European Social Policy area and for more power for the social partners at the European level. This was an active position, not a passive belief that EMU would imply further integration in the social dimension by means of spill-overs. Indeed it was substantiated by the strengthening of the ETUC, which with the election of Emilio Gabaglio as General Secretary, became more sensible to the positions of its Italian component and more prone to follow this proactive strategy.[35]

Concluding, the picture of Italian socioeconomic stance towards the Maastricht Treaty and EMU shows[36] that the Italian government's decision to endorse and actively pursue the policies implied in the Maastricht definition of EMU was based on the consensus of all the components of Italian trade unionism.

It has been on the basis of this consensus, indeed, that the Italian government's commitment to the Maastricht criteria has become credible and that Italy has been able to reach the fervently desired goal of a deficit to GDP ratio of 3 per cent.

The next section will examine the British case to verify to what extent the hypotheses so far devised on the marginalisation of the Trade Unions in the process of European monetary integration may be applied also to the TUC.

7.3.2 The TUC and the Struggle against Exclusion

The limited bargaining power of the British trade unions over macroeconomic issues, particularly at the national level, but also, to a large extent at the European level,[37] was reflected in the position adopted by the British Trade Union Congress in the negotiations over European Monetary Union within the 1991 IGC. In fact, rather than trying to influence the decisions regarding the timing and institutional characteristics of EMU, also the British employees' organisation, like the Italian ones, tended to consider the process leading to a European Single Currency as 'inevitable' and to focus on other aspects of European economic integration.

In its debates on the issue, the TUC was keen to distinguish between areas of policy which were likely to happen 'almost regardless of the views of the social partners'[38] and those which could be influenced at the European level. Indeed, the trade unions tended to include monetary union in the first group, and to exert pressure on the issue of political union and measures to promote economic and social cohesion. This, in turn, was related to progress on the social dimension and on measures to improve productivity, and hence the collective bargaining agenda and the role of trade unions as social partners at both the national and EC levels.

Consistently, the TUC required the IGC to take the economic growth and employment objectives seriously also through the establishment of appropriate institutions, as well as to make provisions for the transfer of resources to member states in economic difficulties, as already set out in the draft Treaty before the IGC.

The TUC stressed the importance of fiscal policy under EMU stage III, pointing out how, within a system of constraints on budget deficits and the level of public debt, structural funds and regional policy became an important adjustment mechanism between the weaker members of the EC but also how they risked recreating the national tensions of the Common Agricultural Policy.

A key element in developing cooperative growth policies, was, then, a clear assessment by the Commission of what affects competitiveness, and how to correct underlying differences in industrial productivity and trade performance.

These, according to the TUC, ultimately depended not on real wages, but on non-price factors, such as quality and R&D, training and investment. The pursuit of similar policies at the European level could represent an important, and perhaps fundamental, corrective mechanism for differences in economic performance between member states as well as the only plausible way, according to the TUC, for companies to deal with the competitive pressures coming from EMU.

Overall, the approach was to ensure that companies became 'resource developers', rather than 'asset strippers' and in this environment legislation following the social charter was considered essential to deal with the thousands of small companies who were hostile to the TUC approach.[39]

The priorities of the TUC in the course of the intergovernmental conference, were thus represented by the social dimension, the Social Action Programme, Treaty revision, social dialogue, and the industrial dimension and trade union links.[40]

With respect to EMU, the General Council of the TUC continued to monitor issues discussed in the intergovernmental conference on European economic and monetary union and made input to the ETUC statement on EMU adopted at the ETUC congress in May 1991. This statement confirmed the trade unions' concern that the aims of EMU should be to promote sustainable economic growth and full employment, as well as to reduce inflation. Moreover it suggested that regional policies should be strengthened, and a common set of social standards be developed, and that weaker economies should be enabled to move to EMU at their own pace.

In discussion with the European Parliamentary Labour party (EPLP) it was noted that there should be a linkage between EMU and institutional change, including such change affecting social provisions. EPLP members had raised the need to promote economic convergence between EC countries as a condition for EMU so as to ensure that peripheral countries also benefited from it. A narrowing of regional disparities was also required before the introduction of a single currency. The EPLP wanted also to ensure political control over decisions of the Central Bank, but there was still a range of views as to how that control had to be carried out. On the other hand, the General Council of the TUC recognised that care should be taken not to set aims for economic convergence which were impracticable and which would, in fact, make it impossible to establish EMU.[41]

That the goal of reaching EMU was not to be questioned also appeared clearly in the report produced by the General Council on the Maastricht Treaty and endorsed by the 1992 Congress which called for, on a clear balance of consideration, the ratification of the Treaty itself.[42] Though growth, unemployment, and social and regional cohesion objectives had not been inserted among the EMU convergence criteria, the TUC did not reject the Maastricht decisions on EMU. Even if the Maastricht fiscal criteria, and, particularly the requirement on the deficit might appear over-restrictive, according to the TUC, the EC Commission's report 'One Market, One Money', had made it clear that a deficit to fund investment would be far more acceptable. In turn, an investment based deficit would imply a long-term fall in the ratio of public debt to GDP and improve the underlying economic growth potential of the economy, thus also increasing employment opportunities.[43]

If interpreted in this way, the fiscal criteria could not be held inconsistent with the TUC objectives. Indeed, the convergence conditions were very similar to policy objectives of the British government in any case, but without EMU there would be no move towards replacing the Bundesbank with an institution responsible to the community as a whole or an enhanced role for ECOFIN.

Of course the TUC would have wished to see different conditions for economic and monetary union, and announced a political battle in the 1990s to ensure that growth and unemployment targets were given proper weight in the move towards EMU. However, they basically accepted the Maastricht way to a single currency since: 'As has consistently been the case in the evolution of the EC, economic union will drive political union.'[44] Therefore, the opt-out clause negotiated by the British government was judged by the TUC inconsistent with national interests since it seemed inconceivable that Britain would stand aside from the progress towards monetary union. In the long run the UK, as with the ERM, would find it untenable to remain isolated from those states joined in monetary union, while in the meantime, the opt-out only restrained the UK from influencing further developments of the project.[45] Instead, the General Council took the view that it was realistic to seek a political commitment from the member states of the Community, with a willingness to adopt positive policies 'in the framework of the move towards EMU'.[46]

This was the strategic objective for the trade union movement in the 1990s to be incorporated in the TUC's developing campaign for full employment.

In fact, immediately after the Maastricht summit, the General Council, through the ETUC, started pressing for a cooperative growth strategy to be agreed by the EC member states to provide the context in which EMU could be achieved through minimum negative effects. On 3 July 1992, a joint statement was agreed with the European employers' organisations in which policies for achieving good results on employment and growth within the process of moving towards EMU were mapped out. The statement said that the strategy would be founded on 'the combination of sound macroeconomic policies and supportive structural policies embedded in a cooperative climate provided by the social dialogue at the national and Community level'.[47] Though the statement was not as fully developed as would have been the case with a purely trade union statement, it was a first step towards reaching the 'right kind of EMU'.

Overall, the TUC position towards EMU appears to be heavily conditioned by their inability to influence the internal macroeconomic decision-making process, particularly after the Thatcher era.

Indeed, the Thatcher government's strategy to reduce to its minimal historical record trade union power was a regular, step-by-step process at the end of which the legal balance between unions and employers had significantly changed. There have been five major pieces of trade union legislation passed since 1979. These five acts (the 1980 Employment Act, the 1982 Employment Act, the 1984 Trade Union Act, the 1988 Employment Act and the 1990 Employment Act) have significantly changed the legal position of unions. The blanket immunity enjoyed by unions, as distinct from unionists, was removed by the 1982 Employment Act; the definition of a legitimate trade dispute has been successively narrowed so as to reduce the immunities enjoyed by unionists; the legal basis of the closed shop was initially restricted by the 1980 and 1982 Employment Acts and subsequently removed in the Employment Acts of 1988 and 1990; under the Trade Union Act 1984 unions are required to hold secret ballots for the election of officers. This legislation also requires unions to conduct political fund ballots. The Employment Act 1988 gives individual unionists a series of rights *vis-à-vis* their unions. It also prevents unions from disciplining members who refuse to go on strike or cross picket lines while the 1990 Act makes unions responsible for their members' unofficial action unless the unions repudiate the strike, or make it official after a ballot.[48]

All this led the TUC to consider EMU as a viable way to shift the decision making process from the national to the European level, where, in the context of the ETUC, it would be possible to exert a more effective bargaining power.

Therefore, the TUC tended to attribute more importance than the Italian Trade Unions to the spill-over effect of EMU.

This different interpretation was indeed also reflected in the different positions adopted by the British and the Italian trade unions within the ETUC in the debate over the definition of the structure and the role of the European employees' organisation.[49]

However, this neofunctionalist interpretation of the process of European integration by the TUC should not be abstracted from the national context nor overestimated. Indeed, much of the rhetoric attached to the automatic spill-overs stemming from the process of European monetary integration was intended to give to the public a sense of inevitability of the process of European social and political integration. This, in turn, was explicitly related to the inevitability of British entry in EMU in the long run, notwithstanding the British government's and the City of London's opposition to it.[50]

The reality was, however, that also the TUC, as the quotations reported above clearly demonstrate, had a very clear idea of the degree of social and political confrontation that the building of the social dimension of Europe would imply. Moreover, it was prepared to actively pursue it at both the national and the European level.

7.4 The European Social Partners and the ETUC Rearguard Battle

Shifting the analysis to the level of European organised interests, it is worth noting that the ETUC actively called on the two IGCs to lay down the concrete bases for the establishment of EMU. However, they also urged that the discussions within the IGCs allowed for the achievement of parallel results in all policy areas: the economic, the political and the social ones. They noted that the unification of the markets and of monetary policy had to be realised together with economic and social cohesion and urged that further steps were taken towards the definition of a common European economic and budgetary policy, based on the harmonisation of national fiscal systems and of structural policies aimed at reaching territorial equilibrium with the final goal of reducing unemployment and defining a true European social regulation. This regulation had to broaden the scope of the Social Action Programme whose implementation, however, had to be hastened and had to become legally binding for the member states. Finally, the rule of majority voting had to be extended to social issues.[51]

Given this starting point, it should not be too surprising that the ETUC welcomed the decisions taken at Maastricht and considered the signing of the Social Protocol by 11 of the European governments[52] as an important step to balance the developments of monetary union.

Indeed, the Social Protocol represented the final outcome of the incessant bargaining activity of the ETUC. This had been going on from the Luxembourg Congress onwards and had resulted in the reaching of an agreement on 30 October 1991, with the UNICE, the organisation representing European industrials, in which a common position on the role of the social partners in the new Treaty was defined.[53]

According to Ettore Masucci, the CGIL official responsible for International Affairs as well as member of the Economic and Social Committee of the European Union, the Maastricht Treaty marked a turning point in the development of the European social policy. In fact, the Social Protocol opened the doors to the definition by the EU Institutions of a true European social policy and allowed the social partners to play an autonomous role in the European context.

In particular, Masucci welcomed the extension of majority voting to the decisions relating to working conditions and to workers consultation and information, even if he lamented the maintenance of unanimity for the questions regarding social security and protection, dismissals, co-management and migrant workers. Also regrettable was the explicit exclusion from the acquis communitaire of everything related to wage policy and trade unions legislation, in particular the right to strike.

However, the ETUC claimed a major victory for the role of the social partners in the European context and for the European collective bargaining. According to the Social Protocol, art. 2.4, a member state might entrust to the social partners, at their joint request, the implementation, through a bargaining process, of EU directives. Moreover in art. 3 the Commission committed itself to preliminary consultation of the social partners on social issues and to delegate to them, on request, the reaching of the agreement (through a bargaining process).

All this was interpreted by the trade unions as a true horizontal extension of the principle of 'subsidiarity' to include the social partners in the European decision-making process on social issues. Moreover, the Social Protocol also opened the way to reach collective agreements at the European level on the subjects listed in the Treaty, agreements, which, through a decision of the Council of Ministers, could even achieve a European legal status.[54] This meant that the door was open to the implementation of a true European bargaining process: a good result, from the trade unions point of view, in exchange for the workers' organisations consensus on the Maastricht way to EMU with all that this consensus implied in terms of relaxing the national political debate on the measures necessary for the implementation of Maastricht criteria, particularly fiscal ones.

On the basis of these considerations, the ETUC were among the social forces promoting the ratification of the Maastricht Treaty in the course of the period of uncertainty of 1992–93. In the words of the ETUC General Secretary:

> We have decided to promote the ratification of it [the Maastricht Treaty] mainly because we believe that the workers would be worst off without Maastricht

than with Maastricht: at least, given the establishment of the Single Market, the Treaty gives to the trade unions some more opportunity to try to balance the market from the social point of view.[55]

Summing up, the provisions of the Social Protocol were considered by the trade unions to be such an important achievement that they overshadowed the negative consequences that the Maastricht way to EMU might have on workers' conditions in the short term and on the power of trade unions.

There is, however, at least another way in which the social policy developments agreed in Maastricht might be interpreted. What the employees' organisations tended to consider as a major success, could be seen, from the perspective of the employers' organisations, as a fair price to pay to gain the social consensus on what was for them a set of extremely beneficial policies. It could be seen as a convenient side-payment.

7.5 Conclusions

In conclusion, the analysis above demonstrate that the neofunctionalist framework is too narrow to give account of the relations between the process of European monetary integration and further developments of European social integration.

Indeed, the notion of spill-overs, institutional, economic or political, would need to be stretched too far to be able to contain and explain the proactive behaviour of both national and European trade unions' organisations. Both at the national and at the European level, in fact, the achievements in the social dimension have been the results of conscious political battle and bargaining with both their social and institutional counterparts. To say that these achievements were the automatic consequences of the steps already taken in other realms of European integration is to underestimate the activity and role performed by the social actors.[56]

However, the notion of side payments may prove useful to define the way in which the bargaining process between social and political actors has been carried out. Indeed, what has been interpreted by the ETUC and by the national trade unions as a major victory, the signing of the Social Protocol by 11 governments over 12 , may conversely be seen as a convenient counterpart to obtain the employees' organisation consensus on the institutionalisation of a set of desired macroeconomic goals.

Notes

1   See, for example, Leibfried and Pierson (1995). See also Leibfried and Pierson (1992).
2   See, for example, Hantrais (2000). See also Lange (1992). Some elements of an intergovernmentalist interpretation are contained also in Streeck (1995), p. 389.
3   For a similar interpretation see Rhodes (1995). For an analysis of the relevance of organised interests see Streeck (1995), p. 389, and Streeck and Schmitter (1991).
4   Some authors do indeed talk about neoconstitutionalism in relation to the establishment of EMU. See, for example, Gill (1997). See also previous chapter.
5   See Leibfried and Pierson (1995), p. 44.
6   See Leibfried and Pierson (1995), p. 45.
7   For a thorough analysis and criticism of these three forms of spill-over in the Common European social policy see Streeck (1995), p. 407.
8   For a knowledgeable discussion of the change of the national welfare state regimes see Esping-Andersen (1996). See also Ferrera and Rhodes (2000); Heywood, Jones and Rhodes (2002).
9   See Rhodes (1995). See in particular Streeck (1995).
10 See Marshall (1975), p. 15.
11 This definition is taken from Rhodes (1995), p. 81. For a complete analysis of the developments of the two pillars see this source.
12 See Streeck (1995), p. 389. See also Tsokalis (1997). For more detailed overviews of the developments of social policy see Hantrais (2000).
13 See Hantrais (2000), p. 3.
14 See Hantrais (2000), p. 4.
15 See Lange, Ross and Vannicelli (1982).
16 See Tsokalis (1997).
17 For a thorough analysis of the impact of EMU on European industrial relations and on trade unions see Rhodes (2002).
18 For a similar interpretation see Streeck (1995), p. 390.
19 For a detailed analysis of the development of this strategy see Talani (2000).
20 The ETUC was created in 1973 to allow the meeting and confrontation of the various European trade unions and to act as a consultation and pressure body at the European level. With the Congress held in Luxemburg on 13–17 May 1991 its Statute was changed to allow the representatives of the different categories to enter the executive Committee and a restricted committee composed by the representatives of the trade union leaders was created to act as the decision-making body. See Gnetti (1991b).
21 See CGIL (1990), p. 55.
22 In the conclusions of the Presidency to the Hannover summit of 27/28 June 1988 it was claimed: 'The European Council underlines the importance of the social aspects in the context of the progresses towards the realisation of the 1992 goal ... the internal market must be conceived in a way to be beneficial for everyone.' See CGIL (1990), p. 56.
23 In the conclusions of the Rodi Summit, 2/3 December 1988, it was claimed that: 'The establishment of the Single Market cannot be considered an aim in itself but it must imply the pursuance of a broader objective, represented by the assurance of the maximum welfare for everyone, in conformity with the social progress tradition characterising European history.' During this summit it was also set the deadline of 1989 for the member states to take the decisions due to 'orient the action of the Member States in the social dimension'. See CGIL (1990), p. 56.

24 In the Madrid Summit, 26/27 June 1989, the need was confirmed 'to attribute to the social aspects the same importance given to economic ones'. See CGIL (1990), p. 56.
25 At the Strasbourg Summit of 8/9 December 1989, 11 member states adopted the so-called 'Social Charter' and the European Council invited the Council of Ministers to deliberate on the proposals of the Programme of Action presented by the European Commission to implement the Social Charter. See Paruolo (1991).
26 See *Conquiste Sindacali*, November 1991, p. 11.
27 See Gnetti (1990).
28 In the words of Giorgio Benvenuto: 'E solo con una maggiore integrazione politica che superi divisioni vecchie e nuove l'Europa potra' trovare e svolgere quel ruolo determinante che I nuovi tempi richiedono. Ma c'e' una ragione ulteriore, per chiedere cio' da parte nostra, non solo come cittadini ma come sindacato. Infatti, in noi resta ferma la convinzione che senza un'autorita' politica, sovrannazionale, in grado di decidere e mediare gli interessi tra I diversi poteri, saranno le regioni o le classi piu' deboli a correre I maggiori rischi.' See Benvenuto (1990), p. 45.
29 See Talani (1997).
30 See Benvenuto (1990), p. 45.
31 See Benvenuto (1990), p. 45.
32 See Trentin (1991), p. 74.
33 See further in this chapter.
34 See Lettieri (1991), p. 75.
35 Indeed, the prevailing of this active definition of the role of the ETUC came out of an heated debate between the different European trade union organisations at the Luxemburg Congress and was partly facilitated by the adoption of a common line by the three Italian confederations which resulted in the election of the CISL Confederal Secretary at the head of the ETUC. In his words: 'La mia elezione è innanzi tutto un riconoscimento del ruolo svolto unitariamente dai sindacati italiani, che hanno insistito sulla necessitá di dare alla CES strategia e strumenti all'altezza dei cambiamenti in atto nello scenario europeo e mondiale. Un ticonoscimento tanto piu' significativo in quanto i nostri orientamenti erano minoritari fino all'ultimo congresso della CES, a Stoccolma'. See Gnetti (1991a).
36 For more details on the position adopted by the Italian industrial and banking sector towards EMU see Talani (1998).
37 For more details on the way the TUC lobbying system at the European level was organised see Trade Union Congress (1991a).
38 See Trade Union Congress (1991b).
39 See Trade Union Congress (1991b).
40 For further details on the way these aims were pursued by the TUC and the ETUC see Trade union Congress (1991c).
41 See Trade Union Congress (1991c).
42 See Trade Union Congress (1992a).
43 See Trade Union Congress (1991d).
44 See Trade Union Congress (1992b).
45 See Trade Union Congress (1992b). See also Trade Union Congress (1991d).
46 See Trade Union Congress (1992a).
47 See Trade Union Congress (1992a).
48 For a further detailed analysis of the impact of Mrs Thatcher's industrial policies on the power of the TUC see Marsh (1992).
49 See Talani (1998).

50 For more details about this see Talani (2000).
51 See Benvenuto (1990), p. 64.
52 The twelfth being the British government.
53 See Masucci (1992), p. 46.
54 See Social Protocol, art. 4.
55 See Gabaglio (1992), p. 33.
56 For similar conclusions see Rhodes (1995).

References

Benvenuto, G. (1990), 'Non vogliamo restare fuori dalla porta', *Lavorosocieta*, No. 12, December.

Esping-Andersen, G. (ed.) (1996) *Welfare States in Transition*, London: Sage.

Ferrera, M. and Rhodes, M. (eds) (2000), *Recasting European Welfare States*, London: Frank Cass.

Gabaglio, E. (1992), 'Dopo la tempesta', *Nuova Rassegna Sindacale*, No. 35, 5 October.

Gabaglio, E. (1990), 'Per ora vince il mercato', *Nuova Rassegna Sindacale* No. 48, 24 December.

Gill, S. (1997), 'An EMU or an Ostrich?: EMU and Neoliberal Globalisation; Limits and Alternatives', in P. Minkkinen and H. Potomaki (1997), *The Politics of Economic and Monetary Union*, Amsterdam: Kluwer Academic Publishers.

Gnetti, C. (1990), 'Per ora vince il mercato', *Nuova Rassegna Sindacale*, No. 48, 24 December.

Gnetti, C. (1991a), 'Pensare Europeo', *Nuova Rassegna Sindacale*, No. 19, 27 May.

Gnetti, C. (1991b), 'Il grande salto', *Nuova Rassegna Sindacale*, No. 19, 27 May.

Hantrais, L. (2000), *Social Policy in the European Union*, 2nd edn, London: Macmillan.

Heywood, P., Jones, E. and Rhodes, M. (eds) (2002), *Developments in West European Politics*, London: Palgrave.

Lange, P., Ross, G. and Vannicelli, M. (1982), *Unions, Change and Crisis: French and Italian Union Strategy and the Political Economy*, London: Allen and Unwin.

Leibfried, S. and Pierson, P. (eds) (1995), *European Social Policy: Between Fragmentation and Integration*, Washington: The Brookings Institution.

Leibfried, S. and Pierson, P. (1992), 'Prospects for Social Europe', *Politics and Society*, Vol. 20 (September).

Lettieri, A. (1991), 'Un nuovo internazionalismo', *Nuova Rassegna Sindacale*, No. 26, 15 July.

Lettieri, A. (1992), 'Sindacati a due velocita', *Nuova Rassegna Sindacale*, No. 47, December.

Lettieri, A (1993), 'Occhio all' Europa', *Nuova Rassegna Sindacale*, No. 25, 5 July.

Marshall, T.H. (1975), *Social Policy*, London: Hutchinson.

Masucci, E. (1992), 'Il ruolo delle parti', *Nuova Rassegna Sindacale*, No. 10, 16 March.

Rhodes, M. (1995), 'A regulatory Conundrum: Industrial Relations and the social Dimension', in S. Leibfried and P. Pierson (eds), *European Social Policy: Between Fragmentation and Integration*, Washington: The Brookings Institution, pp. 78–123.

Sbragia, A. (ed.) (1992), *Institutions and Policymaking in the 'New' European Community*, Washington: The Brookings Institution.

Streeck, W. and Schmitter, P.C. (1991), 'From National Corporatism to Transnational Pluralism: Organised Interests in the Single European Market', *Politics and Society*, Vol. 19 (June), pp. 133–64.

Streeck, W. (1995), 'From Market Making to State Building? Reflections on the Political Economy of Social Policy', in S. Leibfried and P. Pierson (eds), *European Social Policy: Between Fragmentation and Integration*, Washington: The Brookings Institution.

Talani, L.S (1997), *Brussels, Intervista con Dott. Liverani, UIL c/o ECOSOC*, 15 May.

Talani, L.S. (2000), *Betting For and Against EMU*, Aldershot: Ashgate Publishing.

Trade Union Congress (1991a), *Building links in Europe*, London: TUC.

Trade Union Congress (1991b), *Economic Integration in Europe: What 1992 and EMU Mean for Unions*, paper for a conference on 6 June, Congress House.

Trade Union Congress (1991c), *Report of the 123rd Annual Trade Union Congress*, London: TUC.

Trade Union Congress (1991d), *Economic Policy Options in the 1990s: Memorandum by the TUC to the NEDC*, NEDC (92) 1, 18 December, London: NEDC.

Trade Union Congress (1992a), *Report of the 124th Annual Trade Union Congress*, London: TUC.

Trade Union Congress (1992b), *Unions after Maastricht: The Challenge of Social Europe*, London: TUC.

Tsoukalis, L. (1997), *The New European Economy Revisited*, Oxford: Oxford University Press.

Chapter 8

Globalisation and Illegal Migration: A Political Economy Analysis of Migratory Flows from the MENA Area to the European Union

8.1 Introduction

Migratory flows from less developed countries to the first world have become one of the first priorities to be tackled by policy-makers in both countries of origin and host ones.

The dimensions acquired by the phenomenon of mass migration, the degree of involvement of organised crime groups in the smuggling of migrants, the appalling conditions in which immigrants often find themselves in the hosting countries, pose a number of questions which make it imperative to investigate on the underlying causes and consequences of the problem.

There seems to be a certain degree of consensus in the literature on the fact that the process of globalisation has indeed modified the terms within which migratory processes take place.[1] However, scholars are still divided on the assessment of the 'hows' and 'whys' of the impact of globalisation on migration.

This is partly due to the fact that the issues relating to migration tend to be interdisciplinary by their very nature, covering the most various academic fields, from urban studies, to anthropology and from sociology to political economy. Moreover, the definition itself of globalisation seems surrounded by a certain degree of mystery, being often invoked in different contexts or debates without a proper systematic attempt to define it.[2]

As regards this contribution, the first part will set the theoretical context in which to study the issue of illegal migration. In the second part, an analysis of the illegal migratory routes from the MENA area is presented.

8.2   Migratory Flows in Theory

8.2.1   A Qualitative Definition of Globalisation

The notion of globalisation is by no means an uncontroversial one in the academic debate as well as in the wider public discourse.[3] It seems however possible to classify the positions adopted by scholars on the subject into three broad groups:[4] those who deny the existence itself of the phenomenon of globalisation;[5] those who admit it but tend to give only a quantitative definition of globalisation,[6] and those who adopt a qualitative definition.[7]

The thesis denying globalisation rests on considerations about the historical recurrence of periods of increased international and cross-border interactions. In reality, those who adopt a similar perspective deny the 'originality' of globalisation and its characterisation as a 'new phenomenon'. Sometimes, they can get as far as to deny to the current phase of the world economy development any 'global', 'globalised' or 'globalising' nature. It seems however that, whether you multiply the number of 'globalisations' taking place in the course of history or even deny its occurrence in the present historical moment, the question of how to define 'globalisation' remains unsolved and ultimately the terms of the debate rest on the dichotomy between the 'quantitative' and the 'qualitative' definition of the phenomenon.[8]

It might even be suggested that the denial of globalisation stems from the failure to identify the distinctive characteristics of the current phase of capitalist development by adopting a quantitative definition of the phenomenon.

Indeed, from the quantitative point of view, globalisation is defined as: 'The intensification of economic, political, social and cultural relations across borders'.[9] This definition leaves unsolved a number of issues regarding on the one hand, the means by which to measure the degree of economic, social and cultural relations across the border as well as their intensification. On the other hand, it leaves unclear the kind of relationships between the economic, social and political aspects of globalisation, and, indeed, it does not even specify whether there is any relationship at all. Moreover, by accounting for the phenomenon of globalisation only in quantitative terms, one can hardly get to grips with its causes and consequences. This makes it extremely difficult to relate it to other phenomena such as mass migration from less developed countries. It is therefore necessary to deepen the perspective by adopting a qualitative definition of globalisation.

Indeed, from the qualitative point of view, globalisation is defined as a process comprising a number of qualitative transformations, which in turn characterise the current phase of capitalist development. In this context, globalisation is identified as a qualitatively new phenomenon, comprising a number of components all of them concurring to define globalisation as a process or, as Mittleman suggests, a 'syndrome'. Moreover, these components tend to spill over one onto the other without any predetermined single cause/effect relation but in a dialectical way, which makes it possible to identify the direction of the change, if not to react accordingly.

The components included in such a qualitative definition of globalisation are represented by: the technological transformation, the financial transformation, the geographical reallocation of production, the process of commodification, the polarisation of wealth, the subordination of politics to economics and the related decline of the nation state, and the emergence of a new global division of labour.[10]

8.2.2 The New Global Division of Labour and the Increase of Mass Migration

Technological change, as further elaborated in the conclusions of this book, represents the engine of a process of transformation, which interests both the productive and the financial structure. Leaving aside the latter, what is particularly relevant to frame the analysis of migratory flows, is the geographical reallocation of production. This takes place through the creation of export processing zones in developing countries, through a policy of mergers and acquisitions or through straightforward foreign direct investment.[11]

As a consequence of the restructuring of production, also the labour structure changes with a substantial reallocation of labour intensive production in third word countries. However, this outcome is compounded by the opposite effects of technological development in terms of the increase of distant work, and of the increase of labour mobility, including mass migration.

On the one hand, production tends to move to some specialised regions of the globe,[12] where it is possible to exploit the advantages of lower production costs both in the form of lower labour costs and/or in the form of lower costs of primary resources. This phenomenon gives rise to the paradox of regionalisation within globalisation characterised by the creation of economically integrated regions.[13] This further adds to the marginalisation of those zones of the globe which are not interested, for reasons too long to analyse here, by the process of geographical displacement of production nor by the globalisation of financial markets.[14]

On the other hand, however, the populations of those marginalised zones of the globe, whose economic conditions are likely to worsen as a consequence of the process of globalisation, experience an increased incentive to leave their home countries and move to the more developed regions of the world looking for better standards of life.

This produces the two interrelated phenomena of the 'brain drain', when skilled or highly educated labour flees the country of origins, and 'mass migration', when migratory flows interest unskilled labour.

The ensemble of the above described dynamics leads to a new global division of labour whose main characteristics are, thus, on the one hand, the geographical displacement of production alongside regional patterns and the increased use of third world cheaper labour; and, on the other hand, the increase of brain drain and mass migration from the regions left behind by the process of regionalisation within globalisation.

One of the outcomes of this new division of labour is an overall decrease of production costs both in third world countries and in industrialised ones. Indeed, this process not only brings about lower production costs through the reallocation of production abroad or the hiring of immigrants, particularly illegal ones, but it also lowers the prices of domestic labour by putting pressure on organised labour and reducing its bargaining power.

Moreover, mass migration, both legal and illegal, acquires regional patterns, due to historical, geographic, social or cultural reasons. All responses to mass migration, therefore, take the form of regional policies, like the US or the EU immigration policy. Here a fundamental paradox arises. The paradox is between the advantages of immigration in terms of reduction of the costs of production and of contribution to the sustainability of the welfare state (particularly given the aging problem in the more developed world) and the implementation of stricter migration policies at the regional level. In Europe, for example, despite the fact that the implementation of a common migratory policy is still far from being achieved, the outlook of public policy responses to mass migration has accredited the idea of the creation of the so-called 'Fortress Europe', i.e., an area where internal mobility is promoted while barriers are erected *vis-à-vis* countries outside the EU.[15]

Of course the main reasons for the adoption of similar responses to mass migration are the traditional concerns over political unrest, social conflict, cultural clashes, or religious struggles.

However, a further aspect of the issue is represented by the political economy consequences of 'illegal' migration (as opposed to the legal one), in terms of cost reduction and increase of bargaining power *vis-à-vis* organised labour. There seems indeed to be some evidence of the fact that the use of illegal migrant work reduces the wages of legal work and consequently, the power of organised labour. For example, in Germany studies have shown that a 1 per cent increase in the share of less-skilled foreign workers in the labour force leads to a 5.9 per cent fall in the wages of blue-collar workers and a 3.5 per cent increase in white-collar wages.[16] In this context, it would be interesting to carry out further investigation on the economic sectors involved in the use and exploitation of illegal immigration and to assess the political economy consequences of similar practices in terms of shift of power between different socioeconomic actors.[17]

Moreover, analysing the dichotomy between legal immigration and illegal immigration, the second is more favourable to the neoliberal order than the first, because it allows for the flexibilisation of the internal labour market, while legal immigrants should be integrated in the existing welfare state provisions system.

As Saskia Sassen writes:

> Indeed, those who deal with the real political economy of the city already know this: the rhetoric of the law-and-order Republican mayor here in New York City is surprisingly friendly to illegal immigrants.[18]

Summing up, the political economy consequences of the increase of mass migration in the context of globalisation are: a precarisation of working conditions both in developed and in less developed countries; an increase of the power of the transnational companies at the international level and the reaction of the governments through the constitution of regional governance scheme, such as the EU, where the labour/capital dynamics are reproduced but with a strong reduction of power on the labour side.[19]

Concluding, from the theoretical point of view, the following issues appear particularly relevant:

1 the paradox of marginalisation within globalisation and its causes and consequences for the working force of marginalised countries;
2 the paradox of regionalisation within globalisation and the related definition of a new global division of labour;
3 the paradox of the Fortress Europe and the political economy consequences of illegal migration.

In the next section of this contribution attention is drawn to the dynamics of the smuggling of illegal migrants between the two shores of the Mediterranean.

8.3 Migratory Flows in Practice

8.3.1 Smuggling and Trafficking of Human Beings in the Mediterranean Region

The illicit, if not straightforward illegal, exploitation of migratory flows from less developed countries into western, industrialised ones, has acquired, nowadays, worrying dimensions. Indeed, the most common way for migrants to acquire access to more developed countries is through the intermediation of transnational organised criminal groups smuggling them in, or directly trafficking in human beings.

Smuggling involves the procurement of illegal entry of a person into a State of which that person is not a national, with the objective of making a profit. Trafficking is a more complex activity. It involves the recruitment, transportation, or receipt of persons through deception or coercion for the purposes of prostitution, other sexual exploitation or forced labour. In many cases, of course, the dividing line between smuggling and trafficking is unclear.[20]

In general terms it is possible to categorise entry or exit of a migrant as follows:

- *legal-legal*: the migrant applies for immigrant status, gains legal entry and remains in the country as a legal migrant;
- *illegal-legal*: this includes those migrants who enter a country illegally, using false documents or evading immigration restrictions, and who seek to change their status after arrival;
- *legal-illegal*: this group is considered the one including the largest percentage of the 'illegal' migrant population;
- *illegal-illegal* (independent): this group enters the country illegally and remains illegal but without the assistance of organised criminal groups.
- *illegal-illegal* (indentured): this is the most vulnerable category. They are undocumented migrants at the mercy of the criminals who procured their passage and employment. They have incurred large debts for their passage which require long periods of time to repay;

- *legal-legal* (indentured): these are those migrants who paid criminal organisations to gain legal access to and a legal stay in the host country. Legal status may improve job prospects, however the amount of money to pay back still means that crime is a necessary or attractive option.[21]

The phenomenon of illegal migration is particularly worrying in the relations between Europe and its Mediterranean counterparts. Smuggling illegal immigrants into Europe has become a profitable business. It is estimated that illegal immigration into Europe from the south and east raised sharply in the last years. Some 500,000 illegal migrants are believed to have arrived in the year 2000, up from 40,000 in 1993.[22]

There are several favourite routes in: via boat from Albania, Tunisia or Morocco into southern Europe; via Libya through the desert route from sub-Saharan Africa; from Sarajevo airport via Croatia and Slovenia into Italy and Austria; or overland starting from Istanbul and often ending up in Germany.

8.3.2 Mapping the Routes

a) The Spanish route The fastest illegal route from Northern Africa, particularly Morocco, to Europe is the nine-mile sea journey in small boats from northern Morocco to Spain. The Spanish route includes also the smuggling route leading from north and sub-Saharan Africa to the Canary Islands.

In the last few years, both the Canary and the Gibraltar routes experienced the highest number of boat passages and casualties ever.

According to the Delegación del Gobierno para la Extranjería y la Inmigración, in the year 1999 there were 3,569 total intercepted migrants of which 875 were stopped in the Canary Islands. One-third of these migrants were women who, in many cases, arrived in an advanced stage of pregnancy. At the end of December 2000, the number of immigrants who were caught on board small boats trying to enter Spain by sea was around 15,000 (14,893). Of these, 2,387 were captured on the Canary route. These immigrants reached the Spanish shores with more than 780 boats intercepted in the Strait of Gibraltar or in the Canary Islands.

Between January and September 2001, Spanish officials apprehended 13,000 migrants; including 8,500 Moroccans. In 2002, Spanish police intercepted 1,000 boats and arrested 16,504 people.[23]

Furthermore, Spanish officials estimate that 200 people, mainly Moroccans, die every year trying to reach Spain across the Strait of Gibraltar; other estimates put the number of deaths at 1,000 in 1998.[24]

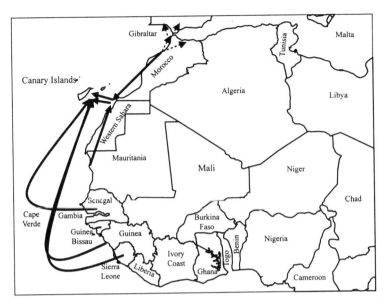

Figure 8.1   The Spanish route

Source: Delegacion del Gobierno para la Inmigracion y Extranjeria.

Table 8.1   Immigrants captured on board small boats

	1999	2000	2001 (Jan.–Sept.)	2002
Total	3,569	14,893	13,000	16,504
(en Canarias)	(875)	(2.387)		

Source: Delegacion del Gobierno para la Inmigracion y Extranjeria.

These figures, however, do not include those who made it without being caught nor those who legally entered the country at the border with a three-month tourist visa and enough money to stay. Nor are included the people who disappeared or lost their lives in the many shipwrecks.[25]

Between 28 January–8 February 2003 ships from five European nations began patrolling the Mediterranean to prevent migrant smuggling, the first time EU members have cooperated in this way. Under Operation Ulysses, Spanish, British, French, Italian and Portuguese police, customs and navy ships are patrolling from Algeciras, Spain to Sicily.

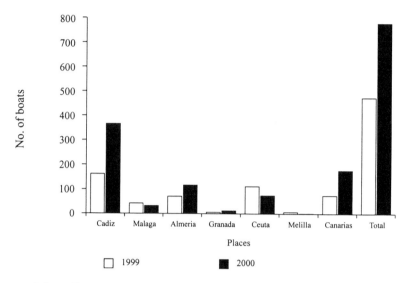

Figure 8.2   Boats detected on the Spanish shores

Source: *El Pais*.

Table 8.2   Casualties on the Spanish route

	1999	2000
Shipwrecks	30	54
Disappeared	23	47
Corpses recovered	29	55
Rescued people	387	1,037

Source: Delegacion del Gobierno para la Inmigracion y Extranjeria.

Despite the fact that small boats are the most common means to reach Spain, there are also other ways, as risky as that, to try and make it to Spain from Northern Africa. Many immigrants, especially young men or teenagers, who do not have enough money to pay the organised crime, cross the Strait of Gibraltar or reach the Canary Islands hiding in the backs of the trucks getting to Spain by ferry. This system, which led Spanish authorities to control vehicles from North Africa more strictly, allows immigrants to get to central and northern areas of the peninsula. Sometimes, however, also the entry by trucks is controlled by the Mafia.[26]

Alternatively, immigrants may stow away on transport or mercantile ships. Those ships are sometimes intercepted by the coastal patrols and the sailors are detained.

Estimates of the number of illegal foreigners in Spain range from 60,000 to 150,000. The majority of them come from Maghreb, around 38 per cent of the total, and from Latin America (25 per cent). Smaller groups are composed by sub-Saharans (12 per cent), Chinese (8 per cent) and Eastern Europeans (8 per cent).[27]

Spain has about 39 million residents, almost 11 per cent of the European Union's population and 10 per cent of its GDP, but accounted for 22 per cent of Europe's immigration in 2002. Some 200,000 Ecuadorians and 150,000 Colombians moved to Spain between 1998 and 2002, and there were additional migrants from Argentina and the Dominican Republic. Between 1998 and 2002, some 100,000 Moroccans arrived in Spain.

Migrants are concentrated in cleaning services, agriculture and restaurants – 27 per cent of legal migrants work in cleaning (compared to 6 per cent of Spaniards); 20 per cent in agriculture (9 per cent); and 11 per cent in restaurants (1 per cent).

In March 2003, 890,000 migrants paid social-welfare contributions of at least E100 a month each, or a total of E1 billion a year.

Latin Americans usually arrive in Spain with tourist visas, and then often work illegally in cities. Moroccans and Eastern Europeans, by contrast, are more often found in agriculture and construction. Critics allege that enforcement is concentrated on Moroccans and Eastern Europeans – 23,400 Moroccans were deported in 2002, followed by 18,900 Romanians – and that the Spanish government goes easy on Latin Americans because they are easier to integrate. Government data found that the 280,000 Moroccans are the largest group of legal foreigners in Spain, but most observers say that there are more Ecuadorians and Colombians than Moroccans.

Together with Spain, France and Italy represent the main destination countries for both legal and illegal migrants from Morocco. A recent Eurostat survey show that 29 per cent of migrating Moroccans head towards France, 28 per cent towards Italy and 20 per cent towards Spain.[28]

According to the same survey, the reasons why so many Moroccan immigrants decide to use the Spanish route are, of course, easily traced back in the physical proximity of the two countries. Adding to this, people from Maghreb also believe that entering Spain, even if clandestinely, is much easier than entering other European countries. Generally, immigrants who arrive in the EU from Maghreb are single males, between 20 and 30, whose motivations

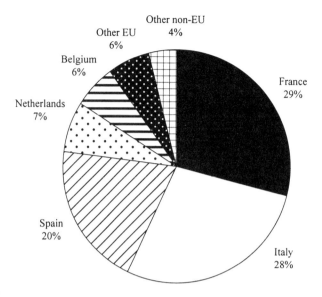

Figure 8.3   Moroccan migrants' destination countries

Source: Eurostat (2001).

are mainly economic. Family reunification is then sought after once they have secured a job in the host countries. Women immigrants are thus much rarer and mainly led by the motivation to join their male relatives. Curiously enough, whereas the majority of immigrants interviewed in the survey claim to be willing to go back to their home countries, only 15 per cent of the Moroccans expatriated to Spain think about going back to Morocco.[29]

Spain has labour recruitment agreements with Romania, Poland, Ecuador, Morocco and Bulgaria in 2004. There are three categories of foreign workers: those with contracts for a year or more, seasonal workers with contracts for less than nine months work in Spain, and young people ages 18–35 who can be employed in Spain up to 18 months. The agreements are reciprocal, and permit Spaniards to work in these countries on the same basis. The foreign workers participate in Spanish social security and health systems on the same basis as domestic workers.[30]

b) The Libyan route   Libya has recently become the main destination for the thousands of sub-Saharan Africans willing to escape from the dire life-conditions of their home countries and work in Libya or fly over to Europe as soon as possible. This happened thanks to the capacity of Colonel Qaddafi, unquestionable authoritarian leader of Libya, to accredit himself as the paladin of the pan-African unity, and thanks also to his open-minded policy towards immigration.[31] Colonel Qaddafi's policy is believed to have increased the flow of migrants, so that more than one million African expatriates are now estimated to live in Libya, which has an indigenous population of five million. Most come from countries on its borders: Niger, Chad and Sudan, whose migrants typically stay to work in Libya. Migrants from other African nations usually use Libya as a springboard to Europe. But how does the smuggling route unfold and what are the conditions migrants have to face to reach Europe?

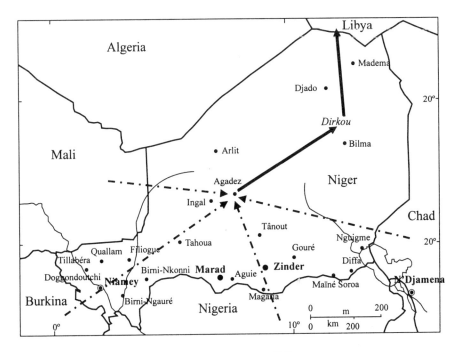

Figure 8.4   The Agadez-Dirkou route to Libya

Source: *New York Times*, various issues.

At the borders of the desert of Niger, where the Sahara unfolds to the end of the horizon, Dirkou, once an abandoned village without any major attractions, is now a thriving town where money circulate in abundance and those who are smart enough can find their fortune. This is just the last outpost on the route from Agadez (Niger) that leads to Tripoli through the desert, but it has now become the symbol of the underground thread linking sub-Saharan Africa to northern Africa and, ideally, to Europe. Dirkou is the last sub-Saharan stop on one of the continent's greatest, and possibly most dangerous, smuggling routes: Africans travel hundreds of miles through desert to arrive there and board Libyan trucks that take them across the remaining expanses of the Sahara into North Africa. There the migrants stay to work, or they save up money to travel to Europe and even America, where some may end up in New York working in restaurants and grocery stores.[32]

This smuggling route was discovered in October 2000, after Libyans killed or hurt thousands of African expatriates, lynching a Chadian diplomat and burning down the Niger Embassy. This outburst of violence was a revenge for the alleged rape of a Libyan girl by a Nigerian immigrant. Thereafter, in a sudden reversal of the exodus, tens of thousands of Africans were herded into buses and trucks, and then dumped in the desert south of Libya or expelled by plane to Nigeria and Ghana. Yet after less then two months, Africans were flocking again to Dirkou on their way to Libya. The surprisingly quick resumption in the exodus has been related to the worsening of the standards of life in sub-Saharan Africa in recent years. Civil wars, diseases and authoritarian regimes are plaguing the continent and even once traditional regional powers like the Ivory Coast and South Africa have been breaking down politically or economically. Ordinary Africans are now finding it hard to survive, much less to have hope of improving their condition with the consequence of a dangerous brain drain to the West. However, the desert of Dirkou, witnesses the exodus of the lowest strata of African society, namely, young African men with little or no education. Some of them border on criminality; others are engaged outright in smuggling substances such as heroin, or just ordinary people looking for a chance to improve their lives.

Before making it there, migrants entering Niger pass through Agadez, about 560 kilometres southwest, which, like Timbuktu in neighbouring Mali, has served for centuries as a gateway between black Africa to the south and Arab Africa to the north. In Agadez, the smuggling system is highly organised. Middlemen from the subregion direct their countrymen to one of the dealers in the Agadez-Dirkou route. At the bus station, dealers hand the middlemen $3 for each passenger they receive. Travellers with passports are charged $15 for a one-way ticket to Dirkou. Since, however, around 80 per cent of the passengers lack papers, most also pay what may be called a corruption surcharge of $7 to bribe the authorities at the four security checkpoints dotting the desert between Agadez and Dirkou.

Migrants are loaded like cattle on open-air trucks charged with goods without any guarantees for them to arrive safely at the other edge of the desert. The cargo is normally composed by Guineans, Nigerians, Ghanaians, Cameroonians, Congolese, as well as Nigerois, who stay in Libya as long as it is necessary to collect enough money to be smuggled to Europe or to the United States. Along the way, some get lost, some die, and some get arrested, for much of the smuggling of migrants goes hand in hand with the smuggling of a number of other products, especially drugs.

Many migrants sail for Italy from Libya in the summer months. Three thousand are believed to have landed in Italy in June 2003. Sicily, is the Italian region more interested in the landing of illegal migrants coming from Libya. In the last years the Libyan route seems to have taken over the Turkish and the Sarajevo ones. Indeed, figures show that in the year 2003 the number of migrants arriving in Sicily (6,286) is by far higher then the number of those arriving in Calabria (177) and Puglia (81), which normally are the final stops of the Balkan routes.[33]

Table 8.3   Number of migrants landing on the shores of Italy, 2001–2003

Years (15 June each year)	Sicily	Calabria	Puglia	Total
2003	6,286	177	81	6,544
2002	6,886	1,442	2,174	10,502
2001	1,334	1,038	5,236	7,608

Source: Panorama, 'Li manda Gheddafi', 16 June 2003.

c) The Turkish route A report published by the *New York Times*,[34] described the Laleli quarter of Istanbul, as a place to buy false passports and visas for prices that range from several hundred to several thousand dollars. An Iranian passport, for example, goes for $250 with the original photograph in it, or $350 with the migrant's own photo inserted and a forged official Iranian stamp applied to it. Western passports are far more desirable and expensive, a Danish one costs $9,000 and an American one $14,000, but the Iranian document might prove extremely useful. In fact, the migrants gathering in Istanbul are likely to use their Iranian passports for a visa-free travel to Bosnia from which illegal access to Europe is easily available.

People choosing this route to Europe are normally from Northern Iraq, northern Africa and Central Asia. Many of the migrants seeking entry to Western Europe are legally in Turkey, arriving by plane, by boat or by land, but they need to be smuggled from Turkey into countries that deny them visas. Istanbul thus becomes a waiting room before migrants travel to Europe via illegal means. From here, migrants can either move to Sarajevo to try the Balkan routes, or sail to Albania and reach Europe via the Italian coast, mainly Lecce and Bari but also, more rarely, via the French coast. Some of them remain stuck in Turkey and live a life of misery and humiliation unable to go back to their own countries of origins or to proceed on the journey of hope to Europe.

A major human disaster in February 2001 showed the entire world the appalling conditions in which migrants sailing from Turkey are brought to Europe. A cargo ship packed with more than 900 Kurdish migrants, mostly from Iraq, ran aground off the coast of France after the crew fled. The journey to Europe cost the Kurds $4,200 per adult to get to Europe, with $1,700 charged per child whose number was around 300. It lasted seven days in the most intolerable conditions, during which the migrants were not even allowed to know where the boat would arrive.[35]

The smuggling of migrants from Istanbul is dominated by Turkish and Albanian gangs, composed of five to 20 members. However, the North African community is huge, not only amongst those trying to be smuggled in, but also amongst those actively participating in the business. Charging between $1,000 and $4,000 to move people to Western Europe from Turkey, those organisations quickly build up large amounts of cash that are invested in stolen luxury cars, property, restaurants and illegal activities including drug smuggling.

Many immigrants borrow money from the same criminal organisations to be able to pay crime gangs to move them. This is actually how migrants add up to the number of the new slaves, tied up to the criminal groups by the debts they incurred to be smuggled in. Indeed, dealing in human beings is a business that, though very profitable, implies few risks on the side of the organised criminal groups, for penalties are much lighter than for other criminal activities like drug smuggling. It is true that Turkey has recently added extra border posts at its frontiers, increased the number of border guards, tightened inspections in various Aegean ports, started sharing intelligence on human smuggling with other countries including Italy and Bosnia, and begun new training for guards. However, this is far from representing a substantial policy against traffickers and smugglers and it is very much dictated by Turkey's will to please the EU in view of its eventual entry.

Turkish authorities apprehended 47,518 migrants in 1999, and 40,245 in the first six months of 2000. In 1997 the number of illegal immigrants captured in Turkey was only 28,439. However, thousands more are never caught.[36]

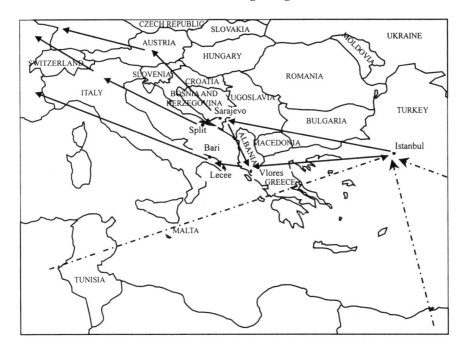

Figure 8.5   The smuggling route from Turkey to the EU

Source: *The Guardian*, various issues.

d) The Sarajevo route For many migrants coming from the Middle East, Northern Africa and Central Asia, Sarajevo is the last stop before Europe. Indeed, the Balkan routes are well established. Chinese via Belgrade;[37] migrants and asylum seekers from the Middle East, Bangladesh and Sri Lanka via Sarajevo, where Bosnian authorities tend to favour fellow Muslims. In Bosnia the largest immigrant groups come from Iran, with Turkish Kurds and Chinese next on the list. Arrivals of smaller groups of Sri-Lankan, Bangladeshi, Afghan Egyptian, Pakistani, Iraqi, Macedonian and Yugoslavian nationals have been also reported.[38]

According to information from the Bosnian authorities and international agencies, more than 5,000 individuals migrate to Bosnia each month with the intention of continuing towards Western Europe. Many of them come from Istanbul, by truck or even by plane. Turkish airlines fly regularly from Istanbul, full of young men with no luggage claiming to be tourists, for tourists in Bosnia do not need visas. The numbers speak for themselves. It is estimated that in the year 2000, 50,000 migrants entered Bosnia through the two main airports; 28,000 are unaccounted for and assumed to be now in Europe.[39]

From Sarajevo, three overland routes sneak them into Italy and Austria via Croatia, Slovenia and Hungary. There are 400 crossing points out of Bosnia and only four of them manned. Croatia and Bosnia, who recently signed a readmission agreement, share 1,200 miles of largely unpatrolled mountainous border. In the first eight months of 2000, the number of irregular migrants caught crossing into Croatia was 11,500, 40 per cent more than in the same period in 1999. Romanians, Turks and Iranians topped the list of nationalities, with 3,640, 2,500 and 2,470 respectively. However, given the thriving trade of Iranian and Turkish passports in Istanbul, it is easy to guess that many nationalities were disguised.[40]

Alternatively, routes lead through Albania or Croatia to cross the Adriatic from Vlore or Split in small boats. It is estimated that more than 130 drowned in the year 2000.[41]

The International Organisation for Migration calculated that the trade of men is worth upwards of £70 million a year in Bosnia alone.[42]

This is not all. In Bosnia the traffic in illegal migrants conceals a second, more venal trade in humans: the trade in sex slaves which lures women and young girls to Bosnia 'mainly from Eastern Europe and former Soviet republics' with the promise of jobs as au pairs or waitresses in the EU.[43] However, in Bosnia prosecutions have been almost non-existent for both crimes; detection is hampered by those willing to help the people-smugglers and these are mainly represented by the corrupted elite of the country. Evidence exists too that the smuggling business is part of a sophisticated international network that also supplies forged documents. The shocking reality of Bosnia today, international officials say, is this. A few years after the Dayton Peace Agreement was signed to bring a genocidal war to an end, a country that has received unprecedented military and economic aid from the international community has turned, not into a model Balkan democracy, but into one of Europe's main hubs for smuggling people.[44]

Notes

1   See, for example, Gardezi (1995), Gosh (1998, 2000), Sassan (1998) and Weiner (1995).
2   See Chapter 9, Conclusions, for a more detailed account of this debate.
3   See Chapter 9, Conclusions, for the debate on globalisation.
4   A similar distinction is contained in Dicken (1998), p. 5.

5 See, for example, Hirst and Thompson (1999).

6 See, for example, Garret (1998).

7 See, for example, Mittleman (2000). For the relations between globalisation and migration. See, for example, Sassen (1998) and Weiner (1995).

8 See Chapter 9, Conclusions, for further details.

9 See Holm and Sørensen (1995), p. 12.

10 For a more detailed analysis of this approach to globalisation see the conclusions of this book. See also Overbeek (2000).

11 Dicken (2003).

12 Scholars refer to the 'triad' to indicate the three main zones of production of the globe, i.e., Asian pacific region, America and Europe.

13 See, for example Breslin Hughes, Philis and Rosamond (2002) and Hettne, Inotai and Sunkel (1999).

14 On this subject see, for example, Mursheed (2002).

15 Though the Amsterdam Treaty moved migratory issues from the third (intergovernmental decision-making) to the first pillar (Community law), there is still no common migratory policy and the member states retain full competence on legislating on migration.The alien model of immigration regime based on soft law is still the one prevailing at the European level. There have been some moves to devise a common policy to combat illegal immigration (see European Council in Tampere, 1999 and European Council in Seville, 2002) but still no concrete measures have been taken.

16 See Overbeek (2000).

17 For some data see Gosh (1998). See also Harris (1995).

18 See Sassen (1998), p. XIII.

19 See, for example, the relations ETUC-European Round Table or UNICE at the European level.

20 These definitions are taken from the UN Convention on Transnational Organised Crime and its Protocols, see ODCCP webpage, http//:www.odccp.org.

21 See UNODCCP (2001), http//:www.odccp.org.

22 See *New York Times*, 25 December 2000, 'Illegal Migration Rises Sharply in European Union'.

23 See Ministeria del Interior, Delegacion del Gobierno para la extranjeria y la inmigracion (2001). See also *Migrant News*, various issues, at http://migration.ucdavis.edu/mn/pastissues_mn.html.

24 See *Migration News*, Vol. 8 (1), January, 2001.

25 See *El Pais* (2001), 'Reportage on immigration. Un viaje desesperado hacia lo incierto', *El Pais* web page, http://www.elpais.es/temas/inmigracion/index.html.

26 Ibid.

27 See *Migration News*, various issues, at http://migration.ucdavis.edu/mn/pastissues_mn.html.

28 See Eurostat (2001).

29 See Eurostat, (2001).

30 See *Migration News*, various issues.

31 See *Panorama*, 'Li manda Gheddafi', 16 June 2003.

32 See *New York Times*, 4 January 2001.

33 See *Panorama*, 'Li manda Gheddafi', 16 June 2003.

34 See *New York Times*, 25 December 2000, 'Illegal Migration Rises Sharply in European Union'.

35 See Morris, 6 January 2001, 'Turkey's Human Traffic, Rescuers Deal with Victims of the Turkish Disaster', BBC webpage at http://news.bbc.co.uk/.
36 See *New York Times*, 25 December 2000, 'Illegal Migration Rises Sharply in European Union'.
37 For more details on the smuggling of Chinese nationals via Belgrade see International Office for Migration (2000).
38 See International Office for Migration (2000).
39 See Bomford, 9 February 2001, 'Sarajevo: Gateway to Europe, For asylum Seekers, Sarajevo is an Easy Crossing Point', BBC webpage at http://news.bbc.co.uk/.
40 See International Office for Migration (2000).
41 See Carroll (2001).
42 See Skeldon (2000).
43 For more information on the subject see International Office for Migration (2000).
44 See Morris, Kaya and Beaumont (2001). See also Travis (2001).

References

Appleyard, R. (1999), *Emigration Dynamics in Developing Countries*, Aldershot: Ashgate Publishing.

Breslin, S., Hughes, C.W., Philis, N. and Rosamond, B. (2002), *New Regionalisms in the Global Political Economy*, London: Routledge.

Carroll, R. (2001), 'Grim War on Human Traffickers', Guardian, 5 February.

Dicken, P. (1998), *Global Shift*, London: Paul Chapman.

Dicken, P. (2003), *Global Shift: Reshaping the Global Economic Map in the 21st Century*, London: Sage.

Eurostat (2001), 'Why do People Migrate', *Eurostat Statistics in Focus, Population and Social Conditions*, Theme 3–1/2001.

Gardezi, H. (1995), *The Political Economy of International Labor Migration*, Montreal: Black Rose Books.

Garret, G. (1998), *Partisan Politics in the Global Economy*, Cambridge: Cambridge University Press.

Gosh, B. (1998), *Huddled Masses and Uncertain Shores: Insights into Irregular Migration*, London: Martinus Nijhoff Publishers.

Gosh, B. (ed.) (2000), *Managing Migration: Time for a New International Regime*, Oxford: Oxford University Press.

Harris, N. (1995), *The New Untouchables. Immigration and the New World Worker*, London: Penguin Books.

Hettne, B., Inotai, A. and Sunkel, O. (1999), *Globalism and the New Regionalism*, London: Macmillan.

Hirst, P. and Thompson, G. (1999), *Globalisation in Question*, London: Polity Press.

Holm, H.H. and Sørensen, G. (1995), Whose World Order? : Uneven Globalization and the End of the Cold War, Publisher: Boulder, CO: Westview Press.

International Office for Migration (2000), 'Trafficking in Migrants – Focus on the Balkans', *IOM Quarterly Bulletin*, No. 22, Autumn.

Ministeria del Interior, Delegacion del Gobierno para la extranjeria y la inmigracion (2001), 'La inmigracion en Espana: Evolucion y perspectivas', Delegacion del Gobierno para la extranjeria y la inmigracion.

Mittleman, J.H. (2000), *The Globalisation Syndrome: Transformation and Resistance*, Princeton: Princeton University Press.

Morris, C., Kaya, M. and Beaumont, P. (2001), 'Bosnia's Corrupt Elite Grow Fat on Human Cargo Smuggled to West', *Observer*, 28 January.

Mursheed, M.S. (2002), *Globalization, Marginalisation and Development*, London: Routledge.

Overbeek, H. (2000), 'Globalisation, Sovereignty and Transnational Regulation: Reshaping the Governance of International Migration', in B. Gosh (2000), *Managing Migration: Time for a New International Regime*, Oxford: Oxford University Press.

Sassan, S. (1996), *Losing Control*, New York: Columbia University Press.

Sassan, S. (1998), *Globalisation and its Discontents*, New York: New York Press.

Skeldon, R. (2000), *Myths and Realities of Chinese Irregular Migration*, Geneva: International Office for Migration.

Travis, A. (2001), 'A Joint Anglo-Italian Initiative to Stem the Flow from the Balkans', *Guardian*, 5 February.

UNODCCP (2001), 'Global Programme against Smuggling of Migrants', ODCCP webpage, http//:www.odccp.org.

Weiner, M. (1995), *The Global Migration Crisis: Challenge to States and Human Rights*, New York: HarperCollins College Publishers.

Chapter 9

Conclusions: Globalisation, Regionalisation and the Nation State: Intergovernmentalism, Institutionalism and Transnationalism Confronted

9.1 Introduction

If the subject European political economy is inserted, as in this book, in the tradition of international relations/international political economy, the analysis of the process of European integration cannot be separated from the analysis of the broader context within which it takes place. This final chapter, therefore, overcomes the borders of the European Union to move to a higher level of analysis in which the EU, its policies, its institutions and decision-making procedures are seen as only a part of a whole, as a mechanism of a bigger machine which both influences and is influenced by the working of the other mechanisms as well as by the working of the machine as a whole.

At the same time, the EU is itself a whole composed of, as this contribution tried to explain in all its chapters, many different mechanisms, many different parts, many different actors. These actors interact not only with the whole represented by Europe, but also, independently or through its mediation, with the bigger machine given by the world, or, in the 'new-speak' by the 'globe'.

Here it is the place to finally address the 'G' word,[1] this globalisation which is denied, exalted, demonised, hated, loved, considered the panacea or the mother of all evils, according to who is speaking, but never ignored in the contemporary IR-IPE discourse. And here is always the place to see how globalisation is related to the process of European integration, and how the latter is similar or different from the process of regionalisation taking place in other areas of the world, and to investigate over the meaning of regionalisation in relation to both globalisation and the nation state.

Of course, there is not only 'one' theory trying to answer these questions, and, as it should be clear by now, different theories, using different initial assumptions produce completely different pictures. This leads not only to different descriptions of reality but also, and, maybe, more importantly for a discipline like political sciences, to different prescriptions on how the world 'should' be. This is clearly not the place to address the question of the normative value of theories, though it is important to remember that each has one. What this chapter will do is only to identify how three different theoretical approaches, intergovernmentalism, institutionalism and transnationalism answer these issues, leaving the reader the possibility to choose which vision of the world looks more convincing. By no means, however, the author believes to have exhausted an argument whose philosophical, ontological and academic boundaries are becoming more and more difficult to identify.

9.2 Intergovernmentalist Approaches: The Myth of Globalisation and the Centrality of the Nation State

Intergovernmentalist or neorealist understandings of globalisation are characterised by a very sceptical attitude towards the very existence of the phenomenon itself, its relevance for the international political economy, or its definition as a new historical phase.[2]

The concept of globalisation is grossly overstated by those who use it either to demonise it as the mother of all evils, or to emphasise it as the panacea for all problems. It is a convenient myth, in the hands of politicians or public opinion makers. In reality, globalisation hardly exists and even where it is possible to identify some new trends in the international political economy, those may be easily explained by making reference to the nation state and the national dimension.[3]

This conception relies on a quantitative definition of globalisation, which tends to 'quantify' the extent of globalisation by identifying measures for all the phenomena that are normally included within its scope. This means that first it is necessary to define the ideal typical notion of globalisation, identifying all its elements and the modalities to measure them. Then, to be able to effect a comparison, it is necessary to make reference to another ideal type, that of a world economy without globalisation. Also this requires the listing of all the components of such a world economy as well as of their measures. Finally, the empirical testing is carried out by producing data on the state of the real economy to show whether this is closer to the ideal type of a globalised economy or to that of a non-globalised economy.

This approach is used, for example, by Gilpin, to demonstrate that the relevance of economic globalisation is very overstated, and that the core of the world economy is still the nation state, though now its interests are better served within integrated regional economic areas. First, Gilpin, defines globalisation as the increase of integration of the world economy resulting from major changes in trade flows, from the activities of multinational corporations and from developments in international finance.[4] Then, the author demonstrates that this increase has been 'highly uneven, restricted to particular economic sectors and not nearly as extensive as many believe'.[5]

In fact, according to Gilpin, the level of economic integration was by far higher during the gold standard, and even in the late nineteenth century, trade investment and financial flows were greater than now, if they are measured in relative terms. Moreover, though in absolute terms these flows are bigger and faster in the twentieth century, they are confined within the borders of regional economic blocks, dominated by powerful nation states. Even the globalisation of financial markets is limited to short-term and speculative investment.

Finally, the most important measure of economic integration and interdependence of different economies, the so-called 'law of one price', according to which economies are perfectly integrated if identical goods and services have the same or nearly equal prices, is not respected around the world.[6]

Also according to Hirst and Thompson[7] globalisation is more a myth than anything else. Globalisation does not exist, not even as the 'end' of an ongoing process. On the other hand, regionalisation is increasing but as a consequence of the desire of the bigger and more powerful states to maximise their interests.

Similar conclusions are reached by contrasting the notion of a 'globalised world economy' with that of an 'internationalised' world economy.[8] An internationalised world economy is, in the words of the authors: 'One in which the principal entities remain national economies, or agents that continue to be primarily located in a definite national territory.'[9]

The main characteristics of internationalisation are therefore the following:

- national economies remain the principal entities;
- agents continue to be primarily located in a definite national territory;
- there is a clear separation between the national and the international arena;
- there is a quantitative increase in the relation between states.

As a consequence, the main actors of an internationalised world economy are multinationals (MNCs) located in nation states and relying on the national economy as their primary source of earnings, personnel and policy-making.

On the other hand, there is the ideal type of a 'globalised world economy', which is defined as:

> An economy that exists 'above' the national economies and agents, autonomously from those national economies, and that bears down upon those economies and actors ... This would be an economy that escapes 'governance' one typified by unorganized and uncontrollable market forces.[10]

Its main components would therefore be the following:

- economic relations are disembedded from the nation states;
- the global economy exists above national economies;
- the global economy is autonomous from national economies and actors;
- the global economy escapes governance;
- the global economy is typified by unorganised and uncontrollable market forces.

In this case the main actors are transnational corporations (TNCs), actors which are disembodied from any nation state and would produce and sell genuinely internationally.

Having identified the main components of the two ideal types of world economy to be contrasted, the authors then move to their measurement.[11]

The first measure of an integrated global economy is the stock of foreign owned productive activity. The data proposed by Thompson and Hirst show that the stock of the inward foreign direct investment (FDI) as a percentage of GDP in the world in 1995 was only 10.1. This, though more than double the 1980 figure, does not seem to the authors to be such a dramatic figure to justify the claim of the death of national economy.

In any case, FDI flows account only for what a multinational company is lending to the affiliated company abroad, and not what they are, at the same time, investing in their home country. Therefore, a second measure of the degree of globalisation of the world economy is given by the assessment of the level of home investment of multinational companies.[12] The main conclusion of this kind of analysis is that multinational companies remain significantly 'home orientated' in their investment activity, though some of this activity is regionally centred. According to Hirst and Thompson, the data show that between two-thirds and three quarters of MNC aggregate business activity remained home or regionally centred in the 1990s.[13]

These results allow the authors to conclude that:

> International companies are still predominantly MNCs, with a clear home base
> to their operations, and not transnational companies (TNCs), which represent
> footloose, stateless companies.[14]

A third indicator of the degree of globalisation of the world economy is given
by the extent of internationalisation in relation to overall national output,
measured by the gross product of foreign affiliates as a percentage of national
or regional GDP. For developed countries this only increased from 5.1 per cent
in 1982 to 5.4 per cent in 1994, from 6 to 9.1 per cent in developing countries
and from 5.2 per cent to 6 per cent for the world total overall.[15]

Similar conclusions can be reached by analysing the degree of global
integration of financial markets, starting from the assumption that the
degree of financial integration between different countries relies upon the
relationship between national savings and national investments. Indeed, in
a completely integrated global financial system, domestic investment would
not be fundamentally constrained by domestic savings, and the correlation
between investment and savings would disappear.[16]

Therefore, a first measure of the degree of financial globalisation is the
correlation (R^2) between savings and investments, which, however, has not
unambiguously declined in the last years.

A second measure of the importance of domestic resources for domestic
investment is the share of inward FDI flows in gross domestic capital formation
(GDCF) for different economies. Also in this case figures demonstrate the relative
unimportance of FDI flows in their contribution to domestic investment.

Another way to look at the globalisation of financial markets is to underline
the extent to which financial markets are controllable by national governments.
On this, the debate is open, but intergovernmentalists remind the audience that
financial markets are mainly financial institutions with a clear national location
and embedded in a national legal framework. Moreover, they raise their assets
in national markets and have to use their earnings to meet their obligations to
depositors, pensioners and life policy holders. Finally, they have to abide national
macroeconomic policy-making, use nationally or regionally defined interest rates
and respect nationally subscribed agreements on the exchange rates.[17]

In a few words, financial institutions are embedded in national political,
legal and economic constraints and therefore are not completely uncontrollable.
Therefore, the only way to achieve a higher degree of regulation and
stabilisation of financial markets is if major states are willing to cooperate

in order to impose common rules to the system. This is indeed a typical intergovernmentalist recipe.

Concluding, by using figures, intergovernmentalists prove that the 'globalised economy' is a myth and the fact that the world economy remains sufficiently concentrated in the key national states allows for intergovernmentalist solutions to international problems to be effective.

There is however a clear trend towards 'regionalisation'. Regionalisation is happening both *de jure*, with the creation of formal regional free trade arrangements, and *de facto*, with the construction of regional economic blocs which do not necessarily coincide with their formal definition.

Focusing on firms' decisions about where to trade and invest, figures show that the triad of the US, the EU and Japan tend to direct its FDI flows and stock towards a fixed cluster of countries, to form three clearly distinguishable blocks of countries. These country groupings tend to be regionally specific and adjacent to one or the other of the triad members.

From the intergovernmentalist perspective, however, regionalisation is just the demonstration of the economic strength of the bigger states which are able to dominate a number of smaller states within a defined regional area. It is not a step towards globalisation. Rather the contrary, since the direction of FDI relationships is first between the triad countries and then between the dominant country and its cluster, but not between the countries within the cluster.[18]

9.3 Institutionalist Approaches: The Transformation of the Nation State in the Global Economy

Whereas intergovernmentalism and neorealism may be classified amongst the 'sceptical' approaches to globalisation, neo-institutionalists are on the opposite side of the spectrum, and have been classified amongst the group of the so-called 'globalists'.[19] Indeed, if for the sceptics globalisation is at best a useful 'myth' which can be used to justify the persistent hegemony of the most powerful nation states, for institutionalists there is no possibility to deny the existence of globalisation nor to juxtapose it to previous historical waves of market integration.

Starting from a definition of globalisation similar to the intergovernmentalist one, neo-institutionalists do however reach opposite conclusions. In particular, they claim that the process of transnationalisation of the world economy is well advanced and that this produces a number of transformations both at the national level of governance and at the level of the international system,

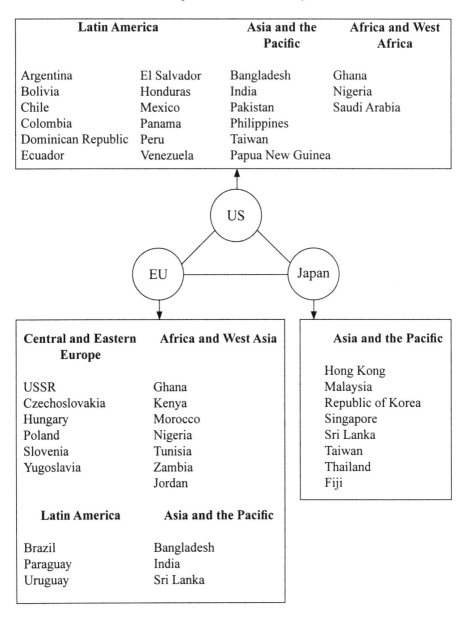

Latin America		Asia and the Pacific	Africa and West Africa
Argentina	El Salvador	Bangladesh	Ghana
Bolivia	Honduras	India	Nigeria
Chile	Mexico	Pakistan	Saudi Arabia
Colombia	Panama	Philippines	
Dominican Republic	Peru	Taiwan	
Ecuador	Venezuela	Papua New Guinea	

US

EU — Japan

Central and Eastern Europe	Africa and West Asia	Asia and the Pacific
		Hong Kong
USSR	Ghana	Malaysia
Czechoslovakia	Kenya	Republic of Korea
Hungary	Morocco	Singapore
Poland	Nigeria	Sri Lanka
Slovenia	Tunisia	Taiwan
Yugoslavia	Zambia	Thailand
	Jordan	Fiji

Latin America	Asia and the Pacific
Brazil	Bangladesh
Paraguay	India
Uruguay	Sri Lanka

Figure 9.1   Foreign direct investment cluster of triad members, 1990 (economies on which triad members dominate inward foreign direct investment stocks/flows)

Source: Hirst and Thompson (1999a), p. 120.

modifying completely the terms of reference of previously well established institutional solutions.

The definition of globalisation offered by this group of scholars is, indeed, again, mainly a quantitative one. Globalisation is, for Keohane: '...The intensification of transnational as well as interstate relations.'[20]

According to David Held, globalisation:

> suggests a growing magnitude or intensity of global flows such that states and societies become increasingly enmeshed in worldwide systems and networks of interaction.[21]

While for Phil Cerny, globalisation is given by the interaction between denser economic relations amongst the states (internationalisation) and denser relations cutting across states (transnationalisation).[22]

However, the evidence produced to substantiate this definition by this group of scholars justify the emergence of a new phase in the development of the world economy, a phase characterised by increase in the economic interaction between states as well as by the increase of economic activities which overcome national boundaries to acquire a new dimension lying above the states. This makes it necessary to adopt new forms of governance, which transcend the nation states. Indeed, the global economy appears as a web of interconnected or, better, interdependent, activities performed at different institutional levels by actors who are increasingly detached from the national level of governance.

Where does this leave the nation state?

Of course, the nation state does not disappear from the picture of the global economy, nor however, does it remain untouched by the wave of transformations enshrined in this notion of globalisation. The nation state survives, but it undergoes a substantial change, which modifies its role, its position in the international system and even its functions.

In particular, transformation of the State encompasses the following two dimensions:

1   there is a different perception of the role of the State in the economy and of the notion of 'public goods';
2   there is a re-orientation of how states interact economically with each other which creates interdependences and international linkages.[23]

As regards the first dimension, given the complex and multilayered institutional framework which is the consequence of the denser international/transnational interactions and their relations, it becomes harder to identify which institution should provide which public goods as well as becoming harder to define the notion of public goods as such.

Taking the main four categories of public goods (regulatory, productive, distributive and redistributive) one by one, it is possible to identify the effect of globalisation on their provision and to reconsider the overall role of the nation state.[24]

Regulatory public goods are defined as those goods relating to the establishment and application of rules for the operation and interactions of both market and non-market institutions. With the advent of globalisation, the ability of firms, market actors and competing parts of the nation state apparatus itself to defend and expand their economic and political reach through activities such as transnational policy networking and regulatory arbitrage has both undermined the control span of the State from without and fragmented it from within.[25] This leads to the necessity to devise new institutional frameworks at the supranational level capable of providing regulatory public goods which can be enforced outside and above the level of the nation states. In a word, it enhances the role and functions of international institutions, including international law,[26] and increases the constraints those can impose on the states.

As far as productive and distributive public goods are concerned, the first are defined as the production of goods and services by the State for economies of scale or normative reasons (e.g., production of energy); the second are defined as the delivery of goods and services by the State given the collective nature of consumers (e.g., transport). In the case of productive public goods, the increased dimension and relevance of multinational companies brought about the possibility of exploiting private economies of scale, thus eliminating the necessity for the State to provide them. While in the case of distributive public goods, it is the individualisation of the consumers through the process of commodification to result in the loss of the *raison d'être* of the State provision

Finally, in the case of redistributive public goods, which are those provided on the basis of a political rationale (e.g., welfare), the impact of globalisation has been dramatic. The power of trade unions as well as the effectiveness of corporatist bargaining weakened as a consequence of international pressures for wage restraint and flexible working practices and this caused a substantial reduction of welfare expenditure.

The new outlook of state intervention into the economy is not any more the welfare state but what scholars have termed the 'competition state'.[27] This is a state able to provide a dynamic 'competitive' advantage in the international economy (as opposed to static notion of 'comparative' advantage), promoting a favourable investment climate to transnational economic actors through the provision of public goods defined as 'immobile factors of capital', like, for example, human capital, infrastructure, support for new technologies, protection of the environment or maintenance of the standards of life for the middle classes.

The transformation of the state from the domestic oriented welfare state to the externally orientated 'competition state' leads to the second dimension of the change in the position of the state as a consequence of globalisation: the reorientation in the way it interacts with the international arena and with the other states. The state changes its international role, shifting its priorities from defence and security, to business. The 'competition state', both in the developed and in the less developed world, attracts business by:

- shifting its public policy-making from the macro to the micro-level: e.g., reduction of labour costs;
- pursuing a 'dynamic competitive' advantage and thus rendering more flexible its structure;
- keeping inflation low and the economy stable to attract foreign investment (neoliberal macroeconomic policies);
- promoting enterprise innovation and profitability at the private and public level.

Summing up, the whole globalisation discourse is taking place within the not yet well defined institutional terrain of the competition state and of a fragmented international regime whose institutions are still in the making. Of course, the process so far described is an ongoing one and the end-result is not yet recognisable. Indeed, the kind of scenario that will prevail at the end of this overall transformation depends on a number of unforcastable factors, including which actors would take the lead of the process.

Regarding this, institutionalists recognise a crucial role as agents of change to political institutions and political agents who act like intermediaries between the international, the transnational and the domestic level in a game which is not simply a 'two level game' but a multilevel one. Indeed, the competition state adds further layers and cleavages to the world economy, which increases the complexity and density of network of interdependence and interpenetration.

In this context, the process of regionalisation is not interpreted as a barrier to globalisation, but as a stage in this process, institutionalising at the regional level new forms of transboundary and supranational governance, which are by no means inconsistent with the institutionalisation of a new international regime.[28]

9.4   Transnationalist Approaches: The Subordination of Politics to Economics

The transnationalist approach differs from the ones analysed so far for the emphasis put on the definition of globalisation as a structural phenomenon, comprising a number of qualitative transformations, which define the current phase of capitalist development.[29] In contrast to quantitative definitions of globalisation, this qualitative definition overcomes the need to measure the phenomena included in the process of globalisation, since it is the mere existence of a series of intertwined structural events that defines the 'ontology' of globalisation.

According to Peter Dicken:

> Globalisation processes are qualitatively different from internationalization processes. They involve not merely the geographical extension of economic activity across national boundaries but also, more importantly, the functional integration of such internationally dispersed activities.[30]

For James Mittleman, globalisation is a 'syndrome',[31] composed of a number of events, which acquire their meaning by the relation with each other and by their co-existence in a specific historical moment. However, these events are not randomly connected. Their relation is defined within a precise framework, which allows transnationalists to overcome the accusation of the 'vagueness' in the definition of the notion of globalisation, often moved against them by more main-stream scholars.[32]

Technological transformation is the central notion of the qualitative definition of globalisation, and it is the factor that brings about the transformation in the realms of financial transactions and of production. This, in turn, triggers related changes in the economic, social and political spheres.

Technological transformation is at the roots of the exceptional developments of financial markets producing what is normally defined as financial globalisation, i.e., the existence of a round-the-clock access to financial transactions all over the world. This, however, does not mean that the physical location of financial markets loses significance or that financial elites become disentangled from national boundaries. On the contrary, their role and their bargaining power inside the national polity increases as their economic position improves, leading to a shift in the power relations between the different socio-economic groups whose relevance can hardly be overestimated. This statement is true both for developed countries (see the growing importance of the City of London for the British economy[33]) and for underdeveloped countries, where the establishment of off-shore markets produces incredible transformations in the local economy and social structure.[34] Moreover, the unlimited, 24 hour access to financial markets leads to a great sensitivity of capital to interest rates, which, in the long run, reduces the scope for the adoption of differentiated national monetary and macroeconomic policies.[35]

Technological transformation

Restructuring of production   **Financial globalisation**

1 Geographical re-allocation of   Round-the-clock/around the world
  production regionalisation: access to financial markets
    foreign direct investment (FDI)   Off-shore financial markets
    mergers and acquisitions (M&A)   Equalisation of interest rates around
    export processing zones (EPZs)   the globe
2 Creation of transnational social   Volatility and uncontrollability of
  classes: international financial markets
    transnational capitalist class   Reduction of effectiveness of
    transnational working class   national macroeconomic policy-
3 Geographical displacement of   making
  labour following regional paths:
  'the triad'
Skilled: brain drain
Non-skilled: mass migration

Socio-political consequences of the quantitative definition of globalisation

1 Commodification
2 Polarisation of wealth (the paradox of marginalisation within globalisation):
    geographical
    social
3 The subordination of politics to economics

Figure 9.2   Components of the qualitative definition of globalisation

Source: Elaboration of the author.

Technological transformation is also the driving force behind the process of transformation of global production and the related global reallocation of production through foreign direct investment, mergers and acquisitions, and the creation of the export processing zones. Indeed, the possibility for multinational companies to modify their productive structure by exploiting geographically displaced cost reduction opportunities is greatly improved by the availability of technological progress. The latter allows for cheap transport costs, distant labour control or economies of scale in specific locations.

This restructuring and geographical reallocation of production, coupled with financial globalisation, spills over on a number of social and political changes affecting all levels of organisation, from the local to the global one.

Amongst the social consequences of the processes so far described, there is the so-called phenomenon of 'commodification' defined as the inclusion in the market sphere of relations previously left outside its boundaries and regulated by different logics.[36] This certainly happens in the western industrialised world, where the number of activities submitted to the market rules of the supply, demand and price tend to increase and include also those spheres of life previously left outside, like, for example, the organisation of leisure time. However, the tendency of multinational companies to move abroad and, mainly, to the less developed countries to take advantage of both lower production costs and market opportunities, brings about the expansion of the phenomenon of 'commodification' to cultural enclaves where the market was traditionally a recessive form of organisation of economic relations, with all that means in terms of cultural clashes and related social and political consequences.

Moreover, the process of globalisation as so far defined, is not neutral in social and wealth terms, but entails new social cleavages and challenges, as well as new winners and new losers. In fact, given the innovative nature of the technological tools necessary to grasp the opportunities of globalisation, the necessity arises for a continuous updating and re-qualification of skills. This poses the problem of the polarisation of wealth both in social and geographical terms, since those who have already the means to access the educational and vocational systems and have the economic possibility to remain in education for longer, if not to stay in education forever (the so-called concept of the 'knowledge society'), will be by far better placed in the global economy. Therefore, the lower strata of society, as well as the weakest ones, like the elders or the women, and, finally, those living in less developed countries, will be increasingly marginalised by the fast moving world of the new skills necessary to keep up with globalisation. It follows, that the social and geographical wealth gap is deemed to increase, leading to the paradox of 'marginalisation within globalisation'.

In political terms, the overcoming of national boundaries for the exploitation of global financial and productive opportunities modifies the existing balance of power between national political institutions and an increasingly globalised economic elite. The latter is placed by globalisation in a position to exert credible pressures at the domestic political level by threatening to move its economic activity abroad in exchange for favourable economic policy measures. The credibility of the threat, in turn, is ensured by the effective possibility to move easily short- to medium-term capital across the border, as well as to displace production and long-term investment.[37] Whether this leads to a *de facto* disempowerment of national politics *vis-à-vis* globalising capital, or there is still a margin for reaction by national political actors, is still the subject of many debates in both academic and political circles.[38] For some authors,[39] indeed, there is the possibility of the activation of a 'double-movement', Polanyi style, according to which, after a phase of triumph of liberalism and of subordination of politics to economics, those who are most affected by these developments will react producing a counter movement and a new social equilibrium guaranteeing a new say to the losers.

The last consideration leads to a further component of the qualitative definition of globalisation. Indeed, globalisation, not only produces the conditions for the creation of a transnational capitalist elite, but, on the other hand, creates the premises for the transnationalisation of the working class through the restructuring of the international labour division and the establishment of a new global division of labour.[40] This might represent the basis for a future reproduction of the class struggle at the transnational level, though, of course, there can be no certainty about the final outcome of this process.

Indeed, the future is open to many possible scenarios, leaving to willing researchers the fascinating task to try and discover where the global shift is leading us all.

Notes

1   See Talani (2003).
2   For a similar interpretation see Held and McGrew (2000), Introduction.
3   A very meaningful example of this attitude may be found in Gilpin (2000).
4   See Gilpin (2001).
5   See Gilpin (2001), p. 364.

6   Gilpin does not show data, however these claims are contained in Gilpin (2001), p. 368.
7   See Hirst and Thompson (1999). In Chapter 8 the authors set their position in the European integration debate clearly endorsing an intergovernmentalist vision of the EU. See in particular: 'Some nation states will remain the crucial actors in constructing a political basis of consent for the macroeconomic policies of the Community .... (p. 253). See also Thompson (1993).
8   See Hirst and Thompson (1999), Introduction.
9   See Hirst and Thompson (1999), p. 140.
10   See Hirst and Thompson (1999), p. 141.
11   All relevant data are contained in Hirst and Thompson (1999), ch. 3.
12   See Hirst and Thompson (1999), ch. 3.
13   See figures in Hirst and Thompson (1999), p. 152.
14   See figures in Hirst and Thompson (1999), p. 152.
15   See figures in Hirst and Thompson (1999), p. 152.
16   See figures in Hirst and Thompson (1999), ch. 3.
17   A similar interpretation is presented in Held and McGrew (2000), Introduction.
18   See Hirst and Thompson (1999).
19   For a similar distinction see Held and McGrew (2000), Introduction.
20   See Keohane (2000), ch. 9.
21   See Held and McGrew (2000), p. 3.
22   See Cerny (1999).
23   See Cerny (1999).
24   See Cerny (1999).
25   See Cerny (1999), p. 99.
26   See Held, McGrew, Goldblatt and Perraton (1999).
27   See Cerny (1999), p. 101.
28   See Held (2000), p. 12.
29   See Mittleman (2000); see also Overbeek (2000) and Dicken (1999).
30   See Dicken (1999), p. 5.
31   See Mittleman (2000).
32   See Hirst and Thompson (1999).
33   For a more detailed analysis of this subject see Talani (2000).
34   See, for example, Lilley (2000).
35   A similar argument is contained in the chapter about EMU.
36   See Mittleman (1999).
37   See Overbeek (1995).
38   See Garret (1998).
39   For a list see Held (2000).
40   For more information see chapter on illegal migration in this book.

References

Buelens, F. (ed.) (1999), *Globalisation and the Nation State*, Aldershot: Edward Elgar.
Cerny, P. (1999), 'Reconstructing the Political in a Globalising World', in F. Buelens (ed.), *Globalisation and the Nation State*, Aldershot: Edward Elgar.

Dicken, P. (1998), *Global Shift*, London: Paul Chapman.

Garret, G. (1998), *Partisan Politics in the Global Economy*, Cambridge: Cambridge University Press.

Gilpin, R., (2000), *The Challenges of Global Capitalism: The World Economy in the 21st Century*, Princeton: Princeton University Press.

Gilpin, R., (2001), *Global Political Economy: Understanding the Global Economic Order*, Princeton and Oxford: Princeton University Press.

Held, D., McGrew, A., Goldblatt, D. and Perraton, J. (eds) (1999), *Global Transformation*, London: Polity Press.

Held, D. and McGrew, A. (eds) (2000), *The Global Transformations Reader*, London: Polity Press.

Hirst, P. and Thompson, G. (1999), *Globalisation in Question*, 2nd edn, London: Polity Press.

Keohane, R.O. (2000), 'Sovereignty in International Society', in D. Held and A. McGrew (eds), *The Global Transformations Reader*, London: Polity Press.

Lilley, P. (2000), *Dirty Dealing: The Untold Truth about Global Money Laundering*, London: Kogan Page.

Mittleman, J.H. (2000), *The Globalisation Syndrome: Transformation and Resistance*, Princeton: Princeton University Press.

Overbeek, H.W. (1995), 'Globalisation and the Restructuring of the European Labour Markets: the Role of Migration', in M. Simai (ed.), *Global Employment. An International Investigation into the Future of Work*, London and Tokyo: Zed Books and United Nations University Press.

Overbeek, H. (2000), 'Globalisation, Sovereignty and Transnational Regulation: Reshaping the Governance of International Migration', in B. Gosh (ed.), *Managing Migration: Time for a New International Regime*, Oxford: Oxford University Press.

Talani, L.S. (2000), *Betting For and Against EMU*, Aldershot: Ashgate.

Talani, L.S. (2003), 'Avoiding the "G" Word in Reinventing European and International Governance', *International Studies Review*, March.

Thompson, G. (1993), *The Economic Emergence of a New Europe?*, Aldershot: Edward Elgar.

Index